THE PURITAN IS POLITICAL

MAPPING ISLAMIC RADICALISM

SANGIT KUMAR RAGI

Vitasta

Published by
Renu Kaul Verma
Vitasta Publishing Pvt Ltd
2/15, Ansari Road, Daryaganj
New Delhi – 110 002
info@vitastapublishing.com

ISBN 978-93-90961-73-3

First Edition 2023
MRP ₹750

All the verses of Quran have been taken from The Holy Quran, King Fahd Holy Qur-ān Printing Complex, Original Version.

Edited by Sudesh Verma
Editorial Support by Shambhavi Mani
Cover and layout by Somesh Kumar Mishra
Printed by Vikas Computer and Printers

CONTENTS

ACKNOWLEDGEMENTS

The idea of this book had been in my mind since long but it started taking shape only in the mid-April 2020s. Corona had spread its tentacles and had the world in its vice-like grip. The Government was grappling to control the spread. In the midst of this came the name of Tablighi Jamaat and its activities which became the main focus of newspapers and news channels alike.

Though founded in India in early 1920s, it remained away from public glare and scrutiny. Interestingly, the Europeans and Americans had been keeping an eye on its activities, suspecting its involvement in radicalising Muslims. Now suddenly the organization was in the limelight and people started digging up its history and ideology.

I had been reading and preparing my notes on political Islam in order to understand the ideology of Islam. I was curious as to what it was that produced such fanaticism among its followers. While working on this project I have delved deep into the history of Islam, its birth and evolution, its journey as a religious-political doctrine and of course the ultimate mission that it defines for itself. The heated debates in Indian media gave me the impetus to actually start writing. The book is not a commentary on Islam as a religion. It focuses on how certain concepts in it have been interpreted in a manner as to invoke violence against non-followers of the religion.

Before venturing on this writing enterprise, I spoke to several friends in the media and the university and they encouraged me to undertake this exercise. I am thankful to each one of them.

I remember today late Bhanu Pratap Shukla, the noted journalist who taught, guided and inspired me to be a fearless citizen and an uncompromising writer when it came to telling the truth, especially when it concerned the national and civilizational cause of India. Without his affection, care, support and encouragement, I would not be where I am today. He taught me skills to theorize a political, social and cultural phenomenon. He would have been very happy to see my work.

I express my gratitude to all members of the team of Centre for Study of Politics and Governance (CSPG) who took out the time to read my draft and point out typos and grammatical errors. I would like to specially mention Raution Thakur, Ashna Monga, Nitesh Rai and Ekta Sheikh who went through the draft and gave valuable inputs.

I also thank the head of the Research Division of NMML, Dr Narendra Shukla who at every stage encouraged me to complete the work. I express my gratitude to my friend Ashok Kawadia who enlightened me on several aspects of Islamic thoughts. I owe a debt to the writings of Sita Ram Goel, which in my formative years nurtured my interests in reading and learning about political Islam.

I have attempted to present facts and analysis in a lucid and simple form. However, it has been made more beautiful and readable through wonderful copyediting by the Vitasta team. I am really thankful to both Sudesh Verma and Renu Verma who accepted my draft for publication. Though I have tried to be faithful to the content, mistakes might have occurred despite my painstaking efforts. I own them without hesitation.

And lastly, I would like to mention my family members Raghav, Madhav and Reena. They are the ones who always suffer on account of my academic writings and readings. Their support has been the strength of my academic enterprise. And blessings of my parents have worked as a catalyst towards fulfilment of the task.

INTRODUCTION

Today radical Islamism and Islamic terrorism are the most talked about terms. Governments are clueless as to how to handle the violence and intolerance that emanates from it. Both Islamic and non-Islamic countries are equally under severe political and civil stress because of rising trends in Islamic radicalism. No country that has a substantial Islamic population is untouched by elements of Islamic zealotry. A careful study would reveal that radicalism is directly proportional to the numerical strength of Islamic population in the society—countries like Syria, Iraq, Sudan, Afghanistan, Algeria, Pakistan and Egypt are a case in point. These Islamic countries are deeply entrenched in a whirlpool of Islamic radicalism as opposed to the United States of America (US) and European countries which are considered enemies of Islam by Islamists. The stories and examples, however, suggest that they have no less enemies among the faith followers. Islamic countries are the worst victims of the radicalisation phenomenon. Contrary to popular belief, Muslims are the biggest victims of Islamic extremism.

As per an estimate, nearly 85 per cent casualties are Muslims.[1]

Muslim society is perpetually at unease. There is constant agitation and warring in societies where Sharia is not practised. In such countries, they want to establish Shariat laws, first for themselves and then for the entire society. But where Shariat law is already at work, the picture is not very different. A section of Muslims feel that in such societies too Shariat is not being followed religiously. And this becomes their excuse to kill even co-religionists. No wonder Islam is at war everywhere and in every society. It does not matter whether its followers are in majority or minority in that society.

There are very few Islamic countries that do not have terrorist organisations claiming to be saviours of Islam. Some of them have turned out to be the core nurseries producing Islamic terrorists. Afghanistan, Pakistan, Iraq and Palestine are classical examples—Jaish-e-Mohammed (JeM, The Army of Muhammad), Hizbul Mujahideen (Party of Holy Fighters), Lashkar-e-Taiba (Army of Pure and Righteous) to name a few. It is proverbially agreed that these countries have pushed themselves into a black hole of death and destruction.

The journey and expansion of Islam has always been rooted in violence and military adventurism. From its first victory at Mecca to its expansion in Asia, Africa and the Southern parts of Europe, the story of Islam has been marked by the use of brutal force and state power. In two hundred years, Islam changed the religious demography of Asia and Africa significantly, reaching right up to the Southern tip of Spain in Europe. For centuries, Christianity and Islam fought against each other for their territorial expansion in the medieval period.[2] While Christianity expanded in Europe, Islam appeared as the most powerful force in Asia and Africa. It started losing its imperial position, with ascendency of European powers after the industrial revolution in the West. Industrial wealth and technological advancements gave Europe an edge over the rest. European countries looked beyond their territorial borders for resources and markets. This culminated in the capture of political and state power to fulfil long-term economic interests leading to colonisation of Asia and Africa. This was when Islamic countries lost political control to the Christian West in many parts of Asia and Africa.

By this time, around 1600, the East India Company had a strong foothold on Indian soil. Initially it had only trade in mind. But soon after the death of Aurangzeb in 1707, when the might of the Mughal empire started crumbling, the Company started looking towards the political control of the country. The Nawabs of the provinces were not really capable. The Battle of Plassey in June 1757 turned out to be a turning point. The joint army of the French and the Nawab of Siraj ud-Daulah was comprehensibly defeated by the East India Company heralding the rule of the East India Company in Bengal which gradually became pan-Indian in subsequent years. The political control of India shifted from the company to the British crown after the Sepoy Mutiny of 1857. The stories of other countries which hitherto were under Muslim rule are not very different. Further, the waves of political democracy post the French revolution brought in new discourses which also impacted the Islamic world where the Caliphate system started weakening and princely kingdoms started making headways. This weakening finally culminated in the disintegration of the Ottoman Empire. After the first World War, in 1922, the Caliphate system officially came to an end.

However, the concept of Islamic brotherhood, integral to theological Islam, gained ground. Its political manifestations appeared when the Jewish state of Israel came into existence in 1947 with division of the former Palestine region into two states—Israel (where Jews dominated) and Palestine (where Arabs dominated). Israel declared its independence on 14 May 1948. The UN resolution on Palestine was not accepted by the Palestinian Arabs. Their groups started attacking Jewish settlements. Finally, the Arab-Israel war broke out. Arab countries such as Syria, Jordan, Egypt and Lebanon staged a joint attack against Israel. Tel Aviv was bombed. Israel defended its border and gained control over some of the territories which were part of Palestine. However, the guerrilla war against Israel continued. Israel finally became the uniting force of the Muslim world. The defeat at the hands of Israel exposed the absence of leadership in the Islamic world and its theological masculinity.

Amidst this, Egypt raised a new hope among Islamic countries when it nationalised the Suez Canal and stopped the navigation of European vessels through it. However, this heroic posture and pursuit did not last long as the combined army of Arabs led by Egypt was again defeated by Israel in 1967. This time Israel captured Golan Heights from Syria and snatched off Gaza Strip from Lebanon. The Egyptian air force was devastated by the Israeli air attacks. In brief, the possibility of the emergence of a powerful Arab force in terms of political, economic, and military power received a major setback. The agony of defeat permeated deep within the Muslim communities and erupted in the form of radical Islamic groups with their aim of liberating the land of Arabs from Israel. However, the Muslim world remained divided despite lending support to the cause of Palestine. Saudi Arabia and many other countries became the ally of Western powers such as the USA and the United Kingdom who were staunch supporters and allies of Israel. Egypt lowered its hostility towards Israel and resumed diplomatic relations.[3] Soviet Union groups and many third world countries sided with Palestine projecting Israel as a bullying nation infringing on the territorial rights of the Arabs.

With Soviet intervention in Afghanistan, the Western powers sought to return the hostility towards the former by using religious Islam. They used Islamic countries such as Pakistan to radicalise Muslim youth in Afghanistan and launch Jehad against the Soviet forces. This is the same radicalisation that later hit the USA with terrorist attacks on 9/11 and brought the threat of Islamic terrorism to the doorstep of Europe. Many people lost their lives in such terror attacks in Britain, France, Germany, Spain and other European countries. This created a sense of fear throughout Europe.

Till the time these radical forces were fighting the Soviets, the USA and other Western powers did not acknowledge the demon they had been nurturing against humanity. India—the worst victim of terrorism—shouted from the rooftops and at various forums raised the issue of Pakistan-sponsored cross-border terrorism in Kashmir. This was never attended to and largely described as 'Islamophobia' in Western discourses.

The 1980s saw the beginning of Islamic radicalism, and in just over a decade, Pakistan and Afghanistan emerged as the nuclei and nurseries of Islamic radicalism and Islamic terrorism. They were followed, subsequently, by other countries of Asia and Europe. Several Islamic terrorist groups espousing the ideology of true and puritan Islam sprung up. The success of these groups in Afghanistan inspired many to form such groups in different Islamic countries. Most of the terrorist organisations emerged after the Arab-Israel conflicts or during and after the Soviet-Afghan war. Taliban, Al-Qaida, Hizbul Mujahideen are the by-products of the radicalisation that followed the Afghan war against Soviet forces from where it travelled to different parts of the world.

This was a new wave of Islamic terrorism which fed on the Petro-capitalism of the Islamic world led by Saudi Arabia, the commercial ally of the USA and the West, but at the same time supporter, funder, and exporter of the radical ideology of Wahhabism. One after another, several countries came under the influence of this new radicalism. As a result, many countries gave birth to radical Islamists organisations which subsequently engaged in violence and terrorism. The weapon of terrorism was used by these organisations not just against the people of other faiths but also against their co-religionists. Their justification for use of violence against Muslims came from their belief that Muslims had got corrupted by the value system of non-Islamic forces and that they had fallen from the practice of true Islam.[4] They reminded such Muslims of the mission of Islam—that of Islamising the entire world—and resurrected the ideology of global Jehad. They sought to enforce the ideology of Puritan Islam by which they meant the practices that were at work during the times of the Prophet and the first four Caliphates. This period of Prophet Mohammad and the immediate years that followed is the phase when Islam originated and expanded as a powerful force in Central and West Asia.

Many countries fell to Islamic military expeditions and adopted Islam as their religion. The Quran and Hadiths were also written during these times. These radicals picked up three aspects: first, they focused on those verses of the Quran which could spark hatred towards other religions and defined it as integral to Jehad. Jehad was not a war of the divine against the demon. It was a war against kafirs, who were those who did not follow or believe in the Quran or believe in God as per the tenets of Islam. This included being unfriendly towards those who do not have faith in Islam. As a result, all idolaters and non-Islamic faiths became enemies who could be conquered and converted. This was precisely the reason for forcing people of other faiths to convert to Islam and to kill them if they refused to do so.

The world witnessed the worst kinds of killings such as, chopping off of organs gradually till the person died, slitting the throat and hanging the body on a tree, publicly gunning down several people in a row, and so on. Boko Haram and ISIS practiced this far more violently than other Islamic terrorist organisations. This was part of their strategy to instil fear in the minds of the apostate and make them fall in line. And they claimed that their real intent was to establish pure Islam and an Islamic state ruled by Sharia.[5]

Secondly, they created a shrunken cell for Muslims by opposing elements of modernity on the one hand, and strictly adhering to medieval Islam on the other. This included strict adherence to dress code for women, almost essentializing the burqa in public places; other social and cultural practices such as a ban on music and films; length and styles of the beard, and so on. This was essentially anti-West. But the thoughts and practices influenced Muslims of Islamic countries as much as the Muslims of the Western world and other non-Islamic countries with Muslim population. There, the focus was on separate Muslim identity and emphasis on goods with Halal certification, burqa, long-beard, Arab style of dressing and stricter adherence to the Shariat practices. The creation of Islamic banks became far more visible than ever.[6]

This was supported and force-multiplied by the rapid growth in communication technology and communication platforms. Television and mobile technologies brought in phenomenal changes in the speed of transmission of news and views across the world. With one click of the mouse, the world got zipped in a small pen drive. Interestingly, it impacted the global ideology differently. It reinforced religious identity which continued to identify with elements of primordial forces. Instead of promoting expansion of markets and spread of modern ideas, the new communication ways enabled

Muslim communities across the world to relate and attach more vigorously with Muslim identity questions. Technology provided platforms for their global network and it immensely expanded the horizontal comradeship at the global level. It's no wonder that Muslims from Kerala in India travelled all the way to Syria to fight for the ISIS.[7] These were not isolated incidents from India. Muslims from other states too joined in. Muslims from several countries joined the Taliban and Al-Qaida to fight the Soviets and then the US forces in Afghanistan.[8]

The radicalisation of Islam became a new global reality. And by this time, it was far more furious and ferocious as it was embedded and equipped with new technology and had acquired sophisticated weapons. Terrorists hijacked commercial aircrafts and attacked the US twin towers on 11 September 2001 deceiving all intelligence networks and technological devices. While one aircraft crashed into the Twin Towers that housed the World Trade Centre and represented the economic might of the US, the other aircraft targeted the Pentagon which symbolised its military might.

Muslims in the US criticised but many of them gave riders too. They explained the reasons and thereby sought justifications for such barbarous acts.[9] Some people could not resist their joy and explained the attack as justice done to the American policies towards the Muslim world. The success in the US emboldened the Islamic radical groups to launch a series of terrorist attacks in different countries of Europe. Every terrorist attack is followed by heated debates on whether or not such acts of terrorism align with the true spirit of Islam.

Those already radicalised endorse it under the broader rubric of Islamic Jehad; such activities are dedicated to the service of Islam. The pacifists within the religion argue that Islam is a religion of peace and does not justify any kind of violence at all. They quote from the Quran wherein it is written in clear terms that 'my religion is my religion and your religion is your religion. Neither you can change your own nor I will'. However, radicals advance the argument that establishment of Global Islam is the mission of Islam; they justify violence and killings of the kafirs for the sake of Islam.

Radical Islamist Zakir Naik quotes from the verses of the Quran to justify the murder of kafirs and idolaters. A reading of the Quran certainly baffles one who does not practice Islam since several verses stand against idolaters and kafirs. This can confuse someone who is tracking Islamic extremism and radical Islamic phenomenon. Certain questions that often strike the mind without exception are: Why is it so that but for few exceptions all the Muslim-dominated countries have Islamic terrorist organisations? Why followers of other religions are not given a fair and equal treatment in Muslim-dominated countries and are subjected to harsh penalties under blasphemy laws? Why is the Muslim population on the rise in non-Islamic countries whereas it is just the opposite in case of Islamic countries?[10] Why is it so that in most of the ethno-religious conflicts in the world, one party happens to be the followers of Islam? Whether Islamic radicalism is a distortion of Islam or it follows and emerges from the religious texts of Islam? Why is it so that invariably Muslim populations everywhere in the world have conflicts with the host and indigenous societies concerning their identity questions? Besides, what are the key schools of Islam which have largely influenced the ideology of radical Islam? How have they inspired the radicals through their teachings?

These are the questions which this book has sought to examine in order to explore plausible answers. It has been argued that the problem is not with Muslims but the ideology of Islam which considers all other religions and their prophets as false and nurtures the arguments and psychology of disrespect and intolerance towards them. The problem is compounded by shrinking the space for reasoned and rational inquiry into key religious texts like the Quran and the Hadiths. Such endeavours are always portrayed as blasphemy inviting exemplary punishments including death. The cases of renowned authors Salman Rushdie and Taslima Nasreen against whom death-fatwas were issued by religious leaders of Islam are telling examples.

The book seeks to discuss and explore the journey of Islam as an ideology from the time of its origin to the present, particularly in respect of three schools namely, Wahhabism, Deoband, and Tablighi which have come to dominate the discourses on the radical stream of contemporary Islam. It explains how the idea of puritan Islam delves into the terrain of political Islam and forms an ideology that is exclusivist in nature and poses a serious threat to democratic pluralism and secularism. It elucidates how the concept of puritan Islam becomes a powerful source for the Islamic organisations to preach, propagate and network the gospel of Islamic terrorism, and how and why the moderate voices from the Islamic communities have failed to respond to these challenges.

The book documents the discourse on Islamic terrorism and brings before readers different models and approaches at a global level to meet the challenges of Islamic terrorism and political Islam. It concludes by arguing two premises; the call for the puritan Islam, broadly referring to the Islam in practice during the times of the Prophet and the subsequent four Caliphates, brings rigidity and hostility in Islam vis-a-vis its relations with other religions. It captures the elements of interfaith amicability because the call for puritanism creates a shell for the ideology. It does not allow the intermingling of cultures, and where it already exists it tears the fabric of social and cultural continuity. Secondly, while Europe and the West will be able to manage the onslaught of political Islam unfolding itself in terms of puritan Islam due to the thin presence of Islamic communities in their countries, it would be a far more complex and a greater challenge for a county like India to tackle the rising radicalisation of the Muslim community in times to come due to rising growth of Islamic population and their polarisation, resulting in ascending counter polarisation by other communities such as Hindus.

The chapters of the book have been designed as follows:

Chapter 1: It contextualises and initiates the debate on political and puritan Islam in the wake of the controversy that centred around Tablighi Jamaat in India amidst the Covid-19 pandemic. Despite being the land of its origin and having its international headquarter right in the middle of the national capital, very few knew about the Jamaat in India due to its ways of preaching and consolidation of Islam away from the public gaze. However, their conduct during the pandemic generated controversy and subsequently triggered the debates on puritan Islam. The chapter explains the historical account of the origin and expansion of the ideology of Islam and seeks to understand the trajectory of sects and schools of thought within Islam. It explains how different sects and traditions in Islam such as Shias, Sunni, and Sufi traditions emerged with time, and how they have different understandings of pure and true Islam, which often leads to conflicts amongst them. The chapter documents further how Islam entered India with the conquest of a part of Sindh and gradually expanded to other parts of the country.

Chapter 2: It discusses the salient features and ideology of Wahhabism and Deoband schools of Islam. These two schools have broadly dominated the contemporary discourses on political and radical Islam in the world and are considered as the source for the rise of the intolerant and radicalised Islam. It is also because most terrorists schools have their roots in their seminaries and schools. It explores why the Deoband Islam in India and Pakistan though sharing the same syllabus for teachings have different interpretations of Islam—the former negotiating for co-existence whereas the latter outrightly supporting elements like Taliban and Hizbul Mujahideen. The chapter further answers why Deoband India passes resolutions against Islamic terrorism whereas Deoband Pakistan supports

Taliban and other terrorist organisations. It seeks to find out whether the Deoband in India gives an accurate analysis or interpretation of Islam or it is constrained by the fact that India is a Hindu majority country where Pakistani version of Deoband would not be accepted?

Chapter 3: This chapter deals with the emergence ofTablighi Jamaat and its functioning. It discusses in detail their ways and methods of teaching Islam. It demonstrates that Tablighis are very much part of the Sunni cult of Islam and they broadly share the same world vision. Tablighis aim at consolidation of the Muslims within the Islamic faith instead of working to increase the numerical strength of its followers through indoctrinations of people of other faiths. This chapter delves into the teaching of puritan Islam which Tablighis propose, and explains how their talks and preaching on the same essentially radicalise the Muslim mind-set and nurture the elements of intolerance and hostility towards people of other faiths. The chapter argues that Tablighis are not directly involved in the terror attacks but they have been found endorsing extremism. Perhaps, this is the reason why governments, barring few exceptions, have kept the organisations on their watch lists.

Chapter 4: Citing examples from different countries of the world it discusses how the world perception of Tablighis has undergone a serious change after the 26/11 Mumbai attack.[11] History bears witness to the terror links of Tablighi—the infamous Coup attempt against Benazir Bhutto in 1995; Richard Reid, the shoe bomber, who sought to bomb the American Airlines in 2001; the London Underground Bombing in 2005 to name a few. The chapter argues how Tablighi is a Deobandi Islamic Movement working as a non-state actor under the façade of spiritual secularism to alter, indoctrinate and target young minds. Their activities have spread in South Asia and the Middle East and also European continents. From their role in Jammu and Kashmir under the sheepskin of the Jaish-e-Mohammed in the tragic Pulwama attack to French Tablighi follower Djamel Beghal who turned out to be a foot soldier of the Al-Qaida, it discusses how Tablighi is a nurturing hub of ideological terrorism creating a threat to the security of the country. The chapter concludes on how Tablighis have been using the curtains of the democratic, liberal framework as a sword for breeding violence, threats, and terror in non-Islamic countries. Its soft alliance with political allies of appeasement is increasing the expansion of Deobandi Islamisation.

Chapter 5: This section debates in detail on the territorial expanse of Islamic terrorism in the world in the last few decades and explains the pattern of violence and identity assertion. It argues that there is a definite stage when the identity questions unfold themselves in the form of assertion and violence. First, the migrant Muslim population seeks concessions for their basics in the host societies. In the second stage, they seek equal participation, and in the third stage they assert their identity demanding to be treated at par with the host society. This happens with the rising numerical strength of the community.

Based on statistical figures, the author argues that followers of Islam are the biggest victims of Islamic terrorism. And yet, there is no effective response from the community against the wild and heinous violence in the name of Islam. It also argues that radical Islamists have used the framework of liberal democracies of the West to freely radicalise their co-religionists. The author argues that the spirit of democracy and democratic values are in danger in such societies with increased appeals of hegemonic Islam.

Chapter 6: In this chapter, the author delves into the idea of puritan and true Islam. The true Islam or the puritan Islam refers to the Islam which was in practice in times of the Prophet and the first four righteous Caliphates. Since all the schools from Wahhabism and Deoband to Tablighis talk about realising the state of puritan Islam, it becomes imperative to understand the terrorists' and extremists' arguments in light of the verses of the Quran. The main argument is that certain verses of the Quran allow its followers and the interpreters to discern that the 'brotherhood of Islam' is not a message of universal brotherhood but merely a brotherhood of Muslims. Accordingly, it divides the entire humanity into believers and non-believers and directs the believers to be hostile to idolaters, polytheists, and other non-believers. This element of exclusivism makes Islam incompatible with democracy and secularism and also breeds intolerance towards other religious denominations.

Chapter 7: Here we discuss the conflicts within Islamic societies. It has been argued that Islamic terrorism is at work not only in plural societies but also in Islamic societies. The Islamic organisations involved in the terrorist activities have killed more Muslims compared to people of other faiths; nearly

85 per cent of the victims of terrorism are Muslims. Also, seven out of ten countries engaged in such violence do come from the Islamic world. It is interesting to note that both the killers and killed are Muslims in such societies and the victims are killed for not practicing true Islam or going against the tenets of true Islam. In Pakistan, every year, there are several acts of violence against the Shias and Ahmadis in which their mosques and followers are targeted by practitioners of the Deoband school of Sunni Islam. They don't consider them Muslim at all. The treatment given to followers of the Sufi tradition is also not very different. This chapter reveals how the proponents of true and puritan Islam, especially followers of Deoband and Wahhabism, are involved in violence against others of the same faith.

Chapter 8: This Chapter analyses the challenge of Islam in plural societies and how these societies are responding to the Islamic threat. It argues that Islam poses a serious threat to plural societies because it propounds and propagates the doctrine of homogenisation of society by converting the 'others' to Islam. This is defined as Pan-Islamism which often leads to conflicts in such societies. Different countries have adopted different approaches to meet the challenge of political Islam that comes in the guise of pure and true Islam, depending on the nature of the political system, the numerical strength of the Muslim community, and the understanding of the nature of the threat. Thus, China has resorted to 'Repressive Non-democratic State Model' (RSM) which includes the exercise of state power to monitor and supervise every movement of the members of the Muslim community. The State uses modern communication and technology to track the activities of every member. Needless to say, this approach violates even the private space of its citizens. Liberal democracies of the West have a different approach. They are struggling to maintain a balance between their commitment to democratic principles and using force while responding to terrorist activities. The Chapter emphasises that the greater the numerical strength of the followers of Islam, the greater are the chances and scope of conflict. And therefore, Europe is capable of tackling the rise of political Islam due to the thin presence of the Muslim population. America has tried to keep it away from its territorial borders. However, challenges are far more complex in the case of India in the wake of historical factors and a numerically large Muslim community.

Chapter 9: This chapter exclusively deals with the challenges of Islam in India. The country was partitioned on religious grounds. It was hoped that the partition would resolve the Hindu-Muslim conflicts in India. But this hope stands betrayed as pre-partition issues and rhetoric have gathered momentum. These are manifested in issues such as cow slaughter, religious conversion, contests over historical figures, and cultural icons. The infiltration from Bangladesh has become a national agenda as the illegal migrants are mainly Muslims who have dispersed across different parts of the country and have altered the religious demography of many parliamentary and assembly constituencies. While the right-wing political and social organisations are campaigning to send them back and take away their citizenship, the Muslim organisations are supporting their stay since it gives them a demographic advantage and increased voice in the political system. The anti-CAA protests were largely a Muslim phenomenon supported by non-BJP political parties. Hindu organisations express fear that if the Muslim population overtakes legislative and parliamentary constituencies in times to come, later on they would also start asserting the cultural and political agenda of Islam in India.

Conclusions: Puritan Islam is both complex and intimidating. It is complex in the sense that it has different meanings for different sects and sets of people within Islam. And it is intimidating because it is in name of the puritan Islam that violence is justified by Islamic terrorists' organisations. When Taliban banned music and forced men and women to follow the norms of behaviour set by them, they justified it on the grounds that it was what the holy Quran mandated. Accordingly, when the ISIS took control of certain areas in Iraq and Syria, they also inflicted similar restrictions on men and women, which they justified in the name of true and puritan Islam. There are Maulanas and preachers of Islam who preach that non-believers are to be treated as enemies according to the Quran. And therefore, any measure of action including violence against them is justified. As Islam mandates realising a global Islamic state, the threat of true and political Islam becomes a dangerous notion. Wahhabism, Deoband, and Tablighi teachings, therefore, become dangerous in pluralistic societies. Their teachings breed exclusivism and intolerance because they don't accept the existence of any other divine incarnation except for the Prophet.

It becomes really difficult to handle such a situation in a plural society like India where one religion is calling for Sarva Dharma Sambhav whereas the other, the second majority religion, holds that it would follow not just religion but also the political and cultural matrix of Islam. It has been seen that the radical forces use the framework of constitutionalism and democracy to promote their radical ideas and consolidate their position. They do not believe in the liberal principles of individual freedom and individual rights but use the same to promote their larger goals and aims.

As facts suggest, it is not difficult to argue that secularism and political democracy is not intrinsic to Islam. The whole notion of puritan Islam is a homogenisation project and it breeds violence across societies. It is this idea that converts into a passionate and emotional mission which the terrorists use to inflict violence against those whom they consider the enemy and obstacles of Islam. The problem, therefore, is not with Islam, but in Islam and Islamic teachings which produces a psyche of not accepting 'others' on the one hand and imposing self on the others. That is the reason Islamic populations are in conflict with other faith systems almost everywhere. The teachings of Deoband, Wahhabis, and Tablighis produce intolerant and exclusivist Islam instead of an inclusive one. No wonder they have emerged as the source of inspiration for radical Islamic organisations. Islam, as espoused in the verses of Quran, is giving fodder to radicalise its followers, a phenomenon which is felt the world over. Islamic terrorism is a global buzzword and countries are struggling to handle the phenomenon of radicalisation and its increasing tilt towards intolerance and violence.

References:

1 According to Daily Sabah, published from Istanbul, 80 Percent victims of Islamic terrorism globally are Muslims. See, https://www.dailysabah.com/islamophobia/2019/11/21/muslims-become-real-victims-of-global-terror-attacks, Accessed on 6 December 2021. Cordesman, Anthony. "Islam and the Patterns in Terrorism and Violent Extremism". October 17, 2017 https://www.csis.org/analysis/islam-and-patterns-terrorism-and-violent-extremism. Accessed on 7 December 2021.

2 Crusades is portrayed as the Christian barbarianism against the Muslims in medieval period in which Christians killed thousands of Muslims till Jehad was launched against them in retaliation.

3 Egypt maintained its full diplomatic relation with Israel in January 1980.

4 Loimeier, Roman. "Boko Haram: The Development of a

Militant Religious Movement in Nigeria." Africa Spectrum 47, no. 2/3 (2012): 137–55. http://www.jstor.org/stable/23350455.

5 https://www.usip.org/sites/default/files/resources/SR308.pdf

6 Imam, P., & Kpodar, K. (2013). Islamic Banking: How Has It Expanded? Emerging Markets Finance & Trade, 49(6), 112–137. http://www.jstor.org/stable/24475284

7 Phillip, Shaju. "Kerala's Islamic State Connection". The Indian Express, Kochi, 5 December, 2019.

8 Hassan, M. H. (2013). Mobilization of Muslims for Jihad: Insights from the Past and their Relevance Today. Counter Terrorist Trends and Analyses, 5(8), 10–15. http://www.jstor.org/stable/26351173. Pp.5-6.

9 The President Trump had alleged this. The Pew Reports however suggest that in survey the American Muslims did not justify any extremism and find their lives better in America than many of the Muslim countries. https://www.pewresearch.org/politics/2011/08/30/muslim-americans-no-signs-of-growth-in-alienation-or-support-for-extremism/, accessed on 15 December 2021.

10 See the Report; https://www.pewforum.org/2011/01/27/table-muslim-population-by-country/. Also See this Report; https://www.pewresearch.org/fact-tank/2017/04/06/why-muslims-are-the-worlds-fastest-growing-religious-group/, Accessed on 15 December, 2021.

11 https://cf2r.org/foreign/tablighi-jamaat-and-its-links-with-islamist-terrorism-2/, accessed on 12 dec 2021.

CHAPTER 1

ISLAM AND ITS EXPANSION IN INDIA

VERY FEW IN India outside the Muslim community knew about the Tablighi Jamaat and Maulana Saad prior to 26 March 2020. Covid-19 virus was spreading its tentacles and everyone was worried how to control it. Nation awoke to shocking news that nearly thousands of Tablighis housed in a Markaz at Nizamuddin in Delhi were not ready to leave the place, and the police, instead of forcefully flushing them out to prevent spread of Covid-19 were persuading them to leave. Probably, Markaz, Maulana Saad, and the Tablighis were making headlines in the news media on such a scale for the first time in the country.

The Tablighis had assembled for a religious congregation at the Markaz which was fixed long back in their calendar.[1] On 26 March 2020, Narendra Modi, the Prime Minister of India declared a national lockdown in wake of the rising threats of the Covid-19 Virus.[2] The sudden announcement brought the country to a standstill. People were expecting measures of this kind but the date and scale were unknown. The number of people affected by Covid-19 was increasing every day. Insecurity had gripped people. None knew what would happen tomorrow. Delhi by then had registered 200 cases.[3] Maharashtra too had witnessed 200 cases and other Indian cities were also moving in the same direction. The day the Prime Minister announced the nationwide lockdown, 800 cases had already been identified in India.[4] Many countries of Europe were facing mounds of dead people whose numbers were rising exponentially day after day. Italy, France, and Spain had already declared national lockdown and United Kingdom was on the way to it. India had started evacuating its students and citizens from Wuhan in China as also from other countries.[5]

The news of Markaz and such a large gathering of people, when caution was needed, stunned the country. Far more disturbing were the videos which showed the police evacuating the Jamatis in the buses for medical examination, and the latter spitting[6] on the roads from the windows of the bus, violating all norms of civilized behaviour. When every section of the society was asked to follow Covid protocol that prevented get together of people, how could these people gather in such large numbers was the question that everyone was trying to ask the government. It fuelled the possibility of spreading Corona faster than expected. Media coined the term 'Corona Jehad' to describe 'intentional violation and then making attempt to spread the disease.'[7] This became a talking point everywhere.

Then came a video in which the Amir of Indian Tablighi,

Maulana Saad, was seen and heard dismissing any such threats from Corona and telling the activists and preachers assembled at the Markaz that 'if death had to come there could not be a place better than the Masjid where they had gathered?'[8] It was horrendous and defied sanity and as expected led to widespread protests in the media and public sphere. People started questioning the role of both the central and the state governments. The question was why did the central government under which Delhi police works allow such events to take place? Such congregations are generally not without knowledge of and permission of the police. Similarly, the question to the state government was that how could the district magistrate which works under and report to the state government did not act in time? Why did the district magistrate not act against the organisation in time? One after another several videos and official notices intended at shifting the blame between the BJP and the state government started coming out in the public.[9]

The government of Delhi issued a press note on 16 March 2020 in which it prohibited opening of gyms, spas, swimming pools, malls, cinema halls till March 31. It also directed to prune social, cultural and religious gatherings limiting the number to 50 except during marriages.[10] Delhi government, however had no answer why it did not activate the district administration headed by district magistrates in each district including Nazimuddin. The three-day (13-15 March) Markaz was in full knowledge of the state government. The central government had issued an advisory to all states on 6 March 2020 asking them 'to avoid or postpone mass gatherings till the pandemic was contained.'[11] But the state government did nothing 'except issuing an order on 13 March prohibiting the assembly.'[12]

Then came a video of Delhi police in which the inspector of the police station was seen and heard talking to the representatives of the Markaz asking them to vacate the place, else he would be constrained to take action as per the laws.[13] He was also seen formally handing over the letter to Jamatis to this respect. The video taken on 23 March 2020 had the inspector saying that 1500-2000 people always remained congregated at the Markaz despite all warnings. The Markaz people also admitted the stay of 1000 Jamatis there.[14] There was more an element of caution and persuasion in the language of the police inspector to the Jamatis against the possible threat from the Corona virus. Media reports suggested that the Tablighis from different countries had attended the Markaz. The Jamaat denied this in the beginning. It informed the police that those who attended the Markaz included people from Lucknow, Banaras and Kanpur etc. and that there were no foreigners. This however, later on, proved wrong.[15]

Amidst all these, news came that Maulana Saad, head of the Markaz, was not ready to vacate the premises and finally, as rumours swelled, the national security advisor of India, Ajit Doval, had to walk down to the Markaz to persuade him[16]. Maulana Saad left the place in the middle of the night for an undisclosed destination. More than a year has passed and there is no clue on where the Maulana has been hiding. From 30 March to 15 May 2020, he issued several voice-recorded statements and messages to his followers. First, he said he was under quarantine and would soon come out.[17] He requested the Tablighis to maintain social distance and follow the government's instructions and cooperate with the doctors and Corona warriors in their fight against the deadly virus. Then came the statement that he had undergone Corona test and the result was awaited.[18] In response, Delhi police served a notice to him seeking response to detailed queries. The Maulana replied that he would file the reply after he would come out of the quarantine and the lockdown would come to an end. But he gave the interview to a Hindi channel Aaj Tak through Skype without revealing his destination.[19]

In the meantime, the Tablighis who had attended the Markaz reached different parts of the country. Many of them went into hiding in mosques and Muslim density areas.[20] It took almost months for the police in different states to detect them and put them under quarantine. But this allowed the virus to multiply the victims at the rate of the geometric progression. Finally, the government of India admitted that out of the total cases, nearly one third were contributed by the Tablighis. Lav Agarwal, joint secretary in India's Ministry of Health, told reporters "Our doubling rate is 4.1 days at present. But had the incident of Tablighi Jamaat not happened, then the doubling rate would have been 7.4 days."[21] In some of the states like Tamil Nadu, 95 per cent of the spread was due to the Tablighis.[22]

It is still baffling why the Tablighis did not come out in open to cooperate with the government and administration? Why did they go into hiding despite public warnings and massive information campaigns and public outrage against them? Their actions of spitting in public were read as deliberate attempt to spread the virus. Media and critics termed it 'Corona Jehad.'[23] Jehad in common sense is a war of Muslims against the infidels. And infidels are those who do not believe in the Quran and the belief that the Prophet is the last messenger of God. Were the Tablighis deliberately acting to spread the disease in India? The behaviour of the Tablighis such as hiding in different parts of the country and their misconducts gave credence to such allegations.

The theological position of Islam against other religious beliefs added weight to it. The theology of Islam divides the world into Dar-ul-Islam and Dar-ul-Harab. Dar-ul-Islam is the land where there is rule of Islam. Dar-ul Harab is land of non-Islam and therefore a place for Muslims to go for Jehad, the holy war against the infidels. India for them is a land of Dar-ul-Harab (World of un-Islam). And creating problems for the infidels in the land of Dar-ul-Harab is also a part of the war against the enemy. It is not known whether the common Muslim on the street thinks in these terms, but the Deobandi and the Wahabi schools of Islam believe in these concepts. They do not believe in Ganga-Yamuna Tehjeeb, which reflect the tolerant cultural mix of Hindus and Muslims. They believe in both the superiority and purity of Islam.

In fact, the Tablighi movement was started in 1926 by Muhammad Ilyas al-Kandhlawi in Mewat region of India. Ilyas al-Kandhlawi was initially associated with the Deoband

School. But he soon parted ways to form the Tablighi Jamaat. It intended to counter the emergence of the very syncretic tradition which Muslims in India claim to be cherishing. He got this impulse when he found that the people who had got converted into Islam were not practicing the Islamic rituals in their day-to-day life. Instead, he saw them continuing with the cultural practices of their Hindu ancestors on occasions of birth of child, marriages and other Hindu customs. Kandhlawi realised that their conversion to Islam was not total and given the call of the Shuddhi movement of the Arya Samaj he feared that the converted Muslims and Christians might go back to their parental religion of Hinduism.

Kandhlawi came from the Mewat region where Muslims converted from Hindu Rajput community continued with their ancestral customs in many ways. He realised that unless the converted ones are completely coloured and drenched in the ideology and practices of Islam in totality it would be difficult to keep them away from their ancestral path. He thought of converting them into Puritan Islam. He worked on the strategy of developing a corpus of dedicated preachers who could go from city to city, village to village and preach Muslims about 'true Islam' and convince them to follow only the Islamic customs, rituals, conducts and even clothing. These preachers coined the slogan 'Oh Muslims, become true Muslims.'[24] They sought to convince Indian Muslims that the moral premises were on decline among the followers of Islam due to neglect of the religion's basic tenets. It was, therefore, important to propagate the true elements of Islam to its followers through the preachers. The Tablighi movement emerged from this thinking. It emerged from the Deoband School with far more focus on puritanism, rigidity and exclusivity.

The Deoband school of Islam represents the Hanafi School of Sunni Islam.[25] The school in India was started in in 1866 at the city of Deoband in Uttar Pradesh. It is argued that after the British occupied the seat of power in Delhi, the Maulanas patronised under the Mughals left for this destination where they started Dini School. In course of time, this school emerged as one of the leading Muslim seminaries of the world. Often Islamic intellectuals compare this with the one in Cairo in Egypt. The Deoband School founded a huge Madrasa to teach and train tenets of Islam to the young minds. In 1919, the school floated a political party Jamiat Ulema-i- Hind. The founders were Islamic scholars like Abdul Mohd Asim Sajjad, Qazi Hussain Ahmed, Ahmed Saeed Dehlvi and Abdul Bari Firangi Mehli etc. Mahmood Hassan, a leading Islamic scholar of that time was the mind behind it.[26] Jamiat Ulema-i-Hind actively participated in the Khilafat movement. But it broke into two factions in 1937.

The breakaway faction formed Jamiat Ulema-e-Islam which was formally established in Dhaka in 1940. It openly supported the cause of Pakistan and aligned with the Indian Muslim League.[27] After the Partition, people of Jamiat Ulema-e-Islam joined Pakistan but they remained in touch of the seminary at Deoband in India. In 2003, even the leader of Jamiat Ulema e-Islam, Fazal-ur-Islam was invited by the Deoband in 2003 to visit its seminary despite knowing it very well that Jamiat Ulema-e-Islam of Pakistan supported terrorists' activities in Kashmir and represented the hardliners in Pakistan who rant against India. The Jamiat Ulema-i-Hind always claims of supporting composite nationalism and cites its association with Mahatma Gandhi to buttress the point. However, it ignores the questions on Hanafi school of Islam which is fanatic and has been the mind and motive behind terrorist's organisations such as the Hakkani Network and the Taliban. The predominant perception about Deoband in South Asia is that it has turned out as to be a 'shorthand for extremists.[28] It is precisely because in most acts of terrorism, the Deoband has been the mind. Giriraj Singh, a senior cabinet minister in the Modi government, therefore, openly called the Darul Uloom of Deoband a 'Gangotri of terrorism.'[29]

In Pakistan, Deoband followers constitute almost 25 per cent of the Islamic population. That they are soft towards Islamic terrorism is known by the fact that the Deoband has never issued any Fatwa against any terrorist. On the contrary, they have come out to oppose any such rare fatwas issued by the Barelvis or the Shias.[30] There are over 26,000 Deobandi Madrasas in Pakistan and they have been supplying the workforce to terrorist organisations in almost all parts of the world. In India also, there is hardly any city where there is no Deoband seminary. From Mullah Umar, who was trained in a Deobandi Madrasa along the Pakistan-Afghanistan border, to Hafiz Sayeed, there is a long list of internationally known terrorists who are products of Deobandi seminaries. Though the Deoband in India dissociates itself from violence, the Indian intelligence and security forces have arrested several extremists from Deoband at Saharanpur in connection with terrorists and violent activities.[31] Maulana Asim Umar, known as Sana-ul-Haq and chief of Al-Qaeda in the Indian subcontinent, who was killed during a US-Afghanistan joint operation in Helmand province, was a resident of Sambhal in Uttar Pradesh and student of Deoband's Darul Uloom. He left India in 1995 to join Harkat-ul-Mujahideen and remained in Pakistan and Afghanistan.[32]

Deoband Islam is very popular among Pashtuns on both sides of the Durand line that divides Afghanistan and Pakistan.[33] The Deoband in India holds that it teaches love and peace, and does not preach fanaticism. But it fails to answer how come the same school have different interpretation of Islam in different countries. It is pertinent to note that all the branches of Deoband seminaries in Pakistan and Afghanistan follow the same core components of the syllabus taught at the Deoband in India. Deoband imparts religious education and focuses on the correct interpretation of the Islamic laws, Islamic Jurisprudence (Sharia) and the Hadith, which are the sayings of the Prophet. The Deoband movement claims to preach puritan form of Islam and it hates the Barelvis and others who talk of syncretic traditions. They also do not like the Sufi traditions. For them, Sufis are Kafirs. The Tablighi movement also talks of preaching the puritan form of Islam and appeals to Muslims to follow the same Islamic practices in their lives, and conducts that were practised at the time of the Prophet.

All Islamists who have taken to terrorism, claim to have

been inspired by the ideology of pure/puritan Islam that was taught at Madrasas; either of Deoband or Salafi School or Wahabi school or Tablighis and their preachers. This applies as much to the Boko-haram in South Africa as to Al-Qaeda, Jaish-e Muhammad, Hizbul Mujahideen etc. operating respectively from Afghanistan and Pakistan. For these organisations, interpretation of impurity in Islam includes the cultural pollution from the West to the political dominance of the latter. And therefore, they justify violence even against the moderate Muslims on the ground that it is intended to establish the rule of pure Islam. In other words, even those who practice Islam become targets of terrorists who have their own interpretation of the faith and consider that their interpretation is the true interpretation of Islam.

Whenever there is an Islamic terror attack against the moderate sects of followers of Islam such as Shias and Ahmadian or other religionists, some Muslim intellectuals often decry and dismiss these as un-Islamic. When 9/11 happened, the clerics in the US declared that it was non-Islamic. There were moderate Muslims who wrote in appreciation of America and criticised the attacks.[34] Many of them were disturbed due to possible insecurity and uncertainty that emerged from this terrorist act. But there was also a section of people who appreciated it.[35] They offered political and emotional explanations for the attacks. For them, America hates Muslims and the Muslim world as evidenced in the US policy towards Israel and the Muslim world, the US presence in Saudi Arabia, attack on Iraq etc.[36] And the attack was the demonstration of accumulated anger of

Muslims. This was not unusual as rationalisation of violence using the logic of victimhood and emotional explanations have been a predominant pattern all over world by most Islamists. For every act of violence, they use this hypothesis to offer justification whether it is in Kashmir in India, Jinjiang in China, Chechnya in Russia or blasts in London metro.

Islamic theologians often argue that Islam is a religion of peace and that violence is not integral to and core of its spiritual ideology and that Jehad (holy war) is not about killing others, it becomes important to understand what is puritan Islam or correct Islam. It becomes far more compelling because Islamic terrorism and terrorist activities are intended either at establishing the rule of Islam where it is not and the rule of Pure Islam where Islamic rule is already there but not implemented in true spirit according to their interpretations. As there are several schools and shades of Islam, it is significant to know which of them become source of inspiration for the terrorists. This understanding becomes all the more important because Islamic tenets also prescribe and define how its followers should conduct themselves Vis-a-Vis followers of other religions. It introduces the concept of Kafirs, Mushrik and infidels for non-Muslims, and prescribes punishment for them. And that is what makes it hostile to the 'others.' Interestingly, none of the Indic religions or their scriptures make such directives for its followers against followers of other religions.

Despite differences, three components are common to all Muslims, irrespective of the cult that they follow and the school they belong to. These three components are the

Quran, the Hadith and the Shariah. The Quran or Koran is the most important scripture which all shades and schools of Islam treat as sacred and divine. The Quran is a Persian term whose literal meaning is recitation or reading. It is a collection and compilation of divine message that Prophet Muhammad received from Gabriel, the messenger of the Allah, from time to time during his life. He had started receiving such messages at the age of 40 (22 December 609 CE) and continued receiving these till his death in 632.

For the benefit of proper understanding, it needs to be put across that the Quran was not compiled during the life of the Prophet. The Prophet uttered the divine messages as and when he received these. His companions used to either record them or memorise them. They put together these verses in the form of Quran after death of the Prophet. There are, however, multiple narratives to it. One school says that on compilation of verses, contradictions were observed between the oral and written records but these were sorted out subsequently at a meeting held in Medina. Another school suggests that the contradiction was not on verses but on their recitals as different people recited the same verses differently. This was leading to confusion and therefore Uthman or Usman, the third Caliphate, after death of second Khalifa, Umar ibn al-Khattab, constituted a 12-members committee to give finality to the Quran.[37]

It is said that when the compilation concluded, Uthman burnt the other versions to avoid confusion, and thus the Quran the way we see today came into existence. There is also another story to this. It is said that Ali who later on became the fourth Caliphate had also assembled the verses and sent to Medina within six months of the death of the Prophet. This was rejected by a large number of people as it differed from Mus'haf (collected written Sheets of verses of Quran) gathered later during the times of Uthman. This was different from the Quran which came into existence during Uthman times. However, there are also those who believe that Quran existed in written form even at the time of the Prophet. It needs to be recorded that Uthman or Osman who was born in Mecca and belonged to the Quraysh tribe was also the son-in-law and companion of the Prophet. Uthman or Osman played a significant role in the expansion of Islamic empire. Uthman was also the brother-in-law of Rashidun another son-in-law of the Prophet, as he was married to Fatimah the youngest daughter of the Prophet.

The second text crucial to followers of Islam is the Hadith. It is the compilation of the Prophet's messages, actions and deeds recorded by his companions. Hadith that comes directly from the Prophet was also, like the Quran, compiled after the death of the Prophet. Hadith becomes the basis for Shariah, the Islamic law. The teachings of the Prophet that have been compiled in the Hadith is called Sunnah. Both the Shias and Sunnis consider teachings of the Hadith important because many times the Quran cannot be understood without the Hadith. Few hold that the Hadith in fact explains the details of what has been written in the Quran. For example, the Quran talks about offering prayers but how the prayer is to be conducted is mentioned in the Hadith. So, Hadith elaborates upon what is discussed in the Quran and therefore is considered as an important text in understanding Islam.[38]

The third is the Shariah. The literal meaning of Shariah is 'The way.' So, it shows the path to the faithful followers to conduct themselves. The Shariah is based on the teachings of the Quran and the Hadith. In essence, it represents Islamic rules which govern not only the religious matters but also the day-to-day life of the followers of Islam. This includes wide range of issues ranging from clothing to the length of beard and lending money to the use of products. In recent times there has been talk of Islamic banking and Islamic trade. In India, recently, news of Halal created a sensation throughout the country. As per this, several organisations have come up which certify the product with a mark that it is Halal i.e., it is according to the Islamic tenets. Earlier this Halal certification was done by the local religious bodies of the Muslims. But given the increasing trend in demands for Halal products in areas like garments and cosmetics, several countries have now come up with dedicated agencies to issue Halal certificates.[39] Over the decades, it has turned out to be the arm and instrument for Islamization of the World and is a form of Jehad. The idea is to use the Islamic population to produce the goods, certify them as halal and sell them to one and all. This is an attempt to run a parallel government. In recent years, Musawamah, Sukuk, Murabaha are the terms which have become known to the bankers and investment companies.[40] Even the Tokyo Stock Exchange started the Shariah index in 2007. The Shariah has always been a rallying and reference points for Muslims in all countries.

However, what constitutes of 'puritan Islam' or practice of true Islam is something for which no linear answer is discernible. Every school claim to represent the truth better than the other schools. For every school, the real essence of Islam is what is in consonance with its interpretations, and whatever is said beyond that is result of external interpolation. Though there are 72 sub-sects (Firake) within Islam but two sects which broadly represent Muslims across the globe are: the Sunni and the Shia. Therefore, a brief note on these two sects along with Sufi tradition becomes relevant to understand the ideological discourse and divides within Islam. The Sufi is a part of the Sunni tradition, but the latter does not recognize the former.

Sects within Islam and their Expansion

The Sunni sect of Islam comprises nearly 85-90 per cent of Muslim population in the world. They believe that the Muslim world should be governed by consensus (Ijma) through an elected head of the state, the Khalifa, according to the democratic principles. Therefore, after the death of the Prophet the system of Khalifa/Caliphate got started.

The Prophet had left no instruction who would succeed him. His death created a vacuum, and the two competing claims came out. Since he had no son, the choice was restricted between Ali and Abu Bakr. Ali ibn Abi, popularly known as Ali, was the Prophet's cousin and also son in law as he was married to Prophet's younger daughter Fatima. Abu Bakr was the Prophet's father-in-law. He came from the Quraysh tribe of Mecca and his younger daughter Aisha was married to the Prophet. Being father-in law, he was also very close to the Prophet who chose him to accompany him to Medina where the prophet spent his last leg of life till June 632 AD.

Ali's supporters wanted him to be declared as the first Caliphate after death of the Prophet. But Abu Bakr with support of elderly and early Muslims managed to get himself designated as Caliphate in a meeting at Saqifah in Medina. This was done in the absence of Ali who was busy in the last rites of the Prophet's body. This was not liked by Ali and his followers who wanted Ali to lead the Muslim world. This resulted into strained relations between Ali and Abu Bakr. It is also charged that the followers of Abu Bakr even had barged into the house of Ali and threatened to burn down the building he was housed in. The followers of Abu Bakr forced him to declare his allegiance to the first Caliphate.[41] This succession tussle created a rift within the Muslim community which got divided into Ali and Abu Bakr camps. Abu Bakr remained Caliphate for little over two years, and died due to illness. It was only during his period that the Quran was compiled in written form after many reciters of Quran had died in in the battle of Yamama, a region of today's Saudi Arabia in December 632.[42]

Abu Bakr was succeeded by Umar-I who was further succeeded by Uthman. Uthman was succeeded by Ali, the son-in-law of the prophet. Ali became Caliphate in 661 AD. Though the periods of the four Caliphates are treated as the 'golden period' by Muslims, the fact is that this period was marked by war and violence. During this period, the successors of the Prophet remained engaged in war in Syria, Jordan, Palestine and Iraq, and conquered all of them.[43] 'Egypt, North Africa, Armenia, and Persia' followed the same. Control of Egypt was taken from the Byzantine Empire in 645 AD.

Nowhere, Islam reached as a spiritual force. It was imposed after military conquests. In fact, all the tribes under the control of the state of Medina revolted after the death of Prophet Muhammad. This further proves that those who had accepted the suzerainty of the Prophet had done so not because of their conviction but due to fear of military invasions and conquests. The Caliphates had to enter into battle to suppress the political and religious rebels.[44]

Umar-I had become Caliphate in 634 AD and remained so till November 644 AD. Major military conquests were initiated and completed during his leadership which included Mesopotamia and Syria. He also initiated the conquest of Iran and Egypt. Umar-I was instrumental in convincing the Muslims of Medina to accept Abu Bakr as the Caliphate. Initially he was opposed to the Prophet but later on accepted Islam in 615 AD and accompanied the Prophet to Medina. He also got his daughter Hafshah married to the Prophet in 625 i.e., seven years before his death. In this sense, Umar who became the second Caliphate was also the father-in-law of the Prophet. Umar-I was assassinated by a Persian Christian Abu Lu'lu'a Firuz. His successor Uthman was also assassinated. It must be noted that all the three Caliphates actually followed Quran and Sunnah of Hadith and they formed the Sunni school of Islam.

It was after assassination of Uthman that Ali become Caliphate of the Muslim world. It is his followers that are known as Shia. He is respected by both the Shias and Sunnis because he was cousin as well as son-in-law of the Prophet. When Muhammad had lost his father, it was Ali's father who had looked after him. Ali's father was a trader and Sheikh of Banu Hasim, a powerful branch of the Qadisiya tribe to which Ali's mother Fatima Bint Asad belonged. Therefore, Ali is also treated as descendants of Ishmael, the son of Ebrahim or Abraham. It is said so since Ali was born inside the Kaaba, in the city of Mecca and Muhammad was the first one to see him after his birth.

Ali stayed with Prophet Muhammad from his childhood. He was just five years when the Prophet brought him home to stay with him. The Prophet was then married and living with his wife Khadija. Ali was just nine when Muhammad declared himself to be the Prophet and propounded Islam as the new religion. It is said that it was Ali whom Muhammad had asked to gather 40 people to participate in a banquet ceremony at Banu Hashim. In the gathering the Prophet had revealed about his receiving of divine messages and asked if anybody was ready to come with him as his Wazir or deputy. But no one responded to his call. Rather one person in the gathering Abu Lahab interrupted the Prophet after which everyone left the banquet.[45]

But this did not deter the Prophet who again called a similar gathering in which he again made the same plea. This time again no one responded except Ali. From then onward,

Ali stayed like a shadow with him till the death. In 622 AD, Prophet Muhammad left Mecca for Medina since none was ready to accept him as a prophet in Mecca.[46] Meccan did not like him and he even survived an assassination attempt. It is said that it was Ali who had slept in his bed and this saved the life of Muhammad. Ali by then was married to the daughter of the Prophet, named Fatima Bint Muhammad. Ali's mother's name was also Fatima but her title was Asad, so she was Fatima Bint Asad. When Ali left for Medina, he took both his mother and wife along.

Ali was the Prophet's trustworthy confidant and accompanied him in all the battles for Islam except the Battle of Tabouk.[47] He emerged as a great warrior after the battle of Badr fought in Mecca in 624. In this battle, Ali defeated Walid ibn Utba, a great Meccan warrior.[48] He also played a major role in the battle of Uhud[49] in which most people in the army of the Prophet had fled in the wake of aggression from the other side. Ali, in fact, had protected the Prophet in this battle.[50] In the battle of Trench, Ali defeated the legendary Arab warrior Abd-al-Wud for which he earned the title of 'Lion of God' (Asadullah) from the Prophet. In 630 AD, Ali also defended Prophet Muhammad in the battle of Hunayn. Ali was instrumental in conclusion of the Treaty of Hudaybiyyah, a treaty between Muhammad and the Quraysh in 628.

Ali was also one of the few who was designated by the Prophet to note down the verses of Quran.[51] He was the key commander of the conquest of Mecca in 630 where on instruction of the Prophet he had broken all the idols worshipped by the Banu Aus, Banu Khazraj, Tayy and others. In 632, Ali was declared Maula by the Prophet before the Muslim gathering while he was on way back from Mecca at a place called Khum which falls today in Saudi Arabia.[52] Shias interpret this event as one in which the Prophet declared his successor. But Sunnis reject this interpretation. For them, it certainly demonstrates the close relationship between them but the same cannot be interpreted as a declaration of political and religious succession to the Prophet after his death. Sufis also differ from Sunnis on this count and for them this was the time when the Prophet had transferred the spiritual power to Ali. Therefore, for Shias, Ali was the first Imam. And for the Shia Sufis he was (Friend and Leader) *Wali*. Amidst this, there is also one school which argues that when this is said to have happened Ali was not with the Prophet but in Yemen for suppressing the political and religious rebels. And thus, they dismiss the whole narrative that the Prophet had declared Ali as his successor in his life time.[53]

Anyway, for long 24 years, Ali did not participate in any of the military expeditions for Islam, and kept himself engaged in taking care of his family which comprised of his children Hasan and Hussain and the wife Fatima Zahra. He did not participate in any of the political activities though he faced the charges of conspiring in assassination of the third Caliphate Uthman.

Although Ali was not the Caliphate, he was always an important figure in the Muslim community of Medina. Ali realised that he could guide the Muslim community as Imam without having the power and title of the Caliphate. He expressed his allegiance to all the Caliphates but his relations with all of them except Umar, the second Caliphate, was strained. He supported Umar in religious and political matters including the beginning of Islamic calendar Hijri. After the death of Prophet Muhammad, Ali and his wife Fatimah wanted custody of the property the Prophet had left behind, specially, the lands of Fadak and Khaybar. Fatimah also had argued with Abu Bakr on this but the latter refused to hand over the properties on the ground that the lands belonged to the Muslim community since the Prophet had no heirs.

Ali's relationship with Uthman or Usman was also not very good. He was unhappy with many of Uthman's decisions on political as well as religious matters, particularly the religious laws. The relations were strained also because Ali was contender for Uthman's position. The second Caliphate, Umar had kept Ali in the council of six members who were appointed to recommend the next Caliphate. Majority of the members were against Ali. Those who supported Uthman were Sa'd ibn Abi Waqqas and Abdur Rahman bin Awf. Both were cousins of Uthman. Also, Uthman was married to Abdur Rahman's sister. Even Umar did not lend total support to Ali. He gave the deciding vote to Abdur Rahman in case of a tie. Rahman offered that he was ready to accept Ali as Caliphate, provided Ali followed the footsteps of previous two Caliphates apart from following the Quran and examples of the Prophet. Ali refused to follow the two previous Caliphates. As a result, Uthman was designated as the third Caliphate.

As the third Caliphate, Uthman had appointed his family members and relatives as Governors. Ali dismissed all of them when he became the fourth Caliphate. However, the relatives of the third Caliphate refused to obey his order, particularly Mu'awiya I who was Governor of Levant, a place which currently is located on 'the European side of Istanbul' in modern Turkey. Ali was the Caliphate between 656 and 661. He also did not meet a natural death but was killed. He was wounded by a poisonous sword by Abd-al-Rahman ibn 'Amr ibn Muljam al-Muradi on 26 January 661, at the Great Mosque of Kufa in present-day Iraq. Two days after that, he died at the age of 59.

Muljam-al-Muradi belonged to the group which had revolted against Ali. The reasons for revolt were that Ali decided to enter into a negotiation with Muawiya after the battle of Siffin (an area near present Iraq and Syria border) which had eroded the authority of Ali and prepared the path for the rise of the Umayyad dynasty. Those who revolted against Ali were called Kharajites. Their position was that Ali should not have compromised with people who were against the Quranic injunctions. Ali, according to them, should have battled out Mu'awiya. The four Caliphates were called the 'righteous Caliphates' or Rashidun Caliphate but we all know how righteous they were and always engaged in war for expansion.[54] After the death of Ali, the Umayyad dynasty took over the reign of power.

The birth of the Shia sect is traced to the period when Ali was denied the position of Caliphate after the death of the Prophet. However, it culminated into the battle of Karbala in 680 AD in which Ali's son Hussain Ali along with his trusted companions were killed. Thereafter, a deep animosity and differentiation started getting sharpened between the Shias and the Sunnis as two different sects. After the death of Ali, his son Hasan Ali was declared as the next Imam or new Caliphate by followers of Ali. It happened because Ali had expressed this openly before his death. But declaration of Hasan Ali as a new Caliphate was not accepted by Mu'awiya, the Governor of Levon, who announced the war against Hasan and proceeded towards Iraq which then was the capital of the Caliphate. Instead of fighting against such tendencies Hasan entered into a deal and accepted Mu'awiya as the Caliphate. An understanding was reached between them that the latter would hand over the position of the Caliphate to Hasan after death and not transfer the same to his son.

Mu'awiya accepted this but broke the accord before his death. He designated his son Yazid to be the successor in 676 AD which angered Hussain, the younger brother of Hasan. Mu'awiya had converted the Caliphate into Kingship. Finally, the armies of both Yazid and Hussain met at the battle of Karbala, which is in Iraq, in which Hussain was killed. This happened on 10 October 680 AD. This day is commemorated by the Shias as the 'Day of Ashura' which marks the sufferings and sacrifice of Hussain. This is called Muharram in which the followers of the sect beat their chest to mark their solidarity with Hussain. From here up to a couple of centuries, the Umayyad dynasty ruled the Muslim world and looked towards territorial expansion.

A brief history of Islam thus explains how the two sects of Islam emerged. This understanding is important because these two sects largely shape Islamic discourses in the world. The trajectory of these developments suggests how Islam evolved as a political religion and expanded through continuous military expeditions. It was not the spiritual strength which brought the Arab and its adjoining areas under its influence but the military raids which had become the order of the day in the Islamic world. All the Caliphates were engaged in the military raids and territorial expansion of Islam. They all fought for power and they all met the fate of protests and rebellion. It was not an easy, peaceful and argumentative discourse which made Islam a religion of Syria, Jordan, Egypt, Iran, Iraq, Yamen, Saudi Arab and many other countries of today's Africa and Asia but the military conquests. It had started with the conquest of Mecca in 630 AD under the leadership of Prophet Muhammad and continued for centuries even after his death.

A new thinking in Islam emerged sometime in the 12th century which focussed less on the traditional prayer system and more on spiritual dimension and inward meditative journey of individuals in pursuit of connecting to the almighty. The followers resorted to devotional music and singing praise of the Almighty akin to the Bhakti movement of Hinduism in India. It was Sufism which brought in a moderate form of Islam to the world. It was unlike the rigid iconoclastic monotheism of conservative Islam. In many places, it accommodated even prophets of other religions and other sects. For example, Indian Sufis accommodated even Hindu gods in their singing.

This made the Dargahs and Majars of the Muslim saints to be more acceptable to Hindus who were liberal and tolerant of other faiths. There are thousands and thousands of Hindus who visit Ajmer Sharif and graves of 10th century Muslim saint Nizamuddin Aulia every year. Scholars of Islam do not consider it as a separate sect but a separate order. This distinction between these sects and the order however is not very relevant for the common man for whom it was a moderate posture of Islam instead of exclusivist Islam of the Prophet and the four righteous Caliphates. Though there is no agreement among scholars as to when and how Sufism emerged, it is agreed that both Shias and Sunni endorse this order. Hardliner Sunnis, however, are against Sufi cult of Nizamuddin in India.[55]

Sufism traces its origin to ascetic life of the Prophet and it departs from the puritan Islam in many ways. It uses devotional music praising the saints and peers, something which traditional Islam does not permit. Like every honest Muslim they commit to five things; belief in one God, Allah, faith in the Prophet as messenger, offering Namaz or prayer five times in a day, doing charity and going for Hajj. Contrary to the common perception which holds that Sunnis are far more rigid, fanatic and violent compared to the Shias, Sufism is more prevalent in Sunnis than in Shias.[56] The Sufis are known as Tasawwuf among Muslims. There are several orders of Sufis-nearly 12 and most of them belong to the Sunni sect. Among the Shias it is called "Tariqa." The spiritual leaders or the saints who inspire and guide them are called 'Murshid.' Sufism unlike the extremist form of Islam does not demonstrate animosity towards other sects or religious beliefs.

Sufi traditions are not homogenous. They differ from country to country and even from region to region within the country. There is hardly any country where this order of Islam does not exist. In the West, the most known 'Tariqa' is the Mevlevi order in which people perform dance in a specific order in devotion. Their logic is to feel and enjoy in devotion which is possible when you have undergone through and realised the self-purification. This order is found in Turkey also. Sufis believe in the Sharia but their focus is on internal purification and raising the individual consciousness in order to connect with the divine. It believes in daily remembering of the God which is called Dhikr. Though Sufism travelled from Africa to Europe to America it makes India a unique place because it is the home of nearly all orders of Sufism.

Islam in India

Islam reached India in 711 AD with the conquest of certain regions of Sindh and Multan by Muhammad Bin Qassim who defeated king Dahir. Muhammad Bin Qassim was an Arab general serving for Umayyad dynasty under the direct command of Al-Hajjaj. The Umayyad dynasty was the ruling dynasty of the Islamic world after the death of Hussain who was beheaded in the battle of Karbala. The capital of the Umayyad dynasty was Damascus unlike Medina which was the capital of all four Caliphates up to Ali. The Umayyad dynasty ruled the Islamic empire for almost 100 years before it came to be replaced by the Abbasids in 750 AD. The Umayyad dynasty is also said to be the second Caliphate tradition. The first had started with Abu Bakr and ended with Ali. Thus, the victory of Muhammad Bin Qassim over Raja Dahir, who was a Brahmin, extended the Islamic Caliphate Empire up to North West of the Indian kingdoms. Both Sindh and Multan today fall in Pakistan. Raja Dahir was killed in the battle. Others who resisted were also killed mercilessly and their wives and children were sent to the service of Al-Hajjaj.[57]

It will be interesting to note that Muhammad Bin Qassim was not the first to attack India. Earlier also, Arabs had attacked but they were pushed back. During the Uthman period, Al-Hakim ibn Jabalah al-Abdi, who was close to Ali, had attacked Makran in the year 649 AD. After Ali became the Caliphate, his two commanders, Harith ibn Murrah al-Abdi and Sayfi Bin Fasayl' al-Shaybani also attacked Makran in 658, though they did not succeed. Interestingly, when the Umayyad dynasty started torturing the Shias in the empire, many of the Shias took refuge in Sindh and Multan, including the families of the Prophet to save their lives and stay in peace. Arabs also had tried to attack India using naval routes through 'Thana, Broach and Debal (Modern Karachi) from 634 to 637 AD.'[58] It was after the failure through the naval routes that they looked for land routes from the North-West side and Makran.

Often the conquest of Arabs of India is projected as a cake walk for the aggressors. But this is untrue and the facts speak differently. Invaders were defeated many times before Sindh and Multan came under their control. It took almost 70 years for the sword of Islam to test victory in India and initially they could subjugate some local kings only. They had almost a cakewalk in their conquests of the Arabs which they accomplished in just a few years. It had started from the Prophet's conquest of Medina and Mecca which soon extended to Syria, Egypt, Jorden, Yamen, Persia etc. Within few decades Islamic Zealots had 'captured' the whole of North Africa.[59] They could not retain this pace once they knocked the Indian borders with a mission to trample India. By the middle of the 8th century, they controlled 'only the highly garrisoned cities of Multan and Mansurah.' And even this was not achieved due to valour or superior military muscle but by exploiting the religious beliefs of the Hindus. Al Kazwin work *Asr-ul-Bilad* unveils interesting facts. It says: "The infidels have a large temple there, and a great Idol.... The houses of the servant and devotees are around the temple, and there are no idol worshipers in Multan besides those who dwell in those precincts...The ruler of Multan does not abolish Idol because he takes the large offerings which are brought to it.... When the Indians make the attack on the town, the Muslims bring out the Idol, and when the infidels see it to be broken or burnt, they retire."[60]

The Hindu resistance was ferocious. As a result, for another 200 years there was no attempt from the Arabs to attack India. However, Sindh and Multan conquest by Muhammad-bin-Qassim showed the path for other invaders and sowed the seeds of Islam on Indian soil. Muhammad Bin Qassim adopted the policy of punishment and rewards. He killed all those who resisted and refused to convert to Islam whereas favoured those who converted to Islam or pledged to work for it.[61]

Between the first conquest of Sindh and Multan in 712 and the first battle of Panipat in 1526 India faced attacks after attacks from Islamic invaders. I have used the word Islamic invaders deliberately because the same tools and methods were used in the war against India as the ones that were used by the Arab world to establish supremacy and expansion of Islam. The second major invasion was led by Mahmud of Ghazni. Ghazni was the capital of Kabul, presently located in South Afghanistan. Mahmud of Ghazni was the son of Subuktin, a Turk who had snatched Kabul from a Hindu king. Ghazni scored several victories in India including getting control over a portion of the Punjab. On the Western side, he reached up to Somnath in Saurashtra, present Gujarat, where he demolished the famous Somnath temple in 1026 AD. The violence and destruction that he inflicted on the people and places reflected the worst of barbarism and animality. Ghazni plundered wealth, killed Kafirs, demolished temples and enslaved countless people.[62]

By the time the Ghazni rule was about to weaken, there came another invasion from across the Western Indian border. It was invasion by Muhammad Ghuri (or Ghori or Gori) who had been defeated several times before his victory against Prithviraj Chauhan in 1192 AD. He started his adventures in 1178 and met several failures. In the first battle of Tarain, he 'was carried half-dead from the battlefield.' The legends suggest that he was reprieved and spared by Prithviraj Chauhan. Chauhan ruled the areas from what is known as Ajmer today and his empire comprised today's Rajasthan, Haryana, Delhi and small portions of Punjab, Madhya Pradesh and Uttar Pradesh. The folktales from *Prithviraj Raso* written by Chandbardayi and other texts provide the accounts of the war, though Western historians consider it exaggerated.

After Ghazni and Ghori, hordes of Islamic aggressors invaded and settled their rule in different parts of India. Hindus resisted, at times defeated the invaders and kept reclaiming the lost kingdoms in intervals but they never waged a united fight against Islamic invaders.[63] As a result, India underwent a chain of violence and destruction for over a thousand years from Muhammad Bin Qasim to Aurangzeb. All measures were undertaken to Islamise India. Cruelty against the Hindus became the order of the day. The killings and conversion of Hindus, destruction of their temples by the Sultans of Delhi Sultanate produced folklores of horrors and disdain in an average Hindu mind. Alauddin Khilji slaughtered 15,000 to 30,000 male Hindus in a day.[64]

Muhammad Bin Tughluq who is infamous for administrative mismanagement was a fanatic Islamist. Durant quotes a historian who notes that thousands of Hindus were killed by him.[65] Firoz Shah Tughluq, Sultan Ahmad Shah, Bakhtiyar Khilji...one after another inflicted death and destruction on India which finds no parallel in history. No wonder Bankim Chandra Chatterjee encapsulated the whole history of medieval India under the rule of Sultans as the chronicle of rape and plunder, killings and conversions, and defilement and destructions of Hindu temples.[66] Sita Ram Goel quotes Bankim extensively, I reproduce: "If I go by the lessons of history, we have to accept that Hindu-Muslim unity is a mirage. When Muslims first entered India, they looted the country, destroyed the temples, broke the idols, raped the women, and heaped innumerable indignities on the people of this country. Today it appears that such noxious behaviour has entered the bone-marrow of Muslims."[67]

Will Durant, an eminent historian summed up the Mohammedan conquest of India being the 'bloodiest story in history' and 'barbarian one.'[68] It was barbaric because unlike the conflicts between the Hindu kings where violence remained limited to the armies of the warring sides, Islamic invaders destroyed the buildings and temples, put the villages and cities on fire, forced people to change their worship styles and so on. India had never experienced such barbarism in its civilisational journey. For the Islamic invaders there was no observance of ethics in the war. The prime and driving motive was to win the kingdom for power and Islam. A historical account suggests that nearly 70 million people were killed in one thousand years of Islamic kingdoms in India.[69]

The killings in war in pursuit of political expansion have been common to all the conflicts in the history of human civilization. But the kind of destruction that was inflicted on India by the invaders and their forces deserves attention to understand the psyche which guided them in their actions. Explorations into the pattern of violence reveal without exception that the raiders were equipped with a kind of hysteria poisoned by Islamic belief that justified the killings of Kafirs and held it as a service to religion deserving praise and love of the Allah. The followers of Islam 'felt convinced that they were carrying the commandments of Allah while they invaded other countries.'[70] The history of Arab and Turkish invasion on India was different from earlier attacks of the Greeks and the Sakas, the Huns and the Kushans. They were political invasions and there were no motives and power of religion behind their expeditions. Therefore, their political conquests did not harm the spiritual and civilizational capital of India. They were ferocious in attacks and invasions but they did not go for demolishing temples, massacring people and converting people into the faith of the invaders.

Islam spread through Sword. It expanded in the Arab world through military conquests followed by mass conversion into Islam. It started with the Prophet and continued under the Caliphates and thereafter, the same pattern was followed in India too. When Muhammad Bin Qasim invaded India and established the flag of Islam on soil of Multan and Sindh, the war cry was Islam and Jehad.[71] The Prophet and subsequent Caliphates destroyed the shrines of other religions and forced their followers to choose between death and Islam. These invaders demolished temples, destroyed shrines and forced people of other faiths to take refuge in Islam. It continued for over one thousand years. Wherever they emerged victorious and as a dominant force, they did it without compunction and remorse. From Multan and Sindh in the North West to Bengal and Assam in the East, from Punjab and Kashmir in the North to Bijapur and Golkonda in the South, the swords of Islam flashed through the necks of the Kafirs.

Muhammad Bin Qassim who defeated Raja Dahir promoted

Hanafi school of Sunni Islam which today guide the Wahabi, the Deobandi and the Tablighis—the three which are largely held responsible for breeding the ideology of Islamic terrorism world-wide. The Hanafi school of Islam refers to Muslims as 'people of the Book.'[72] Hindus for them are Dhimmis. The Hanafi School is one of the four schools of the Sunnis. The other three are Maliki, Shafi'I and Hanbali. Hanafi is the most popular sect, and has the largest number of followers. This school focuses on words of the Quran, the Hadith and customs and traditions at work during the time of the Prophet. And as a true follower of this school, Muhammad Bin Qassim destroyed temples, killed Hindus and forced them to convert into Islam. In doing so, he followed the commander Hajjaj who wrote back to him "not to make distinction between enemy and the friend, give no quarters to infidels but cut their throats."[73] Hajjaj was the one who had ordered Muhammad bin Qassim to punish Raja Dahir who had saved Prophet's family.

Other Arab and Turkish invaders followed the same. Shiva temples at Somnath and Kashi, Ram temple at Ayodhya, Krishna temple at Mathura are few which are known to us because they became part of the political discourse in post-independent India. The truth is that there are thousand others which might not be as big and magnificent as the temples of Somnath or Kashi or Ayodhya but they met the same fate of destruction at the hands of Islamic zealots under the Muslim rule. Cities and temples that came on the way of these Islamic invaders lost their idols and structures along with followers. It is noteworthy why the 6th and 7th century magnificent temples in the South India[74] are found in plenty but it is difficult to find the same in Northern and Western India. It was not that the cult of temples was not in existence in the North. There were many magnificent temples but they were destroyed by Islamic invaders. The degree of destruction and violence varied from Sultans to Sultans, one Mughal to another but from Qasim to Aurangzeb this iconoclasm and forced conversion continued without exception.

The Shia component of the Muslim society in India has relatively been small in number and moderate in interpretation of Islam, though there are scores of examples where Shias also have been part of fanning fanaticism against Hindus.[75] And on many crucial issues they hold the positions different from the Sunnis. The Shias who follow Ali as their first Imam is also not a homogenous category. There are several sub-sects within it such as Zaidis, Ismailis, Usulis, Nizaris, Khojas, Mustalians, Dawoodi Voharas, Ahmadis etc. The Ahmadis and Bohras deserve further explanations because they have been targets of the Sunni sect. Sunni Islamic scholars do not consider them as Muslims at all, though both the Ahmadis and the Bohras claim to be followers of Islam. The Ahmadis are the Muslims who are found mainly in Pakistan. The Sunnis of Pakistan and India do not consider Ahmadis as Muslims. And therefore, we often hear stories of Ahmadis being persecuted in Pakistan. The Ahmadis are followers of Mirza Ghulam Ahmad of Qadiyan (1835-1908) who declared himself to be the last prophet. Both Sunni and Shia Muslims hate them because Qadiyan had challenged the premise that Prophet Muhammad was the last prophet. Similarly, Bohras are mainly found in Gujarat state of India. These Bohras are successful traders in Gujarat and they are not fanatic in their conduct. There is no case of members of Dawoodi-Bohras joining the extremist movement. It has also come to notice that the Shias are rarely found in violent and aggressive hostility towards the Hindus.

As far as the Sufis are concerned, they are generally treated as representative of the liberal syncretic tradition. As mentioned earlier, this impression emerged from the amorphous and wide-ranging Sufism which included localism in terms of customs and practices and adopted a few other practises such as meditation and devotional songs. But this did not mean that they were or they are for the composite culture or syncretic traditions. They were the foot soldiers of Islam which they never hid. They believed in the ideas and practices of the Sunni sect. A syncretic tradition is one which accommodates all prophets and all sects. This is not the case with Sufism. There is no example where a Sufi has given respect to the non-Islamic shrines or their prophets. The entire misconception has emerged from the Sufi music which at times includes even Krishna and Shiva in their devotional couplets. But these are later date entries to make the Sufi tradition look liberal and universal.

A careful examination of the Sufi order reveals some startling facts. First, they entered India with the Islamic state and they adhered to the Islamic principles of having faith in Muhammad as the last and the only prophet. Second, they have been following the larger tenets of Islam. Thirdly, they have been associated with both the liberal and fanatic traditions of Islam. Fourthly, they have acted towards Islamization of the Hindu society in areas of their numerical strength and influence. Though they associated with the devotional music which was not in practice in Islam but there are scores of examples which suggest them following the fanatic path of Islam.[76] One reason why all these have not become parts of the dominant discourse in the Sufi movement is because they have been seen to be largely avoiding violence and application of force to convert non-Islamic people into Islam. Secondly, in their devotional songs they are not seen to be as rigid and fanatic. Their claims of syncretic tradition could find better resonance if they had worked for promoting the common spiritual tradition and worked beyond the fixed precincts of Islam. Historical accounts don't endorse this.

There is no dearth of examples where Sufis saints planned conversion. The common perception is that the Sufis did not work for radicalisation in Islam or applied the concept of Kafir for Hindus. However, there are scores of examples which suggest that the Sufis prevailed on Sultans to use force against the infidels (Indic religionists) to convert them into Islam and force the followers of non-Islamic religions pay religious taxes. It happened in Kashmir and elsewhere. What we know today as Bangladesh can be credited to the Sufis who engineered mass level conversion of Hindus into Islam. Though Kashmiriyat is broadly defined as a combine of Rishi and Sufi tradition where the Sufis are not averse to Hindu idols and Hindu temples but facts suggest that Sufis did allure Hindus to convert. Hazarat Bulbul Shah who is considered as the first Islamic Missionary in

Kashmir was instrumental in converting a Buddhist Rinchana who came to be known as the first Muslim King in Kashmir. Rinchanawas was refused re-entry into Hinduism by the Brahmins of Kashmir.[77]

Kashmir witnessed mass killings and conversions of Hindus and destruction of Hindu temples and idols. Saifud-Din originally Suha Bhatta, was a Hindu and had converted to Islam under the influence of Syed Mohammad Hamdani, son of Hazrat Shah Hamdani, an Iranian spiritual leader. Under the influence of Hamdani, Saifud-Din unleashed terror and carried out wholesale destruction of idols and temples such as Martand Temple, Bijbehara Temple, Ishabar Temple (near Nishat Garden), Triphar Temple (at the foot of Mahadeva mountain) to name a few.[78] He imposed Jazia on non-Muslims and 'compelled thousands of Hindus to embrace Islam.' Those who resisted were killed. Muslim chroniclers have tried to twist history of violence by saying that the said spiritual leader was not happy with Saifu-Din but this is without any basis. Few other examples from other parts of India would help in understanding the mind of Sufis and their service to Islam.

Shah Waliullah was a Sufi and son of a known Sufi Shah Abdur Rahim who was employed by Aurangzeb for compiling Fatwa-i-Alamgiri, a text running in several volumes on Islamic jurisprudence. For Shah Abdur Rahim and his son Shah Waliullah, Sultan Mahmud of Ghazani had done a great service to Islam in India. Waliullah was pained to see the declining trend of the Muslim Raj in India after weakening of Aurangzeb and expanding political clout of the Marathas and Jats. He was so disturbed by the decline of the Mughals that in desperation he wrote to Ahmad Shah Abdali and requested him to attack India.[79] In his letter he said that if the situation continued people would renounce Islam. He called upon Abdali that it was 'his bounden duty' to 'invade Hindustan, to destroy the power of the Marathas, and to free the Muslims from the clutches of the non-Muslims.' He expressed hope that the Muslims would be freed from the stronghold of the infidels.[80]

Waliullah is rated one of the greatest theologians on Islam. He authored more than 71 books. He claimed to have received divine messages from the Prophet in the state of trance or in a meditative state. Waliullah is not the only Sufi who made the distinction between believer in Islam and infidels. Another Sufi Ahmad Sirhindi made it very clear that 'sharia prospers under the shadow of Islam.' He opposed giving high or equal position to the infidels as it would amount to an insult to Islam. He explicitly articulated these in his letters.[81] Sirhindi ridiculed Hinduism and criticised the allegedly liberal policy of Akbar towards Hindus.

Therefore, the dominant perception that Sufism presents a liberal syncretic tradition is far from the truth. All the Sufis worked for Islam. They all adored the Prophet and dictates of the Quran. Sufism cannot be and should not be read from music which is too insignificant to be attended to in the light of Qur'anic injunctions and direction from the Hadith. This cannot be ignored that destruction of Somnath and other temples were appreciated by many Sufis like Nizam al-Mulk Tusi, Sanai and Atar who drew a parallel with destruction of idols of the Arabs by the Prophet.[82] If Jamaat worked for puritan Islam, Sufis worked to initiate people into Islam by making it look more attractive. The movement thus was to entice people to come close to Islam through Sufism, become a Muslim and then the Jamaat would make you a true Muslims by teaching rigours of the faith.

These two sects and the Sufi order basically formed the teachings and guide for the followers of Islam in India ever since footprint of Islam touched the Indian soil. None of these sects and orders treated Hindus as equal. They all accepted Muhammad as the last Prophet superseding all other ones, the Quran as a revealed unalterable religious scripture and the Hadith being the roadmap for conducts and behaviour for every Muslim. Idolatry was condemnable and therefore deserved the wrath of Allah. Islamic invaders followed the same pattern throughout in their religious and political journey in India. First, they demolished places of religious worship of Hindus; second, they forced Hindus to convert into Islam or face death. Those who were considered liberal forced Hindus to pay Islamic tax Jizya. In brief, treating infidels as the enemy of Islam has been the theme common to all.

The increasing radicalisation of Muslim youths under the influence of the Deobandi and the Wahabi sects of Sunni Islam has adversely impacted the Shias, the Sufis, the Ahamadis and the Bohra traditions of the same faith. Their people and shrines have been at the receiving end in Islamic countries. The attacks have come from several extremist organisations such as the Islamic State, Hizbul Mujahideen, Al-Qaeda, Taliban etc.

The Islamic State killed 70 people and wounded nearly other 100 while bombing a 13th century ancient Sufi shrine, Lal Shahbaz, in the Sindh province of Pakistan when people had assembled there for a weekly devotional dance of Dhamal.[83] Often, the militant attacks in Pakistan on Shia Masjids and Sufi shrines are done by extremist Sunni organisations such as the Pakistani Taliban and the Islamic State. Inter-sect disharmony or infighting can be traced in all the religious traditions but the way it has taken toll on human lives in Islam can rarely be found in human history.

Those who compare the religious expansion of Buddhism and Hinduism with Islam to justify violence either reflect their innocence or cunningness. Buddhism spread with the message of peace, without a drop of blood being shed, whereas Islam splattered blood wherever it went. People resisted it everywhere but they fell to the power of the sword. Islam is a revealed religion. And therefore, it does not allow scrutiny of fundamental propositions of scriptures. As a result, it produces followers not seekers of the truth. The Truth has already been revealed. It fails to produce rationality and the tradition of arguments and counter arguments since faith is infallible. It makes Islam a static religion and seeks to pull its followers back to the times of Prophet Mohammad and the Caliphates.

References

1 'Questions Remain About How Delhi's Nizamuddin Became a Coronavirus Hotspot', The Wire, 31 March 2020, https://science.thewire.in/politics/government/delhis-nizamuddin-hotspot-coronavirus/, accessed on 10 April 2020.

2 Hebbar, Nistula. 'PM Modi announces 21-day lockdown as COVID-19 toll touches 12', The Hindu, New Delhi, 24 March 2020, https://www.thehindu.com/news/national/pm-announces-21-day-lockdown-as-covid-19-toll-touches-10/article31156691.ece.

3 'Coronavirus in India Highlights: Delhi reports 183 new cases in 24 hours; 154 belong to Tablighi Jamaat', Business Today, New Delhi, 10 April 2020. https://www.businesstoday.in/latest/economy-politics/story/coronavirus-india-live-updates-10-april-cases-deaths-count-lockdown-odisha-mumbai-delhi-254451-2020-04-10 Accessed on 10 May 2020.

4 'PM Modi announces 21-day lockdown as COVID-19 toll touches 12', The Hindu, New Delhi, 24 March 2020. https://www.thehindu.com/news/national/pm-announces-21-day-lockdown-as-covid-19-toll-touches-10/article31156691.ece Accessed on 10 May 2020.

5 Şencan, Irfan, & Kuzi, Semanur (2020). 'Global threat of COVID 19 and evacuation of the citizens of different countries.' Turkish journal of medical sciences, 50(SI-1), 534–543. https://doi.org/10.3906/sag-2004-21

6 'Tablighi Jamaat attendees misbehave with staffers, spit at doctors at Delhi quarantine units', India Today, New Delhi, 1 April 2020. https://www.indiatoday.in/india/story/coronavirus-india-tablighi-jamaat-attendees-misbehave-staffers-spit-doctors-delhi-quarantine-units-1662322-2020-04-01, accessed on 10 April 2020.

7 Desai, Shweta & Amarasingam, Amarnath (2020). *#CoronaJihad: COVID-19, Misinformation, and Anti-Muslim Violence in India*, Doi- 10.13140/RG.2 2.14215.62889.

8 'Neither leave mosques nor follow doctors' advice: Maulana Saad tells followers in audio tape', India TV, New Delhi, 31 March 2020. https://www.indiatvnews.com/news/india/nizamuddin-maulana-saad-audio-tape-advice-followers-mosques-coronavirus-603296. Accessed on 12 May 2020.

9 'Tablighi Jamaat: How did the government fail to detect a coronavirus infection hotspot?', Scroll, New Delhi, 1 April 2020, https://scroll.in/article/957891/tablighi-jamaat-how-did-the-government-fail-to-detect-a-coronavirus-infection-hotspot, accessed on 12 May 2020.

10 Akhef, Mohammed. 'Swimming pools, gyms, theatres to remain shut amid coronavirus.' The Times of India, 16 March 2020, https://timesofindia.indiatimes.com/city/aurangabad/swimming-pools-gyms-theatres-to-remain-shut/articleshow/74642017.cms, accessed on 12 May 2020.

11 Government of India-Ministry of Health & Family Welfare, https://www.mohfw.gov.in/pdf/SocialDistancingAdvisorybyMOHFW.pdf.

12 'Beyond the blame game: On the Tablighi Jamaat episode', The Hindu, Editorial, 2 April, 2020, Chennai, https://www.thehindu.com/opinion/editorial/beyond-the-blame-game-the-hindu-editorial-on-the-tablighi-jamaat-episode/article31230333.ece. Accessed on 14 May 2020.

13 'Covid-19: Delhi police releases video of March 23 warning over Nizamuddin Markaz', Hindustan Times, YouTube, 1 April 2020, https://www.youtube.com/watch?v=HcaSVvjDDjQ&ab_channel=HindustanTimes.

14 'Delhi Police video shows cops urged Nizamuddin Markaz members to vacate area', Hindustan Times, 1 April 2020, https://www.hindustantimes.com/india-news/coronavirus-update-delhi-police-video-shows-cops-urged-nizamuddin-markaz-members-to-vacate-area/story-zKNftKgzfJluFm85BZItwO.html

15 'Uttar Pradesh: Tablighi links shoot up count to 174', The Indian Express, 4 April 2020, https://indianexpress.com/article/coronavirus/uttar-pradesh-tablighi-links-shoot-up-count-to-174-6346545/, accessed on 15 May 2020.

16 'NSA Ajit Doval intervened to get Delhi's Markaz premises vacated: Govt sources', The Times of India, 1 April 2020, https://timesofindia.indiatimes.com/india/nsa-ajit-doval-intervened-to-get-delhis-markaz-premises-vacated-govt-sources/articleshow/74928442.cms, accessed on 15 May 2020.

17 'Missing Islamic Sect Chief Claims Self-Quarantine In Audio

Message', NDTV, 2 April 2020, https://www.ndtv.com/india-news/coronavirus-in-hiding-delhi-nizamuddin-islamic-sect-chief-maulana-saad-kandhalvi-claims-self-quarant-2204723, accessed on 15 May 2020.

18 I've undergone Covid-19 test, results awaited: Tablighi Jammat chief Maulana Saad, India Today, 25 April 2020, https://www.indiatoday.in/india/video/i-ve-undergone-covid-19-test-results-awaited-tablighi-jammat-chief-maulana-saad-exclusive-1670831-2020-04-25. Accessed on 20 October 2020.

19 In conversation with Maulana Saad, 24 April 2020, AajTak (Exclusive Video), https://www.aajtak.in/coronavirus/video/tablighi-jamaat-maulana-saad-exclusive-interview-aajtak-delhi-police-crime-branch-news-in-hindi-1057550-2020-04-24

20 'Over 500 Foreigners Who Attended Tablighi Jamaat Found Hiding in Delhi Mosques', News18, New Delhi, 4 April 2020, https://www.news18.com/news/india/over-500-foreigners-who-attended-tablighi-jamaat-found-hiding-in-delhi-mosques-2563791.html, accessed on 15 May 2020.

21 'Coronavirus doubling rate in India now 4.1 days from 7.4 earlier: Health Ministry', The Print, 5 April 2020, https://theprint.in/health/coronavirus-doubling-rate-in-india-now-4-1-days-from-7-4-earlier-health-ministry/395747/, accessed on 15 May 2020.

22 'Tamil Nadu is worst-hit by Tablighi Jamaat event, but also seeing men admit participation', The Print, 7 April 2020, https://theprint.in/india/tamil-nadu-is-worst-hit-by-tablighi-jamaat-event-but-also-seeing-men-admit-participation/396619/, accessed on 16 May 2020.

23 'How the coronavirus outbreak in India was blamed on Muslims', Aljazeera, 18 April 2020, https://www.aljazeera.com/opinions/2020/4/18/how-the-coronavirus-outbreak-in-india-was-blamed-on-muslims, accessed on 16 May 2020.

24 Stanly, Johny. 'Explained: Who are the Tablighi Jamaat?' The Hindu, 2 April, 2020, Chennai, https://www.thehindu.com/news/national/explained-who-are-the-tablighi-jamaat-the-organisation-at-the-epicentre-of-coronavirus-outbreak-in-india/article31238915.ece.

25 Hanafi School of Islam is one of the four legal Schools of Islam known after Abu-Hanifa who taught at Kafa in present Iraq around 767 AD. For details see; Warren, Christie S. (2013). The Hanafi School, Oxford Bibliographies. https://www.oxfordbibliographies.com/view/document/obo-9780195390155/obo-9780195390155-0082.xml#:~:text=The%20Hanafi%20School%20is%20one,Al%2DFiqh%20al%2DAkbar.

26 Khan, Ehtasham. 'Why did the Pak Maulana visit Deoband?' Rediff.com, 18 July 2003, https://www.rediff.com/news/2003/jul/17pak1.htm, accessed on 16 May 2020.

27 Pathak, Vishal, 'Century not out, Jamiat still bats for an India with a composite culture', The Hindu, 23 June 2018, https://www.thehindu.com/news/national/century-not-out-jamiat-still-bats-for-an-india-with-a-composite-culture/article24242019.ece

28 Mallet, Victor. 'Madrasas: behind closed doors', Financial Times, 30 0ctober 2015, https://www.ft.com/content/d807f15a-7db0-11e5-98fb-5a6d4728f74e

29 'Deoband is Gangotri of terrorists, produced Hafiz Saeed', says Giriraj Singh, India Today, 12 February 2020, https://www.indiatoday.in/india/story/deoband-is-gangotri-of-terrorists-produced-hafiz-saeed-says-giriraj-singh-1645666-2020-02-12, accessed on 15 May 2020.

30 Madrasas: behind closed doors, Financial Times, 30 October 2015, https://www.ft.com/content/d807f15a-7db0-11e5-98fb-5a6d4728f74e, accessed on 16 May 2020.

31 ATS of the Uttar Pradesh government arrested two Jaishe-Muhammad Islamic terrorists from Hostel of Deoband Seminary and recovered a lot of literature. See; https://theprint.in/defence/no-weapon-jihadi-literature-found-in-our-room-friend-of-jaish-operatives-arrested-in-up/200176/. Accessed on 23 October 2020.

32 Tripathi, Rahul, 'Maulana Asim Umar: Deoband's radical orator who tried to brainwash youths', The Economic Times, 10 October 2019, https://economictimes.indiatimes.com/news/politics-and-nation/maulana-asim-umar-deobands-radical-orator-who-tried-to-brainwash-youths/articleshow/71513518.cms, accessed on 16 May 2020.

33 Puri, Luv (2009). 'The Past and the future of Deobandi Islam, Combatting Terrorism Centre,' 2(11), https://ctc.usma.edu/the-past-and-future-of-deobandi-islam/, accessed on 17 May 2020.

34 Tamney, Joseph (2004). 'American Views of Islam, Post 9/11. Islamic Studies,' 43(4), pp. 599–630. http://www.jstor.org/stable/20837376

35 Musaji, Sheila (2002). 'Muslim reactions to September

11th, 'Islâmic Reflections 2002', https://web.archive.org/web/20021218024208/http://www.crescentlife.com/heal%20the%20world/muslim_reactions_to_sept_11.htm, accessed on 17 May 2020.

36 Geaves, Ron (2004). 'Who Defines Moderate Islam Post-September 11' in Greaves, Ron. Gabriel, Theodore, Haddad, Yvonne, Smith, Jane, Idleman (2004). Islam and the West Post9/11, Ashgate Publications, England, p. 62.

37 Razwy, Sayyid Ali Asghar, 'A restatement of the history of Islam and Muslims,' Uthman, the Third Khalifa of the Muslims, https://www.al-islam.org/restatement-history-islam-and-muslims-sayyid-ali-asghar-razwy/uthman-third-khalifa-muslims, accessed on 17 May 2020.

38 What are Hadith? *Whyislam.org,* https://www.whyislam.org/prophet-muhammad/hadith/, accessed on 17 May 2020.

39 Malaysia was the first country in the world which established Halal Industry Development Corporation in 2006. The UAE also formed agencies for the purpose in 2015.

40 Musawamah is a term used in Islamic finance. It describes a type of transaction in which the buyer does not know the price paid by the seller to create or obtain the good or service being offered. Under the rules of Islamic finance, various conditions must be met in order for Musawamah transactions to be permitted and to meet the standards required under Sharia law. These transactions are regulated under Islamic law; specific conditions must be met in order for a particular transaction to qualify. Sukuk is about the finance provider having ownership of real assets and earning a return sourced from those assets.

This contrasts with conventional bonds where the investor has a debt instrument earning the return predominately via the payment of interest (riba). Riba or excess is not allowed under Sharia law. Murabahah refers to a sale of a good or property with an agreed profit against a deferred or a lump sum payment. There are two contracts in Murabahah: the first contract is between the client and the bank, whereas the second contract is between the bank and supplier. The client (purchaser) orders a certain commodity through the bank, the bank then buys the commodity from the supplier and sells it to the client with specified profit whereby the client can make a lump sum or a deferred payment to the bank.

41 Madelung, Wilferd (1997). The Succession to Muhammad: A Study of the Early Caliphate. Cambridge, UK: Cambridge University Press.

42 The battle of Yamama was fought between the forces of Abu Bakr led by Ikrimah and Musaylimah who claimed prophethood in the region. There was also another commander of Abu Bakr who was defeated by Musaylimah.

43 "Islam as Religion" in E. Lundin and A. Lundin (eds.) Contemporary Religious Ideas, Evergreen, CO: Libraries Unlimited (1993), pp. 131-168.

44 Doak, Robin S (2009). Empire of the Islamic World (Great Empires of the Past). Chelsea House Publications. New York.

45 McManus, John, 'Have pictures of Muhammad always been forbidden?' BBC News, 15 January 2015. https://www.bbc.com/news/magazine-30814555

46 Shamsi, F. A. (1984). "The Date of Hijrah." Islamic Studies,

vol. 23, no. 4, Islamic Research Institute, International Islamic University, Islamabad, pp. 289–323, http://www.jstor.org/stable/20847277.

47 Tabouk is place where the battle between the army of Muhammad and the army of Banzyntine Battle of Taboukwas the last expedition/ battle/Ghazwa of the Prophet that occurred in the 8th month of the Hijri and 7th month of the lunar calendar.

48 Siddiqi, Aslam (1963). *Jih d, an instrument of Islamic Revolution*. Islamic Studies, 2(3), pp. 383–398. http://www.jstor.org/stable/20832700

49 Ghomari, Taibi. (2017). Title: Uhud, the battle of (625C), In. Islam: A Worldwide Encyclopedia.

50 'The Battle of UHUD: The second important war in Islamic history,' Zaahara.com, 29 August 2019, https://zaahara.com/blogs/writers-corner/the-battle-of-uhud-the-second-important-war-in-islamic-history, accessed on 5 June 2020.

51 Afsaruddin, Asma & Nasr, Seyyed Hossein. " Al ": Encyclopedia Britannica. https://www.britannica.com/biography/Ali-Muslim-caliph, Accessed on 5 June 2020.

52 Safvi, Rana, 'How interpretation of the word maula caused the Shia-Sunni schism', Dailyo.in, 7 October 2017, https://www.dailyo.in/lifestyle/prophet-mohammad-muslim-world-shia-sunni/story/1/19373.html, accessed on 5 June 2020.

53 Madelung, Wilfred (1997). *The Succession to Muhammed: A study of the early caliphate*, Cambridge University Press. Cambridge.

54 Sonn, Tamara (2009). *A Brief History of Islam*, Wiley-Blackwell.

New York.

55 Sunni Conference: Neither the Leadership nor the Imamat of Wahabi is accepted. Sunni News. 6 January 2010. https://sunninews.wordpress.com/2010/01/06/sunni-conference-neither-the-leadership-nor-the-imamat-of-wahabi-is-accepted/, accessed on 7 June 2020.

56 Ibid.

57 Ahmed, Nazeer. The Conquest of Sindh. History of Islam- An encyclopedia of Islamic History. https://historyofislam.com/contents/the-age-of-faith/the-conquest-of-sindh/, accessed on 8 June 2020.

58 Goel, Sita Ram (1982). *The Myth of Muslim Empire in India* in The story of Islamic Imperialism in India, p. 68. Voice of India. New Delhi.

59 Ibid, p. 69.

60 Ibid, pp. 69-70.

61 Kennedy, Hugh (2007). The Great Arab Conquests: How the Spread of Islam Changed the World We Live In. Philadelphia: Da Capo Press, Print.

62 'Invasions, Plunders, Loot and Cultural Disintegration: The Chronology of Islam's 800-year-old rule over India,' Organiser, 21 May 2021, https://www.organiser.org/invasions,-plunders,-loot-and-cultural-disintegration:-the-chronology-of-islam's-800-year-old-rule-over-india-1880.html, accessed on 25 May 2021.

63 Ambedkar, Babasaheb (1990). Pakistan or the Partition of India. Education Department, Govt. of Maharashtra. Dr. Babasaheb Ambedkar: Writings and Speeches (8), pp. 60-61.

https://mea.gov.in/Images/attach/amb/Volume_08.pdf

64 Durant, Will (2014). The Complete story of Civilization, Simon & Schuster.

65 Ibid.

66 Basu, Shamita (2002). Religious Revivalism as Nationalist Discourse: Swami Vivekananda and New Hinduism in Nineteenth-Century Bengal. Oxford University Press. New Delhi.

67 Goel, Sita Ram (1983). Muslim Separatism, Causes and Consequences, Voice of India, p. 97.

68 Durant, Will (2014). The Complete History of Our Civilization: Our Oriental Heritage, p.587.

69 Elst, Koenraad (2002). Negationism in India: Concealing the record of Islam, Voice of India.

70 Goel, Sita Ram (1983). Muslim Separatism: Causes and Consequences, Voice of India, p.32.

71 Balouch, Akhtar, 'Muhammad Bin Qasim: Predator or preacher?' DAWN, 8 April 2014, https://www.dawn.com/news/1098562, accessed on 18 May 2021.

72 Bearman, Peri, Rudolph Peters & Frank E. Vogel, eds. (2005). The Islamic School of Law: Evolution, Devolution and Progress, Harvard University Press. Cambridge.

73 Goel, Sita Ram. 'The Calcutta Quran Petition'-Chapter 6: Jihad in Bharat's History. Hindu Post, 21 April 2020. https://hindupost.in/history/the-calcutta-quran-petition-by-sita-ram-goel-chapter-6-jihad-in-bharats-history/, accessed on 19 May 2021.

74 Southern India relatively remained safe because the Islamic invasion could not be as powerful and long as it was in the North.

75 'Kashmiri Pandits offered three choices by Radical Islamists', Col (Dr) Tej Kumar Tikoo, Indian Defence Review, See more at Kashmir: Its Aborigines and their Exodus, http://www.indiandefencereview.com/news/kashmiri-pandits-offered-three-choices-by-radical-islamists/, accessed on 19 May 2021.

76 Sufis involved in fanning fanaticism against Hindus.

77 Ahmad, Aziz (1979). *Conversions to Islam in the valley of Kashmir*, Central Asiatic Journal, 23(1/2), pp. 3-18. http://www.jstor.org/stable/41927246, accessed on 19 May 2021.

78 See 'Glimpses of Kashmiri Culture', Vivekananda Kendra, Kanyakumari, June 1984. https://www.ikashmir.net/glimpses/doc/glimpses.pdf, accessed on 19 May 2021.

79 Goel, Sita Ram (1983). Muslim Separatism, Causes and Consequences, Voice of India, pp. 39-40.

80 Karthikeyan, Ananth, *'An Aborted Afghan.'* DNA, 26 November 2017, https://www.dnaindia.com/analysis/column-an-aborted-afghan-invasion-2562507#:~:text=Shah%20Waliullah%20wrote%20an%20impassioned,Sikh%20units%20harassed%20his%20army, accessed on 20 May 2021.

81 Letters and writings of Sirhindi have been compiled and produced in three Volumes. The letter no. 163 clearly mentions that the Jijya was introduced for humiliating the infidels/Kafirs/unbelievers. Letter No. 81 depicts cow-slaughter as the

noblest Islamic practices in India. For details See: Sita Ram Goel, Chapter 6.

82 Ahmed, Azaz (1964). Studies in Islamic culture in the Indian environment, Oxford: Clarendon Press, p. 79.

83 'At least 70 killed in Sufi shrine bombing in Pakistan', DW.com, 16 February 2017, https://www.dw.com/en/at-least-70-killed-in-sufi-shrine-bombing-in-pakistan/a-37589645, accessed on 19 May 2021.

CHAPTER 2

THE SCHOOLS OF TERROR IDEOLOGY

Wahabi and Deoband Schools

SUNNI ISLAM IN the last three hundred years has unravelled itself in several forms with several preachers and schools of thought across the world such as the Ahle Hadeeth, the Barelvi, the Wahabi, the Deoband and the Tablighi. These schools claim to propagate true Islam as preached by the Prophet and the first four righteous Caliphates. We will limit our discussion to the Wahabi, the Deoband and the Tablighi because these three schools have dominated the Islamic discourse in contemporary world. These are internationally known and have acquired a transnational dimension in terms of expansion and impact. While Wahhabism has Arab origin, the Deoband and the Tablighi have been born in India. Both the schools emerged in times when Islamic rule in India had started waning and Islam was in search of a new identity in the changed political-administrative dispensation under the British rule. These three schools deserve special attention since they have functioned as laboratories of Islamic extremism in the world. All notorious Islamic terrorists from Osama Bin Laden to Hafiz Saeed and Mullah Umar and thousand others have roots in either one or all of them. Similarly, most Islamic terrorist organisations in the world have linkages with these schools that serve as their ideological nurseries.[1]

Wahhabism as a school of thought in Islam emerged in Nejd, a remote and scarcely populated area in central Saudi Arabia. Its founder Muhammad Ibn ʿAbd al-Wahāb was a scholar and jurist who wrote several books on Islam. He advocated the Sunni cult of Islam and insisted on propagation of puritan Islam dismissing all the impurities that had come into practice in last several centuries. He disliked Muslims visiting the Majars and Dargahs to seek blessings of the Peers and the Sufi saints. For him, these were impurities since visiting the tomb or the shrines of the Sufis amounted to idolatry and accepting the supernatural power of saints. Such innovations (Bid'ah)[2] in Islam was unacceptable to him. He insisted on the return to the pure form of Islam inscribed in the Quran and the Hadith. Further, Ibn-Abd – Al – Wahab opposed any attempt to interpret the Quran to suit the changing conditions. This, he said, was distortion of the sacred message of Allah. He asked his followers to read Islam from the original text and spread the same across the world. This Wahabi school has emerged as one of the most conservative and radical schools of Islamic thoughts.

It all started with a covenant between Muh-Ulama Bin Saud and Muhammad Ibn ʿAbd-al-Wahāb under which they agreed to work jointly for emancipation of the states of the Arabian Peninsula from control of the Ottoman Empire and to try to unite them into one state. Saud was not a tribal leader but just a chief of an agricultural settlement near Diriyah. This covenant was concluded in 1744, and the same year the forces of Mohammad Bin Saud took control of Diriyah which is known as Riyad today, the capital of Saudi Arabia. In Saudi Arabia's history, this event is described as the first phase of evolution of the Saudi state and Mohammad Bin Saud is regarded as the founder of the Saudi State.[3] This was made possible because Muhammad Ibn ʿAbd al-Wahāb, who by then had emerged as a known theologian, called upon Muslims to wage a religious war (Jihad) against the Ottoman Empire and support Mohammad Saud. This theological and political relation subsequently transformed into family ties when when Wahab's daughter got married to the son of Muhammad Bin Saud. While Al-Wahab provided religious legitimacy to King Mohammad Bin-Saud, the latter helped Wahab spread the ideology of Islam which he called the most 'puritan form.' Al-Wahab advocated 'austere' practices which attracted the tribes who were his followers. As a result, the ideology of Wahhabism soon became popular in the state of Diriyah.

Muhammad-Bin-Saud died in 1765 after which his son Abdul Aziz bin Muhammad-Al-Saud, popularly known as Abdul Aziz took the reign and ruled the state till 1788. He had seven children: Prince Fahd, Abdul Rahman, Bandar, Badr, Sa'ad, Abdullah and Prince Abdul-Aziz of which Prince Fahd became the ruler as per the succession norm. Though the descendants of Muhammad Bin Saud finally took control of present Saudi Arabia in 1932, which was recognized by the United States in 1933, the period from 1803 to 1932 was marked with conflicts and turbulence.

In 1818, the Ottoman Empire regained its control over Riyadh and executed many religious, political and military leaders close to the Saud kingdom. The king was exiled. In 1902, Abd al-Aziz ibn Saud, who came directly from Muhammad Al Saud, made attempts with his brothers and cousins to win back Riyadh but failed. The Saud family regained its control only in 1924-25 with help of Ikhwan, a brave tribal leader. Abd al-Aziz ibn Saud with help of Ikhwan won many provinces including the city of Mecca and Medina. Ikhwan wanted to go beyond that and expand the empire but the king refused. Ikhwan revolted and was killed. Ulama supported the king's decision to kill Ikhwan. To consolidate the power and win the loyalty of the tribal groups Abd-al-Aziz ibn Saud married one daughter from each tribe and important clerics. The king had several wives but he could not keep more than four at a time in consonance with tenets of the Quran. This gave the king control over the two holy cities of Islam and the two most important mosques. This helped Saudi Arabia to influence the Islamic world.

Saudi Arabs under the leadership of Abd-al-Aziz-ibn-Saud sought to lead the Arab world, both in religious and political matters. In 1933, he established the organisation of oil-producing countries which later on turned into the Organization of Islamic Countries (OIC). He handed over the oil-producing areas to the American companies on lease. This was criticized by many clerics and Islamic leaders but the seat of Wahhabism endorsed it. The money generated was used to run the kingdom as well as to propagate Wahhabism whose impact was felt the world over.

In India too, the Wahabi movement emerged as a revivalist movement. The first to endorse this was Syed Ahmad of Raebareli. He was influenced by Shah Waliullah and his son Shah Abdul Aziz. Shah Waliullah belonged to the Sufi tradition but his interpretation of India as the land of Kafirs had led to controversy. Muslim and Left historians have tried to portray the Wahabi movement as anti-imperialism[4] but it had little to do with independence of India. It worked for the restoration of the seat of power of Islamic rulers who were dethroned by the British. The Wahabis depicted India as a land of Dar-ul-Harab and called upon to convert this into Dar-ul-Islam, a land of Islam. This school opposed Western education and talked about application of puritan Islam in the conduct of Muslims.

The Wahabi Islam divides humanity into three parts: Dar-ul-Harb, Dar-ul Sulah and Dar-ul-Islam. Dar-ul Islam means the land of Islam where Islam dominates and rules. All the countries where Muslim are dominant are the Dar-ul-Islam. Dar-ul-Harb is the land of non-believers in Islam which is also the land of war i.e., Jihad. Dar-ul-Harb has to be converted into Dar-ul-Islam. Dar-ul Sulah is the land which have signed agreement with the World of Islam for peace and non-aggression. The scholars of Quran are divided on the existence of such categorisation. They suggest that such divisions are not integral to the Quran. But there are others who say that the classical Islamic laws accept this division and its roots can be traced to the time of the Prophet who sent out messages 'to the Persian, Abyssinian, and Byzantine emperors' to choose between Islam and war.[5] There are also scholars who trace the use of the term after the Umayyad Caliphate failed to move beyond Spain in Europe. Notwithstanding the different age about the origin, the terms are in use and both the Wahabi and the Salafi schools endorse it. In fact, there is little distinction between them.

The Salafi School emerged in Egypt. Like the Wahabis, they also talk about returning to 'puritan Islam' as practiced during the times of the Prophet and three successive generations of Muslims. The Salafis take up these three generations from the Hadith in which the Prophet said that "the best of my community is my generation, the ones who follow them, and the ones who follow them." They were collectively called 'Salafs.' Thus, 'Salaf' included the Prophet and his companions, next their followers and then their followers. The Salafis like the Wahabis reject any innovation, dislike Muslims going to tombs and shrines, and preach strict adherence to the Quran and the Hadith. They strongly detest and despise the infidels (Kuffar or Kafir) and their value systems including visiting their countries. Salafi Islam seeks to return to the age of early Islam. Generally, it is divided in three categories; those who believe in austere life, don't participate in politics, hate the non-Muslim ideas and value system but don't participate in the war. Some call it Puritan Salafi. The second participate in the political activities and the third seeks and wages physical war against the non-believers. Majority followers of Salafi believe in the third principle.

There was a time when almost all countries of the Persian Gulf were dominated by Sunni Islam. However, 16th century onwards traditional Sunnism started losing followers to Shia sects, and several countries of the Gulf such as Iran, Iraq and Bahrain became Shia dominated. Though the Shia sect made inroads in other countries as well, including Afghanistan, Pakistan and Kuwait, the Sunni Islam continues to be numerically dominant the Islamic world accounting for 85-90 % of the total Muslim population.

Wahhabism can be treated as a stream of Sunni Islam closer to Maliki school of Islam. Maliki school of Islam is a school of jurisprudence founded by Malik Ibn Anas in 8th century. It considers the Quran and the Hadith to be the primary sources of Islamic jurisprudence and rejects the idea of innovation and interpretation. Critics of Wahhabism both within the Sunni and Shia sects consider that this school is based on wrong interpretation of Islam. They therefore, cannot be even described as schools of thought but a Firqua. It is important to note that Wahabis hate Shias whom the founder of the movement had declared to be 'non-believers.'[6] It is said that the founder of the Wahabi cult even permitted the killings of Shias.[7] It was this that recently motivated a Wahabi Sheikh of Saudi, Saad al Durihim, to issue Fatwa on twitter asking 'fighters in Iraq' to kill the Shias, including their children and women.[8] Though this was criticised in the Muslim world, it cannot be denied that the followers of the Salafi and the Wahabi schools have attacked several mosques of Shias and shrines of Sufis in different parts of the world. Pakistani Taliban's attacks on Shia Mosques in Peshawar in 2015,[9] bombing of Shia Mosques in Saudi Arabia in May 2015,[10] ISIS attack on Hazara community tuition center in 2018,[11] attack on Shia Mosque in Afghanistan in October 2017[12] are some of the most talked about cases in recent times. Such attacks and raids against Shias and their mosques are frequent in many Sunni dominated Islamic countries including Pakistan where Shias have to live in perpetual fear. Many parts of India have witnessed Shia-Sunni riots in the past.

Such attacks derive inspiration and strength from tradition and history. The second ruler of the first Saudi State Abdul-Aziz bin-Muhammad, who was also the son-in-law of the founder of the Wahabi school, had attacked Karbala with full force on 21 April 1802 and destroyed the tomb of Hussain Ibn Ali, the son of the Fourth Caliphate and seized valuable items like pearls, gold etc., besides killing nearly 2000 people.[13] This attack was led by son of Abdul Aziz bin Muhammad. This goes to suggest that despite the death of the founder of Wahhabism, the tyranny of the cult continued under the patronage of the royal family. They did not spare the people in the market and their homes. They looted everything they found and the son of Abdul Aziz distributed these among the soldiers keeping one fifth of the booty to himself.[14] Interestingly, the recent tweet of the Sheikh advocating that not all the Muslims would go to Paradise on the day of the Judgment but only the 'saved group'[15] of Najd reflected the influence of Wahhabism.

Saudi Arabia has emerged both as ideological and financial source of Wahabi Islam. When it opened the diplomatic consulates in different countries it appointed a team of clerics whose only job was to fund organizations that would establish Mosques and promote Wahabi Islam. The huge earnings from exports of oil and presence of both the holy cities of Mecca and Medina in its territory enhanced its political and religious clouts both in the Muslim world and the world outside. It established several hundred Islamic colleges, Islamic study centers and thousands of mosques and Madrasas (schools) in the country as well as in foreign countries including non-Muslim dominated countries.[16] The purpose was three-fold; to establish itself as the leader of global Islam, place its own state in favourable terms in the eyes of the Muslims, and to promote Wahabi Islam. Along with money, it also sent the Wahabi literature which was critical of other sects such as the Shias and the Sufis. This resulted into violence against the Shias and the Sufis in those countries. Indonesia is a glaring example of it. A country which has been known for its peaceful existence and also celebrating its cultural icons connected to Hinduism has started experiencing attacks on Shias and their religious establishments on grounds that this school does not represent the true interpretation of Islam.[17]

Saudi Arabia also reached out to other similar ideologies practiced under different names in different countries such as the Salafis and the Muslim Brotherhood in Egypt and the Jamat-i-Islami in Pakistan and India. There was a time (in

2012) when the Salafis, the major beneficiaries of the Saudi funds, were in de-facto control of the Egyptian parliament.[18] The Muslim brotherhood and its Freedom and Justice Party had emerged as a powerful force in Egyptian politics. Once, Egypt had taken upon itself the leadership of the Islamic world when it acted tough against Western powers on the issue of the Suez Canal. But military defeat of the Muslim world in war with Israel left them devastated and devoid of credible leadership. But entry of Petro-dollar in the economy of the countries of the Persian Gulf changed the whole scenario. Muslims workers from Pakistan, Egypt, Sudan, Iraq and other countries started coming to work in Saudi Arabia and when they went back, they returned with both money and radicalism of Wahabi Islam.[19] It gave strength to the extremist Islamic elements in these countries. It was the Muslim brotherhood that killed Anwar Sadat and made several attempts on life of Hosani Mubarak. It was despite the fact that Anwar Sadat had forged alliance with the Muslim Brotherhood. The entire Arab world benefited from the fund of Saudi Arabia but they also came under the grip of Wahhabism.

Saudi Arabia with the help of the CIA funded the Jihadists to fight the Soviet Union in Afghanistan. Thousands of Islamic fighters were sent to Afghanistan from Saudi Arabia including Osama Bin laden. The American government under the regimes of Jimmy Carter and Ronald Reagan took help of Saudi Arab to fund them and establish extremists' network in Afghanistan which could fight the Soviet Army present there. Most of the terrorist organizations today—be it the Al-Qaeda or the

Taliban derive their ideological premise and interpretation of Jihad from Wahhabism which goes essentially against the non-Muslims and softer versions of Islam.

Deoband and Islam

The second school which has impacted the ideological world of Islam the most is the Deoband Seminary of Saharanpur in India's Uttar Pradesh. Established in 1866, it was a revivalist movement which teaches the basic tenets of puritan Islam. Because of its conservative outlook, it is also called 'pink-Wahabis' in India. The Deoband follows the Hanafi School of Sunni Islam and for them the Shias and the Sufis are non-believers i.e., takfir.[20] Deoband's Islamic scholar Arshad Madani, who often hogs the limelight for his controversial statements, rejects Sufism as a part of Islam on the ground that there is nothing like this mentioned either in the Quran or the Hadith. In 2016, when the World Sufi Congregation was organized at the Ram Lila Ground in Delhi, Madani lashed out on the Sufi cult and refused to recognize it as part of Islam. Madani said "Sufism is no sect of Islam. It is not found in the Quran or the Hadith. How the Sufis are different from the rest of Muslims? Don't they follow the same Imam, Muhammad Rasulullah? Don't they follow the same regimen of five prayers a day? Don't they believe in the Quran? So, what is Sufism in itself? This is a thing for those who don't know the Quran and the Hadith."[21] He charged that the organization of Sufi congregation was intended to divide the Muslim community.

The Deoband does not have any better word for the

Shias. For Deobandis, the Shias are 'deviators' who have lost the path of true Islam. The Sunnis always seek to dominate the Shias and they use both their numerical and economic resources to outnumber and out-shadow the latter. There are scores of examples in which Deobandis have funded the Shias's mosques and the appointment of their clerics. But they do so to manipulate and bring such mosques under their control.[22] Deoband's followers do not like to be clubbed with Wahhabism because of the bad name the latter has earned due to involvement in terrorist activities. However, both Shias and Sufis preachers agree that the Deoband has created a chain of Madrasas in India in which they radicalize Muslim youths through preaching hardline Islamic principles akin to the Wahabis.[23]

Interestingly, the Deobandi School appreciates Shah Waliullah Dehalvi as a visionary and a source of inspiration. Shah Waliullah was an Islamic scholar and Jurist who was contemporary of Muhammad Ibn Abd al-Wah b of Saudi Arabia. Waliullah had no big ideological difference with Muhammad Wahab. Waliullah is treated as a great reformist by Islamic scholars. Even Muslim intellectuals Maulana Abul Kalam Azad and Mohammad Iqbal appreciated his works. Abul A'la Maududi, the doyen of Pakistani Deoband, praised him and so did Sir Syed Ahmad Khan, the founder of Aligarh University.

Shah Waliullah had asked for rationalization of the Shariah in the changing context and sought to bring all schools together on one platform. But he hated Shias just like Muhammad

Wahab did and cherished the 'extreme Sunnism of the Sufi tradition.' More importantly, Waliullah was the one who had invited Ahmad Shah Abdali to attack India in wake of declining powers of the Muslims. He apprehended that the Jats and the Marathas were emerging powerful enough to control the power after the death of Aurangzeb and, therefore, requested Ahmad Shah Abdali, the Afghan ruler, to emancipate Muslims from 'rebellious Kafirs' i.e Hindus. He wrote in the letter: "We beseech you in the name of the Prophet to fight a Jihad against the infidels of this region." [24] Needless to say, it is the Hindus who were infidels in the eyes of Shah Waliullah, and Jihad was to be waged against them. Waliullah wanted the restoration of Muslim rule in India and in wake of dwindling power of the Mughals he wanted Ahmad Shah Abdali to come for the rescue of Indian Muslims against the Kafirs. This gives an insight into the mind behind the formation of the Deoband School which came to be known as Dar-ul-Uloom i.e., Seminary of Islamic Teaching. People like Muhammad Qasim Nanauti and Rashid Ahmad Gangohi, the key minds behind establishment of the Deoband School, were supporters of both the Wahabis and Waliullah.

The Deoband came into existence in India after the first war of Independence against the British in 1857. This was being nationally led by Bahadur Shah Zafar that gave a ray of hope to Islamists for restoration of Muslim power in India. But this got shattered with the suppression of the revolt. Establishment of the British Empire had reduced Muslims to status of equality with Hindus who were subject race under the Mughals.[25] The clerics who enjoyed royal patronage during the Mughals were deprived of their privileges under the British. This caused many Ulemas to migrate to several destinations in North India.[26] The Deoband was one of such destination where they established the seminary in 1866.

There is also another theory which says that the Islamic seminary was established at Deoband after some Islamic clerics decided to consolidate Islamic education and religion. They were worried due to the fast-growing use of English education and dwindling patronage to the clerics in the new political set-up.[27] They were equally worried that the advancement of Western materialistic civilization was fast capturing attention of elites across communities and they feared that it would severely dent the religious and cultural identity of Muslims in India.

Although Deoband was a Hindu dominated small town, it had a substantial Muslim population. The Muslim clerics sought to take the Hindus along and tried to maintain a congenial atmosphere. Hindus too responded positively. The Deoband aligned itself with the Indian National Congress in fight against the British but to interpret this as anti-imperialist or fight for democratic values would be farther from the truth. Their anti-imperialist ideology was not intended to liberate India for the Indians but to defeat the forces that had brought misfortunes to the Muslims by crushing Muslim power in India. They harboured the feeling that this was the land which had been won by their forefathers but was in the control of the British.[28] It was in this political and religious context that the school of Deoband was founded. It was aimed at remobilization of followers of Islam in name of restoring the faith to its puritan form as practiced by the Prophet and as described in the Quran and the Hadith in consonance with Sunni understanding and explanations of the texts.

The Deobandi and the Barelavi did not see an eye to eye.[29] Barelvi is a sect within the Sunni cult. The nomenclature Deobandi and Barelvi come from the places of their respective origins. While the Barelavi supported the Partition of India and sided with the Muslim League, the Deoband was vertically split on the issue. There was a strong section within Deoband which supported Pakistan. As a result, the Jamaat-i-Hind which was its political wing got divided and a new split away group was formed as Jamaat-i-Islam which was headquartered at Dhaka. After the Partition, Jamat-i-Islam shifted its office to Pakistan. This division is often interpreted by the scholars of Muslim politics as pro-Indian act of Deoband. It is projected also to suggest that the Deoband in India (closer to Aligarh), which happened to be the centripetal point of pro-Pakistan movement, was untouched from it and always took stand in favour of united India.[30] However, the counter argument is that it is not the love for mother India but the notion that the entire India belonged to Islam was the driving force behind this.[31]

Anyway, after the Partition, Deoband seminaries and schools reached different parts of the World. It emerged prominently in Pakistan, Afghanistan and Bangladesh. There is a strong influence of Deoband among Pashtuns on both sides of the Afghanistan-Pakistan borders. The madrasas which started mushrooming during the Zia-ul Haq regime[32] in Pakistan changed the whole narrative of Islam in the region when arms in the hands became the new saga in name of protecting and fighting for Islam. The alumni of these Deobandi Madrasas supported by the Wahabis both in terms of finance and ideology carried out Jihad against the Soviet Union in Afghanistan.[33] Later on, Muslims inspired by the Deoband and the Wahab formed the Taliban and ruled a portion of Afghanistan for many years. Many leaders of Pakistan, both political and otherwise also are products of Deoband seminaries and schools in Pakistan. It is worthwhile to note that the Deoband in Pakistan has the same syllabus as that of the Deoband in India. Therefore, one may ask how the Deoband of Pakistan and Deoband of India are so varied in their interpretation of Islam.[34] The former subscribes to and nurtures the ideology of terrorism while the latter passes a resolution against it and depicts it as un-Islamic. It needs to be put it on record that Deoband India has been consistent in passing resolutions against act of terrorism and violence in name of Islam.[35] However, it is equally true that the security agencies have been very carefully watching the activities of the seminary. A couple of times, they have nabbed terrorists from its precincts.

It needs to be taken into account that the Taliban applied the most cruel and medieval social and cultural codes on Muslims by banning music, film, issuing dress codes for women, and by issuing new work ethics for men and women etc.[36] In December 1998, Taliban published advertisement in a local newspaper in the city of Herat giving the new code and 'number of unlawful instruments and goods including television, cassettes, musical instruments and their accessories were publicly burnt.'[37] It justified the ban by quoting the Hadith! They demolished the statue of Lord Buddha in Bamiyan in Afghanistan and justified it in name of sanction of iconoclasm in Islam.[38] The Pakistani Deoband and Jamiat-Ulema-Islam maintained a stoic silence and did not issue any fatwa against it. Those who condemned it were condemned by the Deoband and the Jamaat-i-Islam in Pakistan.[39]

Interestingly, the Indian Deoband says that it has nothing to do with Pakistani Deoband seminaries and the Pakistani Deoband says that it (terrorism) is an act of other side of the border i.e., the Afghani Deoband.[40] The fact, however, suggests that there are linkages and many terrorists and extremists who formed the Taliban were taught in madrasas and seminaries of the Deoband on both sides.[41] Mullah Umar was educated in a Deobandi Madrasa in Pakistan. This also raises a question that how could the same syllabus produce terrorists in Pakistan and Afghanistan but not in India? Thousands of clerics assembled at Deoband in India in May 2008 and issued a fatwa[42] declaring suicide bombing Un-Islamic.

There are few takers of the liberal face projected by the Deoband through such fatwas. The problem is in the indoctrination that intends to create radical Islamists. Even progressive Muslim scholar Arif Mohammad Khan does not believe in their being soft. Khan was a union minister in Rajiv Gandhi's Government and had supported the Supreme Court stand on the issue of alimony to Shah Bano and did not toe the Government line. He objected to certain books being taught at the Deoband as a part of the Islamic syllabus. In particular, he referred to a 12th century book *Hedaya*, compiled by the Hanafi School of Sunni Islam. Khan quoted specific references from The *Hedaya* which read as thus: "The destruction of the sword is incurred by infidels, although they be not the first aggressors, as appears from various passages in the sacred writings which are generally received to this effect."[43] The book makes it very clear that war on infidels is a permanent war till the time of judgment. The sacred injunction of the war is, as the book records from Quran, 'slay the infidels.'[44] However, it puts a condition that they should be slayed only after they refuse to accept the Islamic faith. The book notes, "When the Muslims enter the enemy's country and besiege the cities or strongholds of the infidels, it is necessary to invite them to embrace the faith." They should not be slayed without giving them the opportunity to change their faith. The book records, "If they embrace the faith, it is unnecessary to war with them, because that which was the design of the war is then obtained without war."[45] This content of the book taught at Deoband is really volatile and explosive. They preach hate against other religious denominations. Khan pointed out that though the department responsible for issuing fatwa and responding to the queries acknowledged the receipt of his objection and promised to reply back, but it never happened.[46]

The security agencies in India have found the role of the Deoband seminaries dubious, and media reports suggest that its Madrasas are informally on the watch list. On 21 February 2019, Uttar Pradesh Anti-Terrorist Squad (ATS) arrested two 'alleged Jaish-e-Mohammad (JeM) terrorists- Shahnawaz Ahmad Teli from Kulgam and Aquib Ahmad Malik of Pulwama- from Deoband in Saharanpur.'[47] This was not the first occasion when Deoband in India came under the scanners of the intelligence agencies. Harakat-ul-Mujahideen (Movement of Holy Warriors), Harakat -ul- Ansar (Movement of Enablers) and Harakat--ul Jihad al-Islami (Movement for Islamic Holy War)—the terrorist organizations operational in Kashmir have linkages with the Deoband.[48] Though the Student Islamic Movement of India (SIMI) has openly declared India to be a land of war and their aspiration to convert India into an Islamic state, the Deoband has not come out to criticize it. This again raises questions because people with ideology that drive the SIMI have been the products of the Deoband.[49]

Today, there is hardly any city in India where Deoband Madrasas do not exist. When the Deoband celebrated the golden Jubilee of its establishment in 1967, it published a report suggesting the functioning of 8934 Madrasas and Maktabs in India. Ever since then it has now come to cover the entire country. In 1950, there were only 88 Madrasas in India.[50] It rose to five lakhs in 2006, as quoted by Ram Ohri.[51] Majorities of Madrasas and mosques in India are in control of Sunni Islam, and the Deoband is the most important among them due to foreign funding from Islamic countries.[52] There are more than 75 Universities world over including the USA and the UK linked to the Deoband School, and surprisingly India is far ahead of Bangladesh, and even Pakistan on this count. It is important further to note that Indian subcontinent has been the source of teachers to Deoband affiliated seminaries abroad.[53] Few years back, the British secret services revealed that '48 British Madrasas are promoting extreme ideas breeding intolerance and misogyny' and Darul Ulooms Madrasas in London Manchester and Glasgow were included in that.[54] Earlier, it was assumed that it is the teachers from the Indian subcontinent which preach hardline Islam in these Madrasas but reports suggest that the British Muslim teachers are no better as they teach the same 'Dars-E-Nizami syllabus.'[55] Darul Uloom High School in Birmingham is known for imparting extremist ideology.[56] This is the case with all the schools and seminaries run by the Deoband.

Arif Mohammed Khan who is a renowned Islamic scholar has been highly critical of the Deoband School for imparting hate ideology in name of pure Islam. Based on research on terrorism by a Pakistani scholar Sohail Abbas, Khan challenged the peace claims of the Deoband. Sohail Abbas had interviewed 517 Mujahideen who were arrested in Afghanistan and lodged in two Pakistani jails. The study revealed that "barring just a few, all belonged to the Deobandi school of thought."[57] No wonder Mallet Victor argued that the Deoband has become shorthand for terrorism in the South Asia.[58] During the Anti-CAA protests, the Deoband School galvanised Muslims to actively lend support to the cause of illegally infiltrated Bangladeshi Muslims.[59] It never issued fatwa against violence by the Islamic terrorists in the state of Jammu and Kashmir. Instead, it has maintained stoic silence on the issue.

The real intent of Deoband is also reflected in the writings of Deobandi scholars from Pakistan. Scholars of Indian Deoband cannot afford to openly interpret concepts like Jihad and Kafir for the fear that this could offend the Hindu majority population in India. Therefore, they always project a liberal interpretation of Islam in public space. The term 'Kafir' for them is one which is taken from the word Kufra which means ungrateful, and Jihad too has been given a liberal expression. It is not the same expression that radical Islamic organizations use against other religious communities in Islamic countries. They also make a distinction between the offensive and defensive Jihad and justify the latter. However, Pakistani Deobandi scholars are far more forthright in articulating the terms. Abul Ala Maududi, the founder of Jamaat-i-Islam in Pakistan who advocated development of Pakistan as an Islamic state in true sense, is a respectable name in the country as an Islamic scholar, Jurist, historian and theologian. He is also credited with Shariatisation of Pakistan. He profusely persuaded General Zia-ul-Haq for this and it was during Zia's tenure that Pakistan started training and sponsoring terrorism and terrorist activities in Afghanistan and India.

Maududi is credited with several books. How he interprets Islam is interesting. For Maududi 'Islam is a system of life, a complete code of conduct that governs all aspects of human existence.'[60] Then he goes on to say that a person cannot be a true Muslim "if he fulfils Islamic obligation in his personal life but neglects the Islamic teachings in the political and economic behavior."[61] In other words, the liberal understanding of religion that it is purely a matter that deals with the individual and his relationship with God does not hold to be true in Islam. There is nothing like distinction between secular and religious space and the religious is far more sacrosanct than anything else in Islam. Islamic scholar Mumtaz Ahmad quotes Maududi as thus: "The final purpose of all the Apostles of God was to set up the rule of God so that they could implement the entire system of life in the manner ordained by God. They were not prepared to allow the unbelievers to retain the keys of power.... That is why all prophets tried to bring about political revolutions."[62] As Mumtaz argues, Maududi focused on Deen and then argued that the Prophet did not want just to worship one God and observe few sets of rituals and beliefs, but he wanted Islam to do with all aspects of life: cultural, political, legal, economic, judicial etc.[63]

This is possible only when an Islamic state gets established and the state power is used to force individuals to follow Islamic practices. Needless to suggest, the Deoband wants the establishment of an Islamic state and permeation of Islamic values in every aspect of human life; be it social, cultural, political or economic. This homogenizing and hegemonic call of Islamic ideology lays the seeds of conflicts. It makes the religion not just intolerant towards other faiths but also prepares logic against the moderate and liberal elements within Islam. No wonder, statistically speaking, Muslims are far more victims of Islamic terrorism compared to non-Muslims. Followers of sects like Ahmadis and Bohra often face violence from Pakistani hardliners such as the Sunnis Deobandi and the Wahabis.[64] In other Muslim countries where radical

Islam has taken deep roots, moderates are subject to violence and humiliation. This throws a greater level of conflicts and challenges in plural societies where Islam is powerfully organized and numerically strong, but Muslims are still in minority. It becomes further more complex in a society where Islam had been a ruling community and engaged in hostility against the dominant host community, and where they have got reduced to a minority in new democratic set up as is the case with India. It fails to negotiate between the past and the present. There is no dearth of Muslims scholars who still think that this was the country which was ruled by their forefathers and displaced by the British. And therefore, the Muslims should work towards reconverting the land into the land of Islam.[65]

The Islamic ideology followed by the Deobandis and the Wahabis poses a great challenge to humanity because they champion exclusivism. They are not just inimical towards other faiths but also against the sects which do not subscribe to them. This is the reason that we have witnessed attacks on the Shias and their mosques in India and elsewhere. Further, this is the reason that Majars and Dargahs are denounced and subjected to attacks. No wonder, these two schools have produced the largest number of terrorist organizations in the world and have brought bad name for Muslims across the globe.

References:

1 Deoband Islam in India has declared the terrorism and terrorists' activities un-Islamic and have also passed resolutions against it. Sikand, Y. (2008). Reflections on Deoband's Anti-Terrorism Convention. Economic and Political Weekly, 43(12/13), 13-15. Retrieved October 27, 2020, from http://www.jstor.org/stable/40277272. Choksy, C., & Choksy, J. (2015). The Saudi Connection: Wahhabism and Global Jihad. World Affairs, 178(1), 23-34. Retrieved October 27, 2020, from http://www.jstor.org/stable/43555279.

2 Though scholars of Islam do not agree with what Wahabis argue. They make a distinction between Worldly and religious matters wherein they argue that there can be no innovation in the religious matters but innovations and changes in the worldly matters are not prohibited by Quran.

3 Knauerhase, R. (1975). Saudi Arabia: A Brief History. Current History, 68(402), 74–88. http://www.jstor.org/stable/45313238, Accessed on 26 January 2022. P. 74.

4 Scholars who have sought to portray the Wahhabi movement in India anti-imperialist. See Also, Alyahya Mohammed. "Don't

Blame 'Wahhabism' for Terrorism." The New York Times, Oct. 19, 2016.

5 See for this; Esposito, John L. (2004). The Oxford Dictionary of Islam.

6 Mouza hem, Haytham. 'Saudi Wahhabi Sheikh Calls on Iraq's Jihadists to Kill Shiites', AL monitor, 28 April 2013. Darul Islam and Darul Harab categorization in the Islamic texts

7 Founder of the Wahabi Movement had called the Shias Non-believers. De-long Natana J. (2004). Wahhabi Islam: From Revival to Global Jihad. Oxford University Press, New York. Pp.84-87.

8 Mouza hem, Haytham. 'Saudi Wahhabi Sheikh Calls on Iraq's Jihadists to Kill Shiites', AL monitor, 28 April 2013.

9 https://www.bbc.com/news/world-south-asia-31451201, accessed on 26 May 2020.

10 https://www.bbc.com/news/world-middle-east-32843510, Retrieved on 26 May 2020.

11 https://www.bbc.com/news/world-asia-46262269, Accessed on 26 May 2020.

12 Ibid.

13 https://ballandalus.wordpress.com/2014/08/02/the-wahhabi-sack-of-karbala-1802-a-d/ Accessed on 14 January 2022.

14 Khatab, Sayed (2012). Understanding Islamic Fundamentalism: The Theological and Ideological Basis of al-Qaida's Political Tactics, American University Press at Cairo. , p.74

15 This concept of 'saved group' is said to be part of the Hadith in which the Prophet says that there will be altogether 73 groups

in Islam but all will not be going to paradise. Only one of them will make it and the rest will go to hell. Wahabis claim that it is the people of Najd and the followers of the path of Wahabi alone who would go to Jannat not other Muslims. This argument is contested by Muslim scholars who say that it is fabricated statement and the real Hadith does not say this. See again, Mouzahem, Haytham. "Saudi Wahhabi Sheikh Calls on Iraq's Jihadists to Kill Shiites", AL monitor, 28 April 2013 retrieved on 26 May 2020.

16 Kovacs, Amanda. "Saudi Arabia Exporting Salafi Education and Radicalizing Indonesia's Muslims"
German Institute of Global and Area Studies (GIGA) Focus, Vol.7. 2014, p.8. https://www.files.ethz.ch/isn/184727/gf_international_1407.pdf.

17 Ibid.

18 https://thearabweekly.com/egypts-salafists-wary-saudi-arabia-treads-path-reform accessed 0n 27 December 2021.

19 Ibrahim, Youssef Michel. "The Mideast Threat That's Hard to Define." Washington Post, August 11, 2002.

20 Takfir is the term which is used by a Muslim to call another Muslim Kafir. The terms which have often appeared in the Quran is Kufr(unbelief) and Shirk (Idolatry).

21 Rai, Siddhartha. "Modi govt trying to divide Muslims", Mail Today, March 21, 2016. https://www.indiatoday.in/mail-today/story/modi-govt-trying-to-divide-muslims-says-maulana-syed-arshad-madani-314159-2016-03-21. Accessed on 27 May 2020.

23 Shias and Sufis criticism of Deoband.

24 Sookhdeo, P. (2006). Issues of Interpreting the Koran and Hadith. *Connections, 5*(3), 57-82. Retrieved April 1, 2021, from http://www.jstor.org/stable/26323255

25 "The Rise of Mughal Power - De Gruyter." https://www.degruyter.com/document/doi/10.1525/9780520917774-011/pdf. Accessed 1 Apr. 2021.

26 https://ctc.usma.edu/the-past-and-future-of-deobandi-islam/, accessed on 28 May 2020. The Past and Future of Deobandi Islam, November 2009, Volume 2, Issue 11, Luv Puri.

27 Reetz, D. (2005). Dār al-'Ulūm Deoband and its Self-Representation on the Media [Corrected Title: Dār al-'Ulūm Deoband and its Mediatic Self-Representation]. Islamic Studies, 44(2), 209-227. Retrieved October 27, 2020, from http://www.jstor.org/stable/20838962. Accessed on 27 October 2020. Metc.alf, Barbara Daly (1982). Islamic Revival in British India: Deoband, 1860-1900, Princeton University Press.

28 Quote here both Jinnah and Sir Sayed who had argued that the British should handover the power to the Muslims.

29 Behuria, Askhok K. (2008). Sects within Sect: The Case of Deobandi Barelvi Encounter in Pakistan, Vol 32, Issue 1, IDSA, New Delhi, pp.57-58.

30 Deoband supported the Indian National Congress during the freedom movement. Initially they were with the government but subsequently realized that propagation of true Islam was not possible within the British rule. See, Reetz, Dietrich. "Dār Al-' Ulūm Deoband and Its Self-Representation on the Media [Corrected Title: Dār al-'Ulūm Deoband and Its Mediatic Self-Representation]." Islamic Studies 44, no. 2 (2005): 209–27.

http://www.jstor.org/stable/20838962.

31 Those who argue that Deoband was for entire India being converted to Islam See Also, Rahman, Tariq. "Jihad as Anti-Colonial Resistance in India: 1831-1920s." Pakistan Journal of Historical Studies 3, no. 2 (2018): 1–42. https://doi.org/10.2979/pjhs.3.2.01.

32 Deoban Madaras that sprung up along the Pakistan Afghanistan border during the General Zia-ul Haq government. Abdulbaqi, Misbahullah. "Madrassah in Afghanistan: Evolution and Its Future." Policy Perspectives 5, no. 2 (2008): 130–59. http://www.jstor.org/stable/42909538.

33 Deobandi trains young minds to pick up gains in their hands. Templin, J. D. (2015). Religious Education of Pakistan's Deobandi Madaris and Radicalisation. Counter Terrorist Trends and Analyses, 7(5), 15–21. http://www.jstor.org/stable/26351354. Pp.15-16. See also the arguments suggesting radicalisation by Deobandi Madrassas. https://www.efsas.org/publications/study-papers/pakistan-army-and-terrorism%3B-an-unholy-alliance/. Accessed on 24 January 2022.

35 Sikand, Yoginder. "Reflections on Deoband's Anti-Terrorism Convention." Economic and Political Weekly 43, no. 12/13 (2008): 13–15. http://www.jstor.org/stable/40277272. Accessed on 2 January 2022. Also see, "Jamiat endorses Darul Uloom's fatwa against terrorism" The Indian Express, Hyderabad, 8 November 2009.

36 Taliban restricting Radio and TV, films in Afghanistan. See, Wroe, Nicholas. "A Culture Muted." The Guardian, 13 October 2001. Such headlines repeated in news media when

Taliban came to power for the second time in Afghanistan in 2021. "Under Taliban, thriving Afghan music scene heads to silence," India Today, 23 September 2021. https://www.indiatoday.in/world/story/under-taliban-thriving-afghan-music-scene-heads-to-silence-see-pics-1856194-2021-09-23.

37 Roe, Nicholas, A Culture Muted, The Guardian, (International edition, 13 October 2001.

38 On February 26, 2001, and after having consulted a college of 'ulama', Mullah Muhammad Omar, the leader of the Taliban, issued a decree ordering the elimination of all non-Islamic statues and sanctuaries in Afghanistan. https://www.mei.edu/publications/death-buddhas-bamiyan. Accessed on 2 January 2022.

39 "How to Islamize an Islamic Republic: Jamaat-e-Islami in its own words." 25 Apr. 2017, https://www.brookings.edu/research/how-to-islamize-an-islamic-republic-jamaat-e-islami-in-its-own-words/. Accessed 1 Apr. 2021.

40 Jan, Najeeb A. The Meta-colonial State: Pakistan, Deoband Ulama and The Biopolitics of Islam Ph.D. Thesis Submitted to the University of Michigan.

41 Terrorists taught in Madrasas of Deoband both sides of Afghanistan and Pakistan.

42 "Deoband First: A Fatwa Against Terror", The Times of India, 1 June 2008.

43 Hedaya, Vol II, page no 41 and 43

44 Boston, Andrew J (2010). The Legacy of Jihad: Islamic Holy War and the Fate of non-Muslims, Prometheus Books. New York, USA.

45 Hedaya. Vol II P41.

46 Khan, Arif Mohammed. "Silence of The Deoband Lambs", Outlook, 5 June 2008.

47 The Economic Times, 22 February 2019.

48 Haqqani, Husain. "India's Islamist Groups", Hudson Institute, 16 February 2006. Accessed on 29 May 2020.

49 "Jamiat-Ulama-I-Hind Wanted to Convert India into An Islamic state." 14 March 2016. https://swarajyamag.com/politics/jamiat-ulama-i-hind-wanted-to-convert-india-into-an-islamic-state. Accessed 1 Apr. 2021. Also see; Frayer, Lauren. "The Taliban's Ideology Has Surprising Roots in British-Ruled India", 8 September, 2021, North Carolina Public Radio. Morning Edition, https://www.wunc.org/2021-09-08/the-talibans-ideology-has-surprising-roots-in-british-ruled-india. Accessed on 22 December 2021.

50 http://indiafacts.org/galloping-growth-madrasas-india/. Accessed on 29 May 2020.

51 Ibid. Hindusthan Mein Madarase' and Dr. Arjumand Ara, a well-known Muslim scholar in her insightful essay on Madrasas and the Making of Muslim Identity.

52 ohd Dilshad. "Saharanpur lawyer files petition in the Supreme Court Demanding Probe into Foreign Funding to Darul Uloom. The Times of India. 14 June 2020.

53 Zaman, M. (1999). Religious Education and the Rhetoric of Reform: The Madrasa in British India and Pakistan. *Comparative Studies in Society and History, 41*(2), 294-323. Retrieved April 1, 2021, from http://www.jstor.org/stable/179448

54 https://www.thenational.ae/world/europe/imams-promoting-extremism-in-british-madrasas-report-claims-1.857581. Accessed on 29 May 2020.

55 The Daily Mail, 4 May 2019.

56 https://www.thenational.ae/world/europe/imams-promoting-extremism-in-british-madrasas-report-claims-1.857581. Accessed on 29 May 2020.

57 Arif Muhammad Khan. The Times of India, New Delhi, 30 September 2008). Arif quoted this in his article in Outlook also published on 5 June 2008.

58 Mallet, Victor. "Madrassas: behind closed doors: Are south Asia's Islamic schools causing a surge in extremism?" 30 October 2015.

59 Deoband in support of Anti-CAA Rally.

60 Ahmad, Mumtaz (1994). "Islamic Fundamentalism in South Asia: The Jamaat-i-Islami and the Tablighi Jamaaat of South Asia." In Marty, Martin E.; Appleby, R. Scott (eds.). Fundamentalisms Observed Vol I. American Academy of Science and Arts. Chicago: University of Chicago Press, p.487.

61 Maududi quoted by Mumtaz Ahmad (1994). Ibid.

62 Ibid, p.487.

63 Maududi quoted in Ahmad, Mumtaz (1994). pp. 457–524.

64 Time for Shias to leave Pakistan - Pakistan - DAWN.COM." 17 Feb. 2013, https://www.dawn.com/news/786738/time-for-shias-to-leave-pakistan. Accessed 1 Apr. 2021.

65 Mushirul Haq

CHAPTER 3

THE TABLIGHI MOVEMENT

Making Muslims More Muslim

THE TABLIGHI MOVEMENT is a Sunni missionary movement that originated in India in 1927 in Mewat region of present day Haryana. It sought to imbibe 'Puritan Islam' in Muslims who were not following Islamic practices. Muhammad Ilyas al-Kandhlawi, who founded the organization, was an alumnus of the Deoband Uloom, and his interpretation of Islam matched with those of the Deoband. Therefore, The Tablighi Jamaat is also depicted as an ancillary organization of the Deoband that supported the Tablighi in formative years since the latter did not have its own mosques and Madrasas. It was the Deoband which provided its mosques to the Markaz in India and abroad to enable their meetings for teaching and preaching of Islam. This continues even today even as both the Deoband and the Tablighi have been speaking against each other all these years.

There are several stories about its formation. One school suggests that Muhammad Ilyas al-Kandhlawi, who was an Ulema, had differences with top echelons in the Deoband where he could not find a proper role. He also had differences with Deoband's political turn when it founded Jamaat-e-Hind that actively participated in the Khilafat movement. Therefore, Kandhlawi took to a new apolitical path. The second set of people suggest that he was not happy that the Deoband had got limited to teaching and training students in Islam academically and empowering them to become Alim or Hafiz.[1] He realized that the global goal of Islam was not possible through the process of teaching and learning. There is yet another school which concludes that Muhammad Ilyas got inspired from his second visit to Mecca in 1926. After this pilgrimage, he decided to convert Islam into a mass movement to take Islamic teachings from seminaries to the masses.

However, the most prevalent and predominant view suggests that Kandhlawi founded it in response to the Shuddhi movement of the Arya Samaj which was trying hard to win back into the Hindu fold those Muslims who had converted to Islam few generations back.[2] Kandhlawi was worried that Muslim converts continued with their pre-Islamic customs, social and cultural rituals on specific occasions such as birth, marriages and death.[3] He termed them 'borderline Muslims' and feared that due to their Hindu ancestry they might easily fall for the Shuddhi movement.[4] He had seen those experiences in Delhi as well in his home region, Mewat, where a large number of Rajputs who had converted to Islam were practicing the Hindu social and religious rituals. Kandhlawi, therefore, decided to train and educate these Muslims the precepts of puritan Islam as practiced by the Prophet and the four Caliphates after him.[5] In other words, the Tablighi movement emerged out of the fear of loss of Islamic identity of Muslims in the wake of rising powers of Hindus with the ascendency of the British power in India.

The Tablighi was less a 'reformist'[6] and more a 'revivalist' movement that sought to imbibe practices of puritan Islam in Muslim converts from Hinduism. Any idea which seeks to restore a pristine past is based on two interconnected arguments; first, it starts with a premise that a lot of impurities have crept into the original idea of Islam which diminished its true essence; second is the response to the first which follows that it is important to remove the impurities to realize and restore the true and pristine glory of Islam. Kandhlawi held the position that centrifugal forces working on Islam drifted it away from its axis and, therefore, it was important to restore the core elements to realize the equilibrium. Since puritan Islam had a global mission, it would be pertinent to suggest that though the immediate region for founding the Tablighi was to desist the followers to practice un-Islamic rituals and customs, its larger goal was to strengthen the objective of global Islam-Muslim brotherhood with same practices, thinking and rituals.

This was a bold and far more radical step than the Deoband. It rejected the whole premise of syncretic tradition of Ganga-Yamuna Tehzeeb which a section of Muslim intellectuals and political class continue to espouse in public discourse.

Kandhlawi was charmed by the Arab Islam and aspired to build a true Islamic society on the same pattern. It was not possible without insulating the Muslim converts against the obvious impact of their pre-Islamic past in terms of rituals, customs and cultural moorings. The *ghar-wapasi* (return home) campaign of the Arya Samaj was not, therefore, the only factor. The Challenges from market forces, demands of modernity, impact of science and rationalism were equally powerful factors that sought to diminish the Islamic identity. While the economic success of the market in the West overshadowed the glory of Islam, science and rationalism questioned bigotry and irrationality. As expected, the Tablighi movement sought to protect and promote Islam by recoiling itself within its religious shell and promote the same. The Tablighi, therefore, did not enter into the domain of giving commentaries on the Quran and the Hadith to develop a new school of thought but it picked up the goal of world Islam and introduced a purely new methodology of proselytization which they called Da'wa or Dawah.[7]

The Tablighis opposed dilution of Islamic identity under various influences and advocated return to the age of the Prophet to restore the true Islam. They strictly stressed on dress code for Muslims and emulated the style of dressing that was prevalent during the days of the Prophet. Followers were expected to follow Islamic rules and cultures in all walks of life. It is precisely the reason that preachers of the Tablighi movement wear clothes in a typical style. This style later became a part of the Shariat. Muslims wearing the skull cap, trousers above the ankles and beard to the proper Shariat length are all in tune with the provisions within Islam.[8] It was therefore, a new identity formation of religious Islam which was distant from Political Islam and yet it favored the same. It provided far more fanatic and rigid codes for practicing Muslims than what the orthodox Islamic organizations had so far been talking about. It took them to the field and at the grassroots where identity formalization was easy. Thus, the Tablighi movement sought to consolidate the religious and cultural Islam in soil of India where conversion into Islam had failed to disturb the cultural matrix.

The Tablighi chose a new method of propagation which was never used by any sect or order in Islam. It worked to create a pool of preachers who could reach out to the Muslim population and speak to them on ingredients of true Islam rather than waiting for them to come to seminaries or Madrasas to learn the same. The Tablighis assemble in groups that are called Jamaats and travel from one place to another to preach true Islam. This is called Da'wa or Dawah. Da'wa is interpreted as a call or invitation to return to faith. Through Da'wa, the followers of the Tablighi Jamaat transmit the message of Islam and the message of the Prophet to Muslims.

The groups of Tablighi who participate in preaching may be male or female. The female preachers become part of it only when they are accompanied with their husband, or brother, or father in case the girls are unmarried. While the male members stay in the local mosque, the female preachers stay in the home of committed Tablighi followers in nearby villages or colonies. Thus, the Da'wa is for both male and females but for males it is of longer period. Tablighi Jamaat followers in India undertake the task from three days to three months. Every Tablighi preacher is expected to go on Da'wa at least for three days in a month. Forty days long period of Da'wa is called Chilla[9] which members are expected to go, at least once in a year, and three successive Chillas once in a lifetime. Married couples can also go for a Chilla if they chose. Besides Da'wa, the preachers undertake four more tasks which are Gasht, Taleems, Mashwara in a mosque, and prayers and appeal to join the Jamaat.[10] They are expected to make Gashts (preaching visits) at least twice a week; undertake two Taleems, that is study sessions every day in which members recite and read Islamic texts such as the Quran and the Hadith, but mostly the literature related to the Tablighi on Islam. Mashwara is a daily deliberation that takes place in mosques.[11] Further, every Tablighi is expected to offer regular prayers and appeal to other Muslims to join the Jamaat. All these four tasks were developed by Mohammad Illyas, the founder of the Tablighi movement in India.

Tablighi preachers are not the great scholars of Islam yet they preach about Islam. This is the method which they follow throughout the world. They do not carry a luggage of books and classical religious texts, but pamphlets and pocket books which are designed for the purpose of preaching. They vary from country to country but some of them are very common. For example, in India, they follow a book called **Fazail-i-Amal** (Virtues of Everyday Actions). This book "contains a number of stories about the great heavenly rewards (Sawab) that await Muslims if they follow the commandments of the Shariah strictly in their own personal lives and steer clear of worldly temptations."[12] The book lays out a manual of how to be a good Muslim, a true follower of Islam. It contains minute details of the processes and techniques of self-purification i.e., 'how to sanctify everyday actions.'[13] In Pakistan, they carry 'Tablighi Nisab' a compilation of seven essays authored by Maulana Mohammed Zakriya and Maulana Manzoor Nomani which every Tablighi preacher must go through.[14] These essays form the source material which the preachers use while addressing Muslims gathered in the mosques. They are not very educated people who have learned theology or Islamic laws. They are just the laymen who have been trained in the curricula and left free to go for Da'wa (proselytization). Interestingly, they are also discouraged from exposure to modern education and other elements of science. They are not allowed even to read newspapers.[15] Higher ups in the organization think that these things would pollute the minds of the Tablighis and take them away from spirituality. Thus, they are almost cut off from the external world. In brief, they are actually converted into men of the mission rather than men of reason.

The Tablighis argue against intellectualism on the ground that reading books does not make man a true human being. The same applies to the field of religion. Knowledge of religious text does not make a man spiritual and religious. Intellectualism is just a *Kibati Ilm*, only a bookish information that does not have much value in the spiritual world. A true practicing Muslim for them is a better man compared to the one who knows much about religion but does not practice the same in his personal life. Da'wa, for them is a programme to convert an ordinary Muslim into a good Muslim. Attending Da'wa and working for it is the real service to *Din*, they hold.

The activists of the Tablighi generally stay in local mosques. They carry stoves, beddings, toothbrush and all basics amenities required for survival.[16] Usually, they move together in a group of 10-12. When they reach the destined areas, they reach out to Muslims residing in that area and request them to attend the morning prayers and evening sermons in the local mosque. They begin the day with the morning prayers together with assembled people. After the prayers, they read out the relevant aspects of the text. They also emphasize on leading an austere life and focus more on Dini affairs than seeking aggregation of personal interests. They persuade them to follow the path as explained in the texts. In the evening, they give talks on the Quran, the Hadith and the Shariah. This way, they continue their preaching for some time in one mosque and then move away for the next destination.

They stay at one place for a period of ten days to three months, depending on the place and need. There is no big role for Ulema or a theologian for preaching the assembled gathering. Thus, they work as the foot soldiers of Islam at the grassroots. Without spreading hate against followers of other religions, they explicitly bind the followers of Islam with orthodox Islamic missionary movement. They travel from cities to cities, from villages to villages preaching the gospel of Islam and Islamic values.

The whole preaching is meant exclusively for Muslims.

There are clear instructions to Jamaat members not to preach the non-Muslim population.[17] The outsiders or non-Muslims are not allowed to be part of an assembly. They also distance from conversion design deliberately as such acts invite protests and even sometime violent resistance from non-Muslim communities. In their scheme of things, consolidation of Islam by inculcating Islamic values among the Muslims is preferred goal over increasing the numerical strength of the community by converting 'others' into Islam. One does not find incidents wherein the Tablighis have been caught red-handed in 'converting Hindus, Christians and Buddhists into Islam.' The Tablighis also try to stay away from political positioning on different issues. They deliberately keep themselves at an arm's length from political activities because of the fear of political backlash that may harm activities of the mission. They project themselves as an organization intended to 'making Muslim a good Muslim.' They use this phrase to project their identity and image which enable the organization to deeply penetrate into community members on the one hand and insulate the organization against possible hindrances from outside.

However, one should not forget that the Tablighis draw inspiration from the Deoband School which sets its mission to Islamize the entire world. They agree with the Islamic ideology of the Deoband School that seeks to pervade all aspects of human life. It would be also relevant to note that the political arms of the Deoband, the Jamaat-e-Islami-Hind and the Jamaat-e-Islami-Pakistan have not openly declared their intent of not adhering to the Islamists ideology. As the founder of

Jamaat-e-Islami-Pakistan, Maududi comprehensively explains the blue print of the Islamic State (IS) and justifies it on the ground that the Prophet himself led these political changes. Maududi argued that Islam must reflect in every walk of life of Muslim and every aspect of national life; be it politics or economy, science or culture. In fact, Maulana Kandhlawi had good relations with both the Jamaat-e-Islami which worked for Pakistan and Jamaat-e-Islami-Hind. In Britain, the Tabhlighis operate from their European Headquarters located in Dewsbury. This is basically the property of Deoband where there is a grand mosque complex and a residential Dar-ul-Uloom Islamic Seminary. The Tablighis use the mosques of the Deoband for preaching and proselytizing (Da'wa).[18]

Mumtaz Ahmad argues that the Tablighis realised in India that the Partition had already raised suspicion about Muslims' loyalty to India.[19] Therefore, any assertion of the Islamic values or system could have made Hindus hostile to them, as the country was partitioned on grounds of religion. Further, the Partition had changed the numerical arithmetic of the communities. It was clear to the Tablighis that it was not possible to have an Islamic political set-up in Hindu-Majority democratic India.[20] Therefore, it was important and imperative to strengthen Islam and Islamic values among Muslims without articulating the political intents or stating the political positions on every issue concerning the Muslim community or the global goal of Islam. The Tabhlighis in post-partitioned India, therefore, chose to silently work towards consolidating the Islamic identity of Muslims. This does not mean that they are completely into the spiritual domain and have nothing to do with politics or are blind to the political processes. First, the organizations may not necessarily take position publicly on political issues but members always take part in it. Everywhere in the world including India, members of the Tablighi are actively involved in the politics of Pakistan. In India, when the Central government passed the laws on amending Citizenship Act (CAA) in 2019, the Tablighis joined the protests with their co-religionists. This was widely reported in the media, both in print and electronic, when the Tablighis were found assembled at the protests site at Shaheen Bagh on 2nd April 2020.[21] They do not flaunt their political participation and preferences so openly as other organizations do but to suggest that they don't indulge into politics is erroneous. As organization they don't openly declare to be part of it but always allow and encourage the members and supporters to extend support to the Islamic cause. And precisely this is what they did in case of the anti-CAA protests in India. They channelized their human resources but did not lead it from the front so that they could claim themselves to be apolitical.

The Citizenship Amendment Act was intended to give citizenship to the persecuted non-Muslims minorities migrating from predominantly Muslim majority Islamic states such as Pakistan, Afghanistan and Bangladesh, which have lately turned out to be the breeding nurseries of Islamic extremists. These Islamic extremists have made it difficult for others to live in peace. This has led to huge migration of persecuted Hindus, Christians and Buddhists from these countries most of whom have taken refuge in India. However, they are living without citizenship documents and have been asking for citizenship to enjoy full opportunities that life offers. On the other hand, there have been a huge number of migrants from Bangladesh, mostly Muslims, who have sneaked into India as illegal migrants and have settled in different parts of India by procuring Indian documents through illegal means.[22] The Central government also declared its intention to have a National Register on Citizenship (NRC) consisting of data of legitimate citizens which has the potential to expose illegal settlors. Most settlors who are Muslims from Bangladesh have changed the religious demography of several states and act as captive vote-bank for political parties.[23] The infiltration from Bangladesh has threatened the social and cultural milieu and also tries to influence the politics of India.[24] Some Muslim political, social, cultural and religious organizations in India think that increased numerical strength of Muslims would also increase their political weight in the system. They oppose any such attempts which seek to identify, detect and send them back to Bangladesh.

These Muslim organizations try to stall actions against illegal infiltrators claiming victimhood and discrimination against Muslims. They argue that if the Hindu migrants from Bangladesh are given the Citizenship, denying the same to Muslims similarly placed would be a gross violation of the secular spirit of the Indian Constitution. Most such Muslim organizations opposed the CAA, 2019, ignoring the basic fact that this law was not directed against Indian Muslims but favoured merely the persecuted minorities from neighbouring Islamic countries. Muslims staying in these Islamic countries are enjoying all basic rights and security and there is no persecution against them on religious grounds. The very basis of the Partition of India was that Muslim constituted a separate and distinct civilization and, therefore, cannot live with Hindus and hence a separate country should be given to them. Those who fanned the protests failed to see this historical factor and made spurious arguments. The Tablighis were not to be left behind anyone in opposing this law. They fully backed the protests through funds and their supporters.

The political dimension of the Tablighis is often ignored because of their public portrayal that their work is limited to individual spiritual purification and making a Muslim a good Muslim. And their definition of a good Muslim is the one who believes only in Allah and Prophet Mohammad as the last Prophet or the messenger of God sent for the whole of humanity. This is called Kalima. He supersedes all previous Prophets and there shall be no prophet after Him. In other words, they instill a thought in the consciousness of any Muslim that rest other Prophets described in other religions are fake and their teachings do not carry any emancipatory role. And therefore, they are not worthy of any consideration and their thoughts are not to be given any weight. Even Prophet Muhammad had declared this after the victory of Mecca and directed demolition of all existing temples and idols in the city and in its near vicinity.

Obviously, a Muslim impregnated with such ideas would

have no respect for other religions. Secondly, a good Muslim must do Salat or prayers five times in a day. Thirdly, he must have knowledge of and remember Allah (Ilm and Dhikr) and, therefore, he must read the Quran and the Hadith. Fourthly, he should respect the fellow Muslims (Ikramul) and must have good intentions towards Allah (Ikhlas). And finally, preaching the message of Allah (Dawah or Da'wa). These are the six principles on which the discourse of the Tablighi rests.[25] Thus, they restricted themselves to 'strict adherence to the orthodox Deobandi cult of Sunni Islam.'[26] The only difference is that while the Deobandi school interpret the mission of Islam to create an Islam-based society and State in order to pervade Islam in all walks of human life including politics, the Tablighis confine themselves to 'preaching pure Islam and not proselytizing.' In a way, they are silent soldiers of Islam who work on the same premises and prepare in fact the army of Islam who have no respect for other religions.

Like the Wahabis, the Deobandis and the Tablighis look at Sufism with disdain and oppose Muslims who appreciate the Sufi version of Islamic thought, listen to Sufi music or visit Sufi Dargahs and Shrines. If a school of thought which is so contemptuous towards another school of thought within Islam just because the latter publicly tries to be inclusive, it is difficult to expect that they will be accommodative towards other religious denominations. Their orthodoxy and approach make them contemptuous of rational thinking. They do not want 'secular education' for their girls and oppose their schooling in co-educational schools. They even preach that girl should not work in the office with the boys. They reject recreational music and dance and oppose any kind of practices which ordinary Muslims may draw from their social and cultural context.

Their proclaimed apathy to politics is difficult to internalize because there have been several tall leaders in politics who were actively involved in Tablighi activities. Also, although the Tablighis are not an active or frontal part of any political movement or protests they do not keep themselves completely aloof from politics. In India, Maulana Abul Kalam Azad was highly under the influence of the Deoband and the Tablighi schools.[27] He was a religious man with firm belief in the Islamic agenda in India. Azad always claimed that he was against the Partition of India and is known as a Gandhian, but several of his contemporaries questioned his stand on the Partition of India including JB Kriplani who worked with Mahatma Gandhi for decades. Kriplani asserted that Azad never opposed the Partition of the country. Azad's opposition to Hindi in the Constituent Assembly and emphasis on Hindustani for India was beyond comprehension. How could a man who saw the Partition of the country on the basis of religious identity with language as an important component repeat the same issue in post-partitioned India?

In Pakistan, the Tablighis conspired to overthrow the government of Prime Minister Benazir Bhutto when she returned to power in 1993.[28] Benazir did not bother much about them. More importantly, Prime Minister Nawaz Sharif's father was a Tablighi and he used to finance them and give them high positions in the government.[29] This is not the only occasion when the Tablighis tried to interfere in Pakistani politics. It was reported that several high ranking civil and military officers, including those who were members of terrorist organization Harkat ul-Mujahideen attempted to stage a coup in 1998 but it thwarted by the Pakistani Army.[30] The appointment of Muhammad Rafiq Tarar as the ceremonial President in 1998 and Javed Nasir as Director-General of the country's Inter-Services Intelligence (ISI) were also said to be the work of Tablighis in Pakistan. This show how deeply they were entrenched in the political and administrative establishment of the country. There is a big section of the military and civil administration as well as extremist organizations where the Tablighis operate or wield immense influence. Its links with the Taliban in Pakistan were evident when the Taliban nominated the chief of the Tablighi as interlocutor to negotiate with the Pakistani government. When Haji Abdul Wahab, the third Amir of the Tablighi Jamaat, died at age of 92 in Pakistan, thousands of people from all walks of life 'including political and military spectrum participated in his funeral.' Marc Gaborieau, a French Tablighi expert, asserts that Tablighi's objective is not less than "planned conquest of the world" in the spirit of Jihad.[31] There are many who agree that although the Tablighis may not be actively involved in internal politics or disputes at local level or issues, but from a 'philosophical and transnational perspective, the Tablighi Jamaat's millenarian philosophy is very political indeed.'[32]

There seems to be clear discrepancies between what they believe and preach, and what they are in reality. This came to light when seemingly quiet and docile Tablighi preachers possibly infected by the Covid-19 'Corona virus' were kept at the quarantine centres in different states of India. Actions by some of them such as spitting on doctors, passing lewd and lustful remarks at nurses or making objectionable sexual gestures towards them, shitting in open at the centres, disregarding all norms and showing tantrums for food certainly exposed their veiled spirituality.[33] And this was not an isolated example. It happened at many Indian cities. This dented the image built by the Tablighis about their organization, as it demonstrated that the entire claim of inward-looking spirituality was a facade. This image has been largely due to their distance from publicity and working from 'behind the curtain'. They maintain a high degree of secrecy and informality in their work which make it difficult for outsiders to penetrate the organization and know about it.[34] They don't have publications meant for public that could exactly state their real intent beyond the stated objectives and ultimate mission.

The Tablighis do not have an internationally networked organizational structure with a centralized control and monitoring system. Though Markaz at Delhi is treated as the International Headquarters of the movement, it just coordinates with different Tablighi chapters in different nations. It does not have controlling power over them. There are Tablighi movements in 165 countries of the world today but it would be wrong to assume that they all are guided and regulated by the Markaz at Delhi. They are linked to Delhi and interact and coordinate for mutual benefits. The movement has country chapters but they all have independent national centres which are connected with their regional and local centres. The country chapters have their own ways of functioning and decision making. Normally the chief of the organization at the country level is called the Amir and there is a consultative body called Shura which guides the Amir on important questions of religion and preaching. This way it is largely a 'free floating religious movement with little dependence on hierarchy, leadership position and decision-making procedures.'[35] There is no bureaucratic structure but self-imposed religious discipline. This flexibility is both strength and the weakness of this movement.[36] It makes everything informal and driven by the passion for belief in Islam. Thus, the fear of Allah and getting left out on the day of the judgment works as a deterrent against indiscipline in the religious domain.

This self-imposed discipline and non-application of reason and rationality to make scrutiny-based decisions is found generally in traditional societies where level of education and economic status is at a low level. Appeal of the Tablighi movement is limited to specific social and economic class though its appeals are directed at, as Yoginder Sikand argues, 'all Muslims.'[37] Sikand made this observation with specific reference to the United Kingdom but this applies equally to India and elsewhere. It is the 'lower and lower middle-class Muslims'[38] which actually forms the backbone of the Tablighi movement. The cadres in mission are mostly the uneducated, or semi-educated and unsophisticated. The leaders come from sound economic and educational background. The preachers who are less educated and come from the less privileged class find a purpose of working for Din. Besides the bread and butter the kind of attention and respect that they receive in the community act as stimuli for them.

The organization does not reveal their economic background so that they do not fall victim to an inferiority complex of any kind. It is always projected that the work they have chosen for themselves are driven by the spiritual quest and spiritual mission of Islam. They are also told that they have deliberately chosen the path of poverty and, therefore, it is a case of willful renunciation.[39] More importantly, poverty is not rationalized or glamourized in the Tablighi discourse, at least in Indonesia, writes F. Noor. The Tablighis publish such literature which shows that those who are part of the groups for Da'wa are the ones who deliberately have chosen this path. This sermon is found almost in all religious movements but the peculiarity of the Tablighi is that this is linked to the liking of the Prophet. They cite the Hadith to claim that the 'poor will be admitted to paradise forty years before the rich.'[40] These preachers call upon the followers of Islam to make it a world religion for benefit of the world. To them, Western modernity is a major obstacle to it. They are trying their best to destroy or contain the march of Islam and, therefore, it is the responsibility of every Muslim to focus on the unfinished mission of the Prophet. Tablighi preachers try to convince and attract Muslims towards the philosophy that 'possession and earning of wealth' is not and should not be the end of the life. They should rather work for a world beyond this world describing this as the service of Islam. In other words, they talk and take the followers to the narratives of the world that confront the individuals after death.

Many Muslims do not like this contempt for wealth and modernity. The well-to-do families and their educated children generally maintain a distance from the Tablighis. They would prefer to participate in political protests for the cause of the community but would not come nearer to the Jamaat. In Tablighi, they sense a lack of masculinity to defend their identity. Muslims, particularly the first-generation migrants in overseas countries do not affiliate to it because the movement does not address their existential and day to day challenges. Those who are struggling to establish themselves as professionals or entrepreneurs keep away from it. Sikand notes, the Tablighis talk either about invisible life that exists beyond the layers of sky or the grave deep inside the earth. This is unacceptable for many who have several responsibilities to discharge. The Tablighis always seek to discourage worldly affairs calling them 'lower grade desires.' People exposed to Western education and new sets of modern skills find it irrelevant.

This used to be the situation in the past. At least in European countries, as the movement has gone into the hands of the younger generation, even educated Muslims are getting involved in preaching and proselytizing works. The ethnographic study of the Tablighi movement in the United Kingdom by Riyaz Timol, who had made a very comprehensive and extensive studies, reveals that college going students are very much part of the Da'wa in Britain.[41] The strength of home grown Tablighi Muslims in Britain picked up particularly after 1994 World Congregation (Ijtima), at the Dewsbury headquarters. This works as the headquarters of the Tablighi movement for the entire West, including Europe, North America and some parts of the South America. This headquarters has a huge Mosque complex and the office of 'Anjuman-e-Islahul Muslimeen of United Kingdom' (The Society for the Reformation of Muslims in the United Kingdom), a registered body under which Tablighi activities are carried on in Britain. Hafiz Muhammad Patel, a person from Gujrat served as chief (Amir) of the Tablighi activities in Britain. And, therefore, Gujrati Muslims are also part of it in huge number. Like Tablighis, Gujaratis are great travelers and despite achieving economic success and prosperity, they remain attached to the religious activities. And being a peaceful and well-connected community, they prefer to associate with the Tablighi movement which does not overtly support or espouse violence and terrorist activities.[42]

Women in Tablighi Movement

Contrary to general perception, the Tablighi movement also has women activists. Maulana Muhammad Illyas Kandhlawi provisioned Da'wa for girls and women too. This was a break from the past that included the Prophet's injunctions who restricted the role of women to raising children and household affairs. During the times of the Prophet and successive Caliphates, their participation in Jehad was limited to taking away their husbands or children who got wounded in the battle for Islam. The Prophet, however, provisioned for Haj for the women. Women in Islamic society played very limited role in the field of science, medicine, trade and other professions. The

Tablighi movement allowed participation of both unmarried and married women.

This worked well in some countries such as Indonesia where Islamic boarding schools (Pesantren) were set up for both boys and girls. The word Pesantren refers to the place of students. In Indonesia and Malaysia, they are used to indicate low cost boarding schools for students. This was initiated with the aim to provide education to children of poor Muslims. Actually, in the beginning it started from madrasas where there were boarding facilities for both for male and female. The literature of the Tablighis was made part of the curriculum. However, these Pesantren gained prominence after two most famous Pondok Pesantren, Al-Fatah and Sunanul Husna al, converted into Tablighi Pesantren and started wielding authority in the Tablighi world. Normally, such boarding schools are located in areas which are treated as the stronghold of the Tablighi constituents. Those parents who are committed to the cause of the Tablighi send their daughters to such boarding schools. Fees vary from children to children depending on their incomes. If somebody does not have parents, their fee is waived off. Most female students who join such boarding schools come from the poor families.[43]

These schools sustain through donations. Field studies on Pesantren reveal that after the 9/11 in the USA, some donors withdrew their patronage to such boarding schools because of alleged involvement of Pesantren of the Tablighis[44] in terror activities. These Pesantrens serve as hub for "spreading Islamic knowledge for Tablighi activities."[45] They train the female students and prepare them to work for Da'wa (Proselytization). Normally, during the school holidays both male and female Tablighi preachers move around and appeal to community members to join the Jamaat for transmitting the message of puritan Islam. The female Tablighis like to be part of the Global Tablighi because this allows them to travel and meet people beyond the national boundaries. Another important facet of the Tablighi Pesantren in Indonesia is they follow the national curriculum apart from the Tablighi curriculum. This is not in Madrasatul Niswan—a Tablighi boarding school in Delhi in India.[46] Moreover, while there is subject distribution of 30:70 to religious and other teachings respectively in the Tablighi Pesantren, it is hundred per cent 'only religious' in case of Madrasatul Niswan in Delhi. These two institutions of Indonesia and India are in touch with each other but that relation is only informal.[47]

Tablighi as a Transnational Movement

Maulana Illyas did not plan to make the movement international and had limited his efforts to Indian Muslims. Gradually, it spread to other countries and by the 1930s preachers from other destinations had already started making moves. The overseas expansion started in the 1940s after World War II and after Maulana's son took over the Tablighi movement. He started sending preachers to different parts of the world in which South-East Asian countries and the United Kingdom were the immediate targets. In the Arab World, it could not spread its wings because there were far more competing schools within the Sunni Islam. Wahhabism dominated the Arab world. As a result, the Tablighi movement has come out to be powerful influence in England after India, Bangladesh and Pakistan. It faced tough resistance in Pakistan because the Deoband School there had different posturing towards non-Muslims in pursuit of building an Islamic society. Everywhere, the movement followed its fundamentals of Da'wa. The Tablighi movement is not monolithic and there are variations. Indonesia is a glorious example where they accept the methods but also introduce different texts and local cultures.

Within four decades of its establishment, the Tablighis grew phenomenally. When the organization held its annual meeting in 1941, there were 25,000 delegates. Today it is spread over more than 165 countries with almost 12 to 80 million followers according to the Pew Research Centre. In Bangladesh, the annual Tablighi congregation, Vishwa Ijtema in 2011 near Dhaka was so large that the organizers decided to hold it twice unlike once in a year. Bangladesh is second after India in terms of number of Tablighi Jamaat members. When the annual World Tablighi Jamaat Conference was held at Raiwind in Pakistan in 1988, nearly one million people from 90 countries attended.[48] In Indonesia in 2009, nearly eight lakh Muslims attended the annual meeting.[49] Indonesia is a very popular stronghold of the Tablighi movement. There is hardly any region in Indonesia where the Tablighi is not there.[50] Southeast Asian countries have a huge Tablighi mass base in countries like Malaysia, Indonesia, Thailand and Singapore.

As explained earlier, England is the second most popular

stronghold of the movement after the Indian subcontinent. The Markaz at a Deobandi complex in Dewsbury serves as headquarters for the Tablighi movement for entire West including Europe, North America and certain parts of South America. This headquarters has a huge Mosque complex and the office of 'Anjuman-e-Islahul Muslimeen of the United Kingdom' (The Society for the Reformation of Muslims in the United Kingdom), a registered body under which the Tablighi activities are run in the UK. Spain, France, Italy, Germany and other European countries too have Tablighi presence. There are over 2.5 lakh followers with a network of well knitted and lubricated organization. In the United States too, their strength is increasing.

England witnessed a very embarrassing situation in 2007, when the Tablighis planned to construct an 18-acre mosque complex in Stratford, East London. This site is very close to the place where Britain organized the Olympic Park that came up in 2012. The Tablighis wanted to erect a huge structure where 9000 people could assemble and take part in prayer at a time. It would have been the largest religious complex in England. This created furor in the British society, particularly the Christians who opposed it. And they forced the Tablighi to take back the project.[51] After 9/11, the security agencies in the United States started keeping watch over this organization. That dented its image and many people withdrew funding to the movement. The Federal Bureau of Investigation in the United States believes that nearly 50,000 people in the country are associated with the Tablighi mission and they run several mosques/Markaz in cities such as California, Texas and New York.[52] The Al-Falah Mosque in New York is the headquarter from where the Tablighi Jamat runs the movement in the US.

Conclusion:

The Tablighi Movement was and continues to be an extended arm of the Deoband. The movement fulfils the role which Deoband did not take in its mission. The Deoband School believes in the Islamic state and Islamic society where there are no infidels, no shirks. They are not very different from Wahhabism except for one thing that they could not demolish the places of religious worships of faith of others in India. In Pakistan, they did. The Deobandis were not less influenced by the Wahabis but they did not appreciate that the Wahabis had demolished several Islamic structures in Saudi Arabia.[53] They could not do so in Hindu dominated India because after the decline of the Mughal Empire it was not possible to do so.

In terms of ideological similarities, "both the Taliban and the Tablighi espouse Deobandi teachings which inculcate a purification of society to replicate the time of the Salaf-i-Saliheen and the institution of a version of Shariah in which women are strictly segregated and cultural practices like music, dance, and soccer are prohibited."[54] Public appreciation of the work of the Tablighis by late Saudi (Wahabi) Sheikh Abd al Aziz ibn Baz and his appeal to Wahabis followers to join the Da'wah mission indicate that the difference in the Tablighis and the Wahhabis is only of degree. The Saudi organizations such as World Muslim League that earlier funded part expenses of the Markaz[55] in London also funded the travel and other costs of the Tablighi missionaries. However, the present crown prince of Saudi Arabia has banned the working of the Tablighis in the country on the ground that the latter preaches hate and extremism!

Between the Islam and the creation of Global Islamic State, the Tablighi fulfils the role of the consolidator. It has chosen a path which no other sects or order of Islam does. It takes the Islam to social and cultural realm and preach an ordinary Muslim how to become a good Muslim. And a good Muslim is one who does not believe in or recognize any other God or religious faith except Allah and his messenger, Prophet Muhammad. It is this conception of puritan Islam which makes the Tablighis exclusivist and dangerous for a pluralist society. Any doctrine that considers another faith system its enemy carries inherent potential of preaching hatred against others. The puritan Islam they espouse is a problematic concept because The *Quran* suggests that Muslims should not befriend the non-Muslims.[57] Islam teaches that those who do not adhere to Islam are Kafirs and deserve punishments even if the followers of the Islam do not like it. No wonder, radical Islamists organizations may have quarrels with the Shias sect but they are comfortable with the Tablighis. Furthermore, there are several such examples in public domain which suggest that terrorists belonging to a radical Islamist group had cozy relationships with the Tablighis and their preachers.

References:

1 'Alim' refers to religious scholars whereas 'Hafiz' is one who has memorized the Quran.

2 Metcalf, B. (2003). Travelers' Tales in the Tablighi Jama at. The Annals of the American Academy of Political and Social Science, 588, 136-148. Retrieved June 1, 2020, from www.jstor.org/stable/1049858. P.137. She also argued that there was a massive ethnic cleansing after partition which accelerated its work.

3 Ahmad, Mumtaz (1994). "Islamic Fundamentalism in South Asia" in :The Jamaat-i-Islami and the Tablighi Jamaaat of South Asia." In Marty, Martin E.; Appleby, R. Scott (eds.). Fundamentalism Observed, Vol. II, University of Chicago Press, p. 511.

4 Ibid. Also see, Metcalf, B. (2003). Travelers' Tales in the Tablighi Jamaat. The Annals of the American Academy of Political and Social Science, 588, 136-148. Retrieved June 1, 2020, from www.jstor.org/stable/1049858. P.137. Noor, F. (2012). Learning to Be: The Foundational Literature of the Tablighi Jama'at and Its Role in Defining the Movement. In Islam on the Move: The Tablighi Jama'at in Southeast Asia (pp. 63-88). Amsterdam: Amsterdam University Press.

doi:10.2307/j.ctt46mzqq. p.

5 Ibid.

6 There is a distinction between reform and revival. Reform is always forward looking whereas revivalism tends to resurrect the past. The Tabligh movement was not to make changes in the religion in light of new circumstances and opening of new areas of rationality and questioning but it was anti- reform in entirety.

7 http://www.internationalbulletin.org/issues/2012-04/2012-04-189-hauser.html

8 Ibid, p.517.

9 Chilla is a Persian term which means forty days of renunciation and spiritual life for self-purification.

10 P1, Bulbul Siddqui, Becoming good Muslim: Tablighi Jamaat in the UK and Bangladesh, Springer, Singapore, 2018. P. Introduction.

11 Ibid. B. Siddiqui.

12 Sikand, Yoginder S. The Origins and the Growth of the Tablighi Jamaat in Britain, 18 April 2007. Islam and Christian Muslim Relations, 9:2, Online Journal.

13 Winkelmann, Mareik J. "Women Studying for the After Life" in Marranci, Gabrielle (2014). Studying Islam in Practice, Routledge, London, pp. 214-216.

14 Ahmad, Mumtaz (1994). "Islamic Fundamentalism in South Asia" in The Jamaat-i-Islami and the Tablighi Jamaaat of South Asia." In Marty, Martin E.; Appleby, R. Scott (eds.). Fundamentalism Observed, Vol. II, University of Chicago Press, p. 516.

15 https://thewire.in/diplomacy/tablighi-jamaat-india-indonesia-relations-diplomats-asean

16 Tablighi Jama'at, Pew Research Centre, 15 September 2010.

17 P1, Bulbul Siddqui, Becoming good Muslim: Tablighi Jamaat in the UK and Bangladesh, Springer, Singapore, 2018. P.

18 Riyaz Timol. Structures of Organisation and Loci of Authority in a Glocal Islamic Movement: The Tablighi Jama'at in Britain, School of History, Archaeology and Religion, Cardiff University, Cardiff, 14 October 2019. Online accessed on 2 June 2020.

19 https://www.sciencespo.fr/mass-violence-war-massacre-resistance/fr/document/hindu-muslim-communal-riots-india-i-1947-1986.html

20 Ahmad, Mumtaz (1994). "Islamic Fundamentalism in South Asia" in The Jamaat-i-Islami and the Tablighi Jamaaat of South Asia." In Marty, Martin E.; Appleby, R. Scott (eds.). Fundamentalism Observed, Vol. II, University of Chicago Press, p.522.

21 Tabhlighis joining the Protests at Shahinbagh.

22 Lt Genberal Sinha Report and Report of T V Rajeshwar, Governor of West Bengal.

23 Ibid.

24 Ragi, S. K. (2022). *RSS and Gandhi: The Idea of India* (1st ed.). SAGE Publications Pvt. Ltd.

25 https://www.aa.com.tr/en/middle-east/haji-abdul-wahab-and-tablighi-jamaat-pakistan-/1315219. Accessed on 29 May 2020.

26 Tablighi Jamaat, Pew Research Centre, 15 September 2010.

27 Tablighi and Maulana Azad connection

28 Alexiev, Alex. "Tablighi Jamaat: Jihad's Stealthy Legions," Middle East Quarterly, Vol 12, No.1. Winter 2005, pp. 3-1.

29 B Raman referred to Alexiev, Alex ibid.

30 The News, 13 February, 1995 quoted by Alexiev, Alex Ibid.

31 Alexiev, Alex. "Tablighi Jamaat: Jihad's Stealthy Legions," Middle East Quarterly, Vol 12, No.1.

32 Pew Research Institute.

33 https://www.outlookindia.com/newsscroll/tabligh-jamaat-members-misbehave-with-nurses-up-govt-to-invoke-nsa/1789994. Outlook 3 April, 2020. Also See The Print 03 April 2020.

34 Riyaz Timol. Structures of Organisation and Loci of Authority in a Glocal Islamic Movement: The Tablighi Jama'at in Britain, School of History, Archaeology and Religion, Cardiff University, Cardiff, 14 October 2019. Online accessed on 2 June 2020. p.1.

35 American Academy of Science and Arts. Fundamentalism Observed, Vol. I, University of Chicago Press, p.459.

36 Sikand, Yoginder S. (2007). "The Origins and the Growth of Tablighi Jamaat in Britain." Islam and Christian Muslim Relations, Routledge, London, Online, Vol 9, No.2,

37 Ibid, 181.

38 Ibid, 183.

39 Noor, F. (2012). Learning to Be: The Foundational Literature of the Tablighi Jamaat and Its Role in Defining the Movement. In Islam on the Move: The Tablighi Jamaat in Southeast Asia (pp. 63-88). Amsterdam: Amsterdam University Press.

doi:10.2307/j.ctt46mzqq. p. 90.

40 Ibid, 92.

41 Structures of Organisation and Loci of Authority in a Glocal Islamic Movement: The Tablighi Jamaat in Britain, Riyaz Timol, School of History.

42 Yoginder Sikand, p.182, The Origins and Growth of Tablighi Jamaat in Britain.

43 (NISA, E. (2014). Insights into Lives of Indonesian Female Tablighi Jamaat, p. 477).

44 Ibid.

45 NISA, E. (2014). Insights Into the Lives of Indonesian Female Tablighi Jamaat. Modern Asian Studies, 48(2), 468-491. Retrieved June 1, 2020, from www.jstor.org/stable/24494587, p.472.

46 Ibid, 473.

47 Ibid. p. 473.

48 Mumtaz Mahmud, Fundamentalism Observed Vol I, p. 510.

49 (NISA, E. (2014). Insights Into the Lives of Indonesian Female Tablighi Jamaat. Modern Asian Studies, 48(2), 468-491. Retrieved June 1, 2020, from www.jstor.org/stable/24494587, p. 469).

50 (Ibid).

51 Pieri, Zacharias P. (2015). Tablighi Jamaat and the Quest for the London Mega-Mosque: Continuity and Change-Palgrave Macmillan, US.

52 Zahid, Farhan. "Tablighi Jamaat and Its Links with Islamist Terrorism." Foreign Analysis, No.19, March 2015. https://cf2r.org/foreign/tablighi-jamaat-and-its-links-with-islamist-

terrorism-2/#_ftn16.Accessed on 5 June 2020.

53 Burki, Shireen Khan. "The Tablighi Jamaat: Proselytizing Missionaries or Trojan Horse?" Journal of Applied Security Research, Volume 8, 2013 - Issue 1, Taylor and Francis Online pp. 98-117. Published online:19 Dec 2012.

54 This was reported in The Financial Times 12 April 1982. Burki, Shireen Khan has referred to it by quoting Alexiev, Alex, Ibid.

55 As quoted in Quran (Surah 8, Ayat 12)
Remember thy Lord inspired
The angels (with the message):
"I am with you: give
Firmness to the Believers:
I will instil terror
Into the hearts of unbelievers:
Smite ye above their necks
And smite all their
Finger-tips off them."

CHAPTER 4

THE TABLIGHI JAMAAT AND ITS TERROR LINKS

BEFORE THE 9/11 terrorist incident in the US, most of Europe and the West had not come to identify the Tablighi movement with terror activities either directly or indirectly. The security agencies had suspicions and cynicism about the Tablighi activities due to their secretive ways of working. The Tablighis deliberately kept a distance from public attention and did not participate in public discourses. Absence of published materials that could expose their design and considered policy of non-engagement with non-Muslims compounded the cynicism.[1] It was also because the Tablighis never figured directly in any of suicide bombing incidents or explosions. They did not take public stand on even highly contested issues which have been close to the hearts of all Muslims cutting cross territorial boundaries such as Palestine and the American war in Afghanistan. Occasionally, they came out and criticized the far more radical Islamists and their organizations in the Muslim world. All these made it difficult for scholars monitoring Islamic ideology to assess its true character and place it on scale of Islam ranging from moderate on the one end to radicals on the other.

Despite being an extended arm of the Deoband and closely linked with radical elements such as the Jamaat-e-Islami of Pakistan and dozen other radical organizations across the world, the Tablighi had succeeded in projecting itself as a representative form of spiritual Islam which had nothing to do with religion-based sectarian political activities. The public denouncements of the Tablighis and attack on their establishments by the Wahabis in initial years helped it in accentuating and strengthening the moderate image of the Tablighis.[2]

The 9/11 attacks in the US, however, changed the perception of security agencies and the people about the Tablighis. The Federal Bureau of Investigation (FBI) found some leads that pointed to the links of the Tablighi Jamaat to the incidents. It had 'serious reservation' about the role of the Tablighi and put the organization on its watch list.[3] This news took the entire world by surprise and security agencies in other countries too started linking dots and revisiting the files. The Tablighi Jamaat all of a sudden came on the radar of security agencies all over the world. This dented the organization's image and people started distancing from it. Thousands of miles away from the US capital, donors started withdrawing funds that were sanctioned for the Tablighi seminaries in various countries.[4] Administrative agencies all over the world started looking at the organization with contempt and people started protesting against its activities. When the Tablighi Jamaat sought permission to build a grand Mosque in East London, local Christians and their organizations[5] protested and got the work stopped. The proposed Markaz was planned to host 9000 preachers at a time, and it was close to the Olympic Park of London which was established only in 2012. The local authorities preferred to give the 17 acres of land for housing, retail, office and community facilities.[6]

Several countries in the world such as Uzbekistan, Russia and China have already banned the Tablighi Jamaat because in their eyes it is a radical organization.[7] The Russian Government banned it in 2009 after it received intelligence inputs that the Jamaat was involved in violent activities. It was, later, endorsed by the country's Supreme Court. This ban was extended to Crimean Peninsula from Ukraine in 2014 after Russia annexed it. The Court accepted the arguments and facts presented by the government that the Tablighi Jamaat's activities were 'violating Russia's territorial integrity and lending support for 'international terrorists' organizations.'[8] Muslim organizations accused Russia of violating the basic human rights of Muslims and also alleged that the judge was politically motivated. But these did not deter the political leadership from taking decisions against the Tablighi Jamaat. When Renat Suleimanov, a local Muslim in Crimea organized a gathering of the Tablighis in the mosque in 2017, he was arrested and sent to jail. The argument that they had gathered just to discuss the religious issues was dismissed by the Supreme Court which went with law enforcement agencies.

The status of the Tablighis in China is little ambiguous.[9] There is no formal ban on the organization but they are also not free to exercise their religious preaching and proselytization as in European countries or India. Further, there are instances of the Tablighis getting arrested and put in the prison for practice of their cult of prayers in China. They "wear the loose, white, South Asian-style clothing common to the movement…" but they don't have exclusively dedicated mosques or institutes for large gatherings as one finds in other countries.[10] When they move from one place to the other for preaching, they take care of the fact that they don't walk in large groups. The reason may be the strong monitoring of the Chinese state and its officials on the activities of Muslims. The Chinese government considers Tablighis activities as a matter of big concern for the nation. The arrest of a few Chinese nationals[11] from Nizamuddin Markaz surprised people in the beginning because there was general perception that the Tablighis are not active in China. Since there were delegates from Uzbekistan and Kazakhstan at the Markaz in Delhi, BJP leader Subrahmanyam Swamy raised the issue with the Ministry of External Affairs. He raised a fundamental question that how could the central government allow the Markaz to take place[12] more so since the anti-CAA (Citizenship Amendment Act) agitation was going on in the country and also the news of the pandemic had started pouring in from different parts of the world.

In India, the demand for ban on the Tablighi Jammat

gathered momentum after the news of clandestine and objectionable activities of the Tablighis came into the open through various television new channels. They were reported to be hiding and fleeing from one part of the country to another, misbehaving with doctors and nurses at the Covid-19 quarantine centres and spitting at public places in order to spread Corona. Uttar Pradesh government invoked the National Security Act against six Tablighis who created ruckus and misbehaved with doctors and nurses in district hospital of Ghaziabad.[13] The popular sentiment demanded strong action against the Tablighi Jamaat. A seasoned politician and former foreign Minister of India, K Natwar Singh writing in a leading daily of the US pleaded for ban on the organization.[14] He articulated the mood of the country after assessing the activities of the Tablighis. The central government did not work on it although it went ahead to ban the entry of 2000 foreign Tablighi into India.[15]

The understanding of the security agencies and their response to the Tablighis stands in sharp contrast to the intellectuals who look at the working of the organization in the framework of constitutionality and liberal democracy. The liberal constitutionalists argue that the Tablighis have the right to exercise their freedom of religion so long as they work under the ambit of the constitution. They defend the rights of the Tablighis to preach and offer prayers and oppose the idea of a ban. Most scholars who have done ethnographic studies on the Tablighis also take forward the arguments of the organization that it aims at promoting true and puritan

Islam. Therefore, they defend their rights against too much intervention from the state. Whether they are from the West or the Indian subcontinent or South-East Asian countries, most of the scholars converge on this.[16] Scholars who have done ethnographic studies on Tablighi anywhere in the world have arrived at the same conclusions. Some of them have even gone to the extent of suggesting that it carries the legacy of spiritual tradition of Hinduism and Sufism.[17]

However, security agencies in the West and elsewhere, including America, Europe, Australia, India and other non-Islamic countries, have arrived at a new understanding about the Tablighis.[18] The US security agencies hold that although the Tablighis are not directly linked to terrorism like members of Al-Qaeda and the Taliban, they are the easier target of recruitment to these terrorist organizations.[19] The indoctrination in fundamentals of Islam, detachment from worldly pleasures and inculcating the psychology of sacrificing everything for Din made the Tablighis easy prey to be recruited into the ideology of extremism. The American agencies have found significant presence of the Tablighi Jamaat cadres of the US recruited into the ranks of the Al-Qaeda. This information and analysis were revealed by the then Deputy Chief of the FBI Michael J Heimbach who handled the section on International Terrorism.[20]

Countries such as Spain, France, Germany, England, Australia and India have witnessed the same phenomenon. The stories of Tablighis being recruited by Pakistani Inter-Services Intelligence (ISI) for fighting Jihad in Kashmir has come to the notice of those who have been monitoring international terrorism.[21] The Al Qaeda and Taliban, both in Pakistani and Afghanistan, recruited their cadre from the Tablighis to fight against America led Northern Alliance forces in Afghanistan. The Western media has many stories depicting the Tablighis joining ranks with the terrorists to fight for Islam in different parts of the World.[22] Several such cases have been resolved where the links to the Tablighis were established.[23] These confirm that the Tablighis are not as apolitical as they claim. Security agencies have realized their mistake in assessment of the organization. The new assessment says that the Tablighis are an integral part of the fanatic orthodox Sunni Islam which shares the larger mission of converting the entire world into Islam and influence all walks of human lives in the light of the tenets of Islam. As it believes in puritan Islam and rejects any kind of deviation it breeds fanaticism and intolerance towards other faith systems which subsequently breeds terrorism and violence. Before we engage in critical analysis and move towards conclusions, a limited mapping of news and literature published so far would give significant insights into the functioning of the Tablighi members.

Victoria Burnett filed a news story on 20 January 2008 in *The New York Times*, with a headline captioned: '14 terror suspects held as Spanish police raid mosque.'[24] The police had arrested 14 suspected militants accused of 'plotting an attack on Barcelona.' The police found out that it was a well calibrated attempt to use violence and terror attacks before the parliamentary elections in the country. The police had raided several apartments, two mosques and a bakery in Barcelona.[25] All of them were from the Indian subcontinent; 12 Pakistanis, one Indian and one Bangladeshi. The arrest was made on the basis of inputs from a foreign agency that a known Pakistani militant had left Pakistan for Barcelona to 'execute a terrorist plan in the country.' The mosque, the adjacent prayer hall, and the apartments raided and people arrested belonged to the Tablighi Jamaat.[26] The materials recovered from the mosque and the apartments were time devices, a bag containing ball-bearing, batteries and cables supposedly meant for making and detonating bombs. The mosque which was raided was 'Torek Bin Ziad Mosque', one of the city's most prominent mosques[27] named after an aggressor who had attacked Spain in 711 AD and had brought havoc in the name of Jihad. This mosque and nearby vicinity were the epicentres of Islamic activities in Spain. Spain had fast emerged as a terrorist hub in Europe and the major contribution came from Pakistani Muslims who were engaged in radicalising Muslims. In 2004, 11 Pakistanis were arrested for plotting bombs to destroy 'several landmarks in the city.'[28] The Pakistani population living in Spain has become a nightmare for the police and security agencies which look at them with a sense of contempt. Indigenous Spanish population has now developed immense trust-deficit against Muslims in general and this reflects in the media reporting as well. Now, the Tablighis are on the watch list of the police.

A Congressional debate reveals how Tablighis are being watched over by the security agencies in the US and how Americans view their activities with suspicion after 9/11 terrorist attacks on the World Trade Centre. Congressman Louie Gohmert while initiating a debate on the growth of rising radical

Islam in the US charged the Obama administration for taking a casual and softer approach to the challenges from the ISIS. He even alleged that the white House and the Department of Justice were soft on terror as these elements had access to these institutions.[29] He also charged that the Homeland Security Department was not screening the migrants who entered the country. He referred to an instance where a radical Islamist was issued American Visa despite his radical posts on the social media. He spoke about the linkages the Tablighi Jamaat had with terror and radical elements.[30]

During his interaction with Megyn Marie Kelly on Fox News, senior official of the US Homeland Security, listed out a number of cases from different parts of the world to suggest that the government should take the terror links of the Tablighis seriously.[31] The list included terror connection of Tablighi Jamaat members in the assassination attempt on Benazir Bhutto, 1995; Coup attempt against Mrs. Bhutto, 2001; Case of John Walker Lindh, 2001; Richard Reid, the shoe bomber, 2002; Jose Padilla, 2002; Portland Seven, 2002; Lackawanna Six, 2005; London Underground Bombing, 2005; airline bombing plot, 2008; and the Barcelona plot, 2017.[32]

He also confessed that not everybody in the Tablighi Jamaat was a radical Islamist or a terrorist but revealed that "Tablighi officials invite recruits to the Tablighi centre in Raiwind in Pakistan for four months of additional missionary training and representatives of terrorist organizations approach these students at the Raiwind centre and invite them to undertake military training."[33] He was speaking on the basis of information published on the Tablighi Jamaat in the Middle East Quarterly in 2005.

Muslims number 3.4 million in the US which is 1.1 per cent of the country's population.[34] It is the third largest religion in the US after Christianity and Judaism (Jews) and is the fastest growing. Majority Muslim population there belongs to the Indian sub-continent. And they brought with them the radicalized form of Deobandi Islam. The number of mosques in the US was 962 in 1994. It increased to more than 2100 in 2019. This means that there is one mosque for every 1650 Muslims in the US. With an increase in population, the society has witnessed an increasing trend towards radicalization. This is evident from increasing use of burqua and scarfs by girls in the public space including universities.

This has often led to public reaction against the community. Al-Huda institute has a global network of the Islamic religious schools including in the US. It is run by a lady, Farhat Hashmi, from Pakistan who has the backing of the Pakistani military establishment and the Jamaat e-Islami.[35] This institute hogged the media when a lady from Karachi, Nosheen Ali Irfan, withdrew her two daughters from the school within five weeks on the ground that they radicalize young minds which is the most suited for breeding terrorists.[36] This further came to prominence when a 29-year-old Tashfeen Malik of Pakistan, educated from Al-Huda's Karachi branch, executed the California killings in America. She was a thoroughly radicalized girl.

The Tablighis in the US have good links with this seminary which is based on Ahl-e-Hadith that has inspired several terrorist organizations and their supporters including the Jamaat-e-Islami. Islamic scholar Phil Haney estimated that over 300 Tablighis in the US had possible terror links.[37] The FBI calculates that there are over 50,000 Tablighi workers who are active in the country on Islamic missions.[38] This explains the reason for increasing American hostility towards Muslims. This led to a sharp rise in attacks on mosques and Muslims in the US.[39] This was for the first time in the last two decades, the White House did not host the Ramdan party in 2017, breaking two decades precedents[40] and signed the executive order to ban entry of Muslims into the US from Muslim dominated countries.[41] Even in 9/11 attacks, Zacarias Moussaoui who was charged with being involved in the attack was 'once upon a time a Tablighi adherent in France.'[42] The Jamaat's 'links to Al Qaeda became known' when arrested terrorists belonging to Al-Qaeda confessed before the police officials in the US that they had 'attended Jamaat camp' in Pakistan.[43]

In France, officials conceded sometime back that nearly 80 per cent of the Islamic radicals they encountered with had direct or indirect links with the Tablighi Jamaat.[44] There were scores of pointers that indicated involvement of Tablighis in terror activities and for providing 'fertile ground for breeding terrorism.'[45] News reports suggested that over 100 French Muslims who fought with Al-Qaeda against the US forces in Afghanistan had Tablighi background.[46] For example, Hervé Djamel Loiseau, a French Muslim who died during a bombing in Afghanistan had stayed in a Pakistani village with his French identity card. He was a young man who was imbibed in the best liberal culture of France. There was no ground for radicalization at home because his father was not very religious. Loiseau liked music and fun. But after he came in contact with the Tablighis, he started acquiring the Tablighi trend. He started visiting Mosque regularly at 5 am and gradually stopped listening to music. Few years later, he went to fight for Al-Qaeda in Afghanistan.[47] Importantly, he was buried in Pakistan where his dead body was given full respect by the locals. The story of Loiseau is not an isolated example. An Algerian born French Muslim Djamel Beghal, who was convicted for planning to blow up the American Embassy in Paris, was a follower of the Tablighis and later joined and started working for Al-Qaeda.[48]

The stories in other Western countries are not very different. The Tablighi connection, directly or indirectly in terms of indoctrination, has come to the notice of the British officials too. Amjad, the brother of Assad Sarwar who was arrested in connection with the plot to blow the transatlantic airliner, admitted that his brother was at Tablighi Jamaat and he thought that it was better to serve the religion than pursuing study.[49] There are a series of similar such arrests in England which have found connections with the Tablighis. Prior to the arrest of Assad, police had arrested another 23 people all of whom were connected with the Tablighi Jamaat. Waheed Zaman, arrested in the same case was also found to be a follower of the Tablighis. The suicide bombing of London Bridge in which 56 people lost their lives in 2005 and about 700 were injured was led and teamed by people associated with the Tablighi Jamaat.[50] Mohammad Sidique Khan who led the attack was a

Tablighi follower. Besides, Youssef Zaghba, a Moroccan who was part of the attack and Shehzad Tanweer had participated in the Tablighi meetings at Mosque in Yorkshire. Richard Reid, from Brixton, South London, who tried to detonate explosives packed in his shoe during a flight from Paris to Miami in 2001, was also a Tablighi follower.[51] All these had a cumulative impact on the British society and when the Tablighis decided to go ahead with their plan to have construct a huge Markaz complex in Central London, it evoked a strong protest.

People in England have started questioning the motives of the Tablighis. Indigenous population concludes that the main objective of the Jamaat is 'to rescue the Ummah from the culture and civilization of the Jews, Christians and other enemies of Islam to create such hatred for their ways, as human beings have for urine and excreta.'[52] They work with Deobandis who are just 20 per cent of British Muslims but control 40 per cent of the mosques.[53]

Germany has started scrutinizing the activities of the Tablighi Jamaat after 9/11 terrorist attacks in the US. The planning for the said attack was designed in Germany raising many eyebrows in the country. For the first time in its history, in the annual report on security in 2004, the Tablighis appeared under the title 'Foreign Extremist Efforts Ominous to Security.' This report normally lists out terrorist and extremist organizations of all kinds which pose potential threat to Germany and its constitution. In 2005, the Federal Interior Ministry of Germany categorically stated that radical Islam was the biggest threat to Germany.[54] Germany has 3.3

million Muslim population. They come from the diverse ethnic background, but Sunni cult is a predominant majority accounting for 75 per cent of Muslim population. Ahmadiyyas are very small numbering 50,000 and they are mostly the refugees from Pakistan. They have not found to be involved in any activity linked to terror. In the last few decades, the Tablighis have spread their activities in Germany.They have deliberately targeted South Asian and Maghreb guest workers. They have several mosques in cities such as Munich, Nurnberg, Erfurt and Cologne.

Europe has started expressing concerns on the rise of Muslim migrants and the accelerated pace of their radicalization. Earlier, the Tablighi preachers coming from first or second generation migrants had language problems. Now, the Tablighis get followers from third and fourth generation of Muslim population who are able to converse in local language. This has helped them make inroads in the local population. The Tablighis and other extremist Islamic organizations find the democratic space and constitutionalism of the European countries fertile ground for construction and consolidation of their religious identity and pitting the same against the host country. They use the basis of individual rights and freedoms to preach the ideology of Islam and gradually move towards community consciousness and consolidation. Thereafter, the argument of discrimination and victimization is brought in place to assert the community identity in the cultural and political space. Violence and aggression become the by-products of such a heightened sense of identity and victimization.

Tablighi in Pakistan

Tablighis are deep entrenched in Pakistan's civil and military administration. They are acting as powerful non-state actors supporting Islamic radicalization and serve as a precursor to militant Jihad outside the country and covert operations inside Pakistan. Tablighi supporters have served in high positions in the government of Pakistan ranging from intelligence chief to the Prime Minister and the President.[55] Although the Tablighis gained international prominence after 9/11 incident in the US, they were already working to radicalize Muslim minds in Pakistan and sending them on missions in different countries. The process intensified during General Zia-ul-Haq's presidency when the Tablighis were invited to address military establishments in Pakistan. It was the time when the Pakistani Army and the young radicalized Afghans were fighting together against the Soviet Union in Afghanistan. After the death of General Zia-ul-Haq, they continued to remain close to the Pakistani establishment. Father of Nawaz Sharif, Muhammad Sharif was a follower of the Tablighi Jamaat. And so was the case with the Chief of the Inter-Services Intelligence (ISI), Lt General Javed Naser.

The Tablighis had tried to overthrow Benazir Bhutto as the Prime Minister. It also figured in the assassination attempts on Benazir Bhutto in 1995. Earlier, it was considered to be the handiwork of Harkat-Ul-Jihad-Al-Islami (HuJI) but later on it turned out to be the work of Jihad bi-al Saif which was said to be closely associated with the Tablighi. Even the HuJI was close to the Tablighis. The HuJI also belonged to the

Deobandi school founded by former Tablighi members such as Qari Saifullah Akhter and Fazal ur Rehman Khalil. This organization fought against the Northern Alliance forces in Afghanistan and also in Kashmir in India.[56] It is operational in Bangladesh too. The organization describes itself as second line of defence for every Muslim and aims 'to establish Islamic rule by waging war.'[57] In Bangladesh, it gave a slogan of 'Amra Sobai Hobo Taliban, Bangla Hobe Afghanistan'(We will all become Taliban and we will turn Bangladesh into Afghanistan). The group that operates in Bangladesh is named as HuJI-B and has the same objective of establishing Islamic rule in the country by waging war. It openly supported Osama bin Laden and the Taliban in both Pakistan and Afghanistan.

Tablighi's penetration and influence in the Pakistani establishment was evident when Prime Minister Nawaz Sharif visited the Tablighi headquarters at Raiwind near Lahore to meet the Jamaat Leader Omar Palanpuri and request him 'to convince Sipah-e-Sahaba and its splinter group Lashkar-e-Jhangvi (LeJ) to end their anti-Shia terror campaign.' Sipah-e-Sahaba (SS)[58] is a sectarian Sunni outfit which wants Pakistan to be declared a Sunni Islamic State and it also contests elections. The far more radical wing of the SS formed the LeJ after splinting in 1996. Many of their cadres were also members of terrorist organizations such as the Harkat-ul-Mujahideen (HuM) and the erstwhile Taliban regime in Afghanistan.[59] It also has a close link with Jaish-e-Mohammed (JeM), a Pakistan-based terrorist outfit active in Jammu and Kashmir.[60] In short, these two organizations are radical Islamist organizations. However, the most shocking of the talk was the reply of Palanpuri that "there should always be a hot wire along with a cold one to light up the bulb."[61] In a way, the Jamaat leader endorsed the attack. The visit of the Pakistani Prime Minister clearly pointed out to the links that the Tablighi leaders had with terrorist groups.

The Tablighis' links with terror outfits have repeatedly been acknowledged by Pakistani officials and constitutional authorities. Interior Minister of Pakistan, Abdul Rehman Malik, in his talk with a UK based think tank in 2011 had said that 'all terrorists arrested in Pakistan had visited the Tablighi Jamaat Centre at Raiwind, near Lahore.'[62] Malik was admonished for his comments throughout Pakistan. But he was not the only one to hold such views. Tariq Pervez, former Director General of National Counter Terrorism Authority (NACTA) of Pakistan also confessed that "the Tablighi Jamaat attracts youth and brings them into the mosque" where "people associated with Jihad and sectarian groups, and, in some cases, their networks are also present. Most vulnerable are the new entrants to the Tablighi fold."[63] This happens in full knowledge of leaders of the Tablighi jamaat. And therefore, to argue that the Tablighis are engaged purely into spiritual Islam is a misplaced notion.[64]

Over the last so many years, Pakistan has become the 'hub' of nurturing extremist elements through the Tablighi Jamaat. Radical Islam has converged with the military and bureaucratic state complex by which both reinforce each other.[65] Pakistan chose militant Islam as its doctrine and made it integral to its foreign policy. It sought to damage India, legitimize the existence of a separate homeland for Muslims and enhance Pakistan's position in the Islamic world. It suited the Western powers which wanted to fight the Communist regimes of China and the erstwhile Soviet Union. The Tablighis got a free hand in indoctrinating youths in the name of puritan Islam who later fought against the Soviets in the name of Jihad. The Tablighis in Pakistan started the largest number of missionaries in different parts of world for Islamic indoctrination to be harvested by terrorist organizations. In Pakistan, Jihadi outfits and Tablighi Jamaat have overlapping membership and they are in close touch with each other. Tablighi's taller claim of being non-political has few takers today in Pakistan. In 2002 general elections, the Tablighis supported the Muthaida Majlis-e-Amal, the alliance of Islamist parties. It is said that after coming into power in KPR province, the MMA alliance advanced Islamists agenda which had tactical support from the Tablighis. It was as a result of this that both the Afghan Taliban and Tehrik-e-Taliban Pakistan could revive themselves.

Tablighi Jamaat in India

Like in other democratic countries of the West, the predominant perception about the Tablighis in India has been that this is a spiritual organization aimed at 'making Muslim a good Muslim.' Despite being born in India in 1926, very few people outside the Islamic world knew about this organization before March 2020. The security agencies had started taking note of the Tablighi activities but they never came out publicly against the organization. Security personnel functioning in Kashmir have admitted that extremist organizations working in North Kashmir were in touch with the Tablighis and they have been sending their cadre for religious indoctrination for 40 days.[66] The Hizbul Mujahideen accepts them in the rank only after they complete such training programmes. They have observed that members of the Tablighis do not face any inconvenience while working in North Kashmir. The areas that have strong presence of the Deobandi Sunni Islam have also emerged as the strongholds of the Tablighis. This is not a mere coincidence. Marhama village in the Anantnag district, where the Pulwama suicide bombing conspiracy was hatched, has a powerful Deoband Madrasa, whose faculty includes Tablighi Jamaat preachers. As Assad Bashir notes, the area is a stronghold of Deobandi terrorist group Jaish-e-Mohammed.[67]

Conclusion: Gate Way to terrorism

The Tabligh movement is not what was generally perceived about and understood by the World some two decades back. It is an outfit based on the philosophy of Deoband Islam. It is not at all a self-searching inward-looking spiritual journey of individual for self-purification and making this world a better place to live in. Tablighi members are the foot-soldiers of Islam that seeks to have a global Islamic state and a global Islamic society. They are not in conflict with any Islamic organization or sect. They never have criticized any suicide bombing or any violence perpetrated by the Islamist Jihadi terrorist organizations. On the contrary, they have radicalized Muslim youths who become easy recruits for terrorist organizations.

The Tablighis have full knowledge of this but they claim to be at an arm's length from such recruitments.

The spiritual training of making a good Muslim provides a fertile soil for seeds of political Islam that believes in physical conquest of the world in the name of Islam, as the Prophet and his successor Caliphates did in their lifetimes. There is credible evidence to establish that membership of terrorist organizations of global network have overlapping membership of the Tablighi. There are several terrorist organizations whose members have undergone the ideological and religious indoctrination sessions of the Tablighis. Funding of the Tablighi activities by the World Muslim League, an organization of the Wahabis, point out that the initial hiccups and animosity between Wahhabism and the Tablighis no longer exists. The arrests of John Walker Lindh, Jose Omer Padila and many others such as David Hook, Richard Reid, the shoe bomber,[68] prove that the Tablighis are conduits in the crime of Global Jihad.

In many cases the Tablighis have facilitated the movement of sleeper cells of terrorist organizations in different parts of the World. From the US and Europe to Australia and India, there is convergence on one point that the Tablighi Jamaat radicalizes Muslims in name of true and puritan faith. The organization tactically, informally and secretly lends support to militant radical forces of Islam whose doctrine is to wage a war against non-Muslim Kafirs and infidels. Its ideology of puritan Islam to fulfil devotional and spiritual quest is a façade which allows it to use the democratic and liberal framework of constitutionalism in non-Islamic countries to develop and expand its network. Its cosy alliance with fanatical Islamic political parties and organizations is not a matter of chance but a considered understanding and concurrence with an exclusivist doctrine of Islam. It is not a progressive reformist Islamic movement.

Reference:

1 Alexiev, Alex (2005). Tablighi Jamaat: Jihad's Stealthy Legions, Middle East Quarterly 12(5), pp. 3-11.https://www.meforum.org/686/tablighi-jamaat-jihads-stealthy-legions.

2 Wahabbism propagates an Islam which is very sectarian, fanatic and intolerant to other faith systems. Their attack on Tablighis gave the impression of latter being liberal in thinking which it is not.

3 Alexiev, Alexander (2011). The Wages of Extremism: Radical Islam's Threat to the West and the Muslim World, Security and Foreign Affairs, Hudson Institute. p. 84.

4 Tell the 'gate of terror' that the noose has been tightened on the Tablighis, now Saudi Arabia will also stop terror funding? Hindustan News Hub, 12 December 2021. https://hindustannewshub.com/india-news/tell-the-gate-of-terror-that-the-noose-has-been-tightened-on-the-tablighis-now-saudi-arabia-will-also-stop-terror-funding/. accessed on 19 December 2021.

5 Iqbal, Sajjid (2018). Setback to Tablighi Jamaat Plan to Build a 'Mega Mosque' in London, The Dawn, Pakistan, 30 January 2018. https://www.dawn.com/news/1386043, accessed on 29 October 2021.

6 Plans for 9,000-capacity mosque in east London rejected, The Guardian https://www.theguardian.com/politics/2015/oct/29/plans-for-9000-capacity-mosque-in-east-london-rejected

7 'Explained: Saudi Arabia's ban on the Tablighi and Da'wah group,' Mehr Gill, The Indian Express, 14 December 2021, https://indianexpress.com/article/explained/explained-saudi-arabia-ban-on-tablighi-dawah-group-7670780/, accessed on 17 December 2021.

8 Coynash, Halya. 'New weapon of religious persecution and arrests in Russian-occupied Crimea,' 4 October 2017, http://khpg.org/en/index.php?id=1507082183, accessed on 29 October 2021.

9 Stewart, Alexander (2018). 'TablighJama'at in China: Sacred self, worldly nation, transnational imaginary' Cambridge University Press. *Modern Asian Studies*, 52(4), pp. 1194-1226. doi:10.1017/S0026749X17000658. https://www.cambridge.org/core/journals/modern-asian-studies/article/tabligh-jamaat-in-china-sacred-self-worldly-nation-transnational-imaginary/B0C0F70D0686E4A7BAA390E39531014.

10 Ibid.

11 Tablighi Jamaat: Muslims from China were involved, ABP Special, 02 Apr 2020. https://news.abplive.com/videos/news/india-tablighi-jammat-muslims-from-china-were-involved-abp-special-1188010, accessed on 30 October 2021.

12 Many delegates came from nations which banned Tablighi Jamaat: Subramanian Swamy, seeks MEA clarification, Times Now Digital, 1 April 2020, https://www.timesnownews.

com/india/article/many-delegates-came-from-nations-which-banned-tablighi-jamaat-subramanian-swamy-seeks-mea-clarification/572653, accessed on 30 October 2021.

13 Rashid, Omar & Kumar, Anuj, '6 Tablighi Jamaat-linked persons to be booked under NSA for misbehaving with nurses in Uttar Pradesh's Ghaziabad', The Hindu, 3 April 2020. https://www.thehindu.com/news/national/other-states/6-tablighi-jamaat-linked-persons-to-be-booked-under-nsa-for-misbehaving-with-nurses-in-uttar-pradeshs-ghaziabad/article31247168.ece, accessed on 30 October 2021.

14 Singh, Natwar K, 'Tablighi Jamaat Should be Banned.' The Sunday Guardian, 4 April 2020. https://ww, w.sundayguardianlive.com/opinion/tablighi-jamaat-banned, accessed on 4 June, 2020.

15 'Over 2,000 foreign Tablighi Jamaat members banned from entering India for 10 yrs', Hindustan Times, 4 June 2020, https://www.hindustantimes.com/india-news/960-blacklisted-foreign-nationals-banned-from-entering-india-for-10-years-for-involvement-in-tablighi-jamaat-incident-report/story-EsWvpuvF5Uf2yIAQ3WVxUL.html, accessed on 5 June 2020.

16 Metcalf, Barbara D. (1982) Islamic revival in British India: Deoband, 1860-1900. Princeton, NJ: Princeton University Press.

17 Siddiqi, Bulbul (2018). Becoming 'Good Muslim.' The Tablighi Jamaat in the UK and Bangladesh. Singapore: Springer.

18 'Policy Brief 10 – Tablighi Jamaat and its role in the Global

Jihad', South Asia Democratic Forum, 11 December, 2020, https://www.sadf.eu/policy-brief-10-tablighi-jamaat-and-its-role-in-the-global-jihad/. Doi: 10.48251/SADF.ISSN.2406-5625.PB.10, accessed on 6 June 2020.

19 Sachs, Susan. 'A Muslim Missionary Group Draws New Scrutiny in U.S' The New York Times, July 14, 2003. https://www.nytimes.com/2003/07/14/us/a-muslim-missionary-group-draws-new-scrutiny-in-us.html, accessed on 6 June 2020.

20 Ibid.

21 Taylor, Jenny. 'Understanding and Engaging with the Tablighi Jamaat,' *Lausanne Global Analysis*, 4(6) November 2015, https://lausanne.org/content/lga/2015-11/understanding-and-engaging-with-the-tablighi-jamaat , accessed on 6 June 2020.

22 Marino, Francesca (2020). Tablighi Jamaat, an 'antechamber of terrorism' in Europe? 02 April 2020, https://www.aninews.in/news/world/europe/tablighi-jamaat-an-antechamber-of-terrorism-in-europe20200402214459/, accessed on 7 June 2020.

23 Haar, Kathryn. 'Spanish Police Arrest Jamaat al-Tabligh Members in Bomb Threat.' The Jamestown Foundation. February 13, 2008. https://jamestown.org/program/spanish-police-arrest-jamaat-al-tabligh-members-in-bomb-threat/, accessed on 7 June 2020.

24 Burnett, Victoria. '14 terror suspects held as Spanish police raid mosque.' The New York Times, 20 January 2008. https://www.nytimes.com/2008/01/20/world/europe/20iht-spain.4.9357125.html, accessed on 8 June 2020.

25 Burton, Fred & Stewart, Scott (2008). 'Tablighi Jamaat: An Indirect Line to Terrorism,' Security Weekly, Jan 23, 2008. https://worldview.stratfor.com/article/tablighi-jamaat-indirect-line-terrorism, accessed on 7 June 2020.

26 Ibid.

27 This Mosque is in the name of Tariq Bin Ziad who attacked Spain in 711 AD as a commander of the Umayyad Dynasty in Arab world which had taken the role of Caliphate after the killing of Ali the fourth Caliphate. Ziab was an Algerian and was a slave who after converting to Islam had occupied import role in Umayyad dynasty. His famous words of Jehad are still the source of Inspiration. After entering Spain, he asked his soldiers to burn the boats. It was symbolic to suggest that there is no retreat on the path of Jihad. Before the battle began it is said he was inspired with words that "we are here to spread the message of Allah. Now, the enemy is in front of you and the sea behind. You fight for His cause. Either you will be victorious or martyred. There is no third choice. All means of escape have been destroyed." For details see: https://www.arabnews.com/islam-perspective/news/750016.

28 Burton, Fred & Stewart, Scott (2008). 'Tablighi Jamaat: An Indirect Line to Terrorism,' Security Weekly, Jan 23, 2008.

29 "Co-conspirators in supporting terrorism", Congressional Record Volume 161, Number 182 (Tuesday, December 15, 2015). Pages H9324-H9326. From the Congressional Record Online through the Government Publishing Office [www.gpo.gov], https://www.govinfo.gov/content/pkg/CREC-2015-12-15/html/CREC-2015-12-15-pt1-PgH9324.htm. accessed on 8

June 2020.

30 Ibid.

31 Ibid.

32 Ibid.

33 Ibid.

34 Fadel, Leila (2018). 'How Muslims, Often Misunderstood, Are Thriving in America,' The National Geographic Magazine, May 2018, https://www.nationalgeographic.com/magazine/2018/05/being-muslim-in-america/, accessed on 9 June 2020.

35 Ahmad, Imtiyaz (2015). 'Al-Huda: Pakistani institute that 'radicalised' thousands of women.' Hindustan Times15 December 2015. https://www.hindustantimes.com/world/long-before-tashfeen-malik-pak-institute-blamed-for-radicalising-women/story-URzRLlvzbb3npYJY5I9ycN.html. accessed on 9 June 2020.

36 Nazish, Kiran (2015). 'Is Pakistani religious school a terrorist breeding ground?' USA Today, 12 December 2015, https://www.usatoday.com/story/news/world/2015/12/12/pakistani-religious-school-terrorist-breeding-ground/77149880/, accessed on 9 June 2020.

37 "Co-conspirators in supporting terrorism", Congressional Record Volume 161, Number 182 (Tuesday, December 15, 2015). Pages H9324-H9326. From the Congressional Record Online through the Government Publishing Office [www.gpo.gov], https://www.govinfo.gov/content/pkg/CREC-2015-12-15/html/CREC-2015-12-15-pt1-PgH9324.htm, accessed on 9 June 2020.

38 Zahid, Noor &Takar, Nafees (2016). 'Are Conservative Muslim Tablighi Jamaat Pacifists or Extremists?', 15 January 2016, https://www.voanews.com/a/conservative-muslim-movement-tablighi-jamaat/3148033.html, accessed on 10 June 2020.

39 Revesz, Rachael. 'US Islamophobia: Threats and acts of vandalism against mosques double so far in 2017.' The Independent, 15 March 2017, UK.

40 Hunt Elle and Smith David.'Donald Trump Abandons Traditional White House Ramadan celebrations.' The Guardian, 26 Jun 2017.

41 Siddaqui, Sabrina and Lauren, Gambino. 'Trump Travel Ban: New Order Targeting Six Muslim Majority Countries Signed.' The Guardian, 6 March 2017.

42 Smit, Craig S. 'Muslim Group in France Is Fertile Soil for Militancy,' The New York Times, 28 April 2005, https://www.nytimes.com/2005/04/28/world/europe/muslim-group-in-france-is-fertile-soil-for-militancy.html, accessed on 10 June 2020.

43 Dutt, Vijay, (2006). 'UK terror suspects' faith made in India, ' Hindustan Times, 19 August 2006.https://www.hindustantimes.com/india/uk-terror-suspects-faith-made-in-india/story-qmugBJEqFFyeZKk31npIFL.html. accessed on 11 June 2020.

44 Burton, Fred & Stewart, Scott (2002). 'Tablighi Jamaat: An Indirect Line to Terrorism' World View, Jan 23, 2008. https://worldview.stratfor.com/article/tablighi-jamaat-indirect-line-terrorism, accessed on 11 June 2020.

45 Smit, Craig S. 'Muslim Group in France Is Fertile Soil for

Militancy,' The New York Times, 28 April 2005.

46 McNeil Jr. & Donald G. (2001). 'A Nation Challenged: The Foreign Soldier; Body Confirms Suspicions About Frenchmen in Al Qaeda.' The New York Times, 28 Dec 2001, https://www.nytimes.com/2001/12/28/world/nation-challenged-foreign-soldier-body-confirms-suspicions-about-frenchmen-al.html, accessed on 12 June 2020.

47 Ibid.

48 Beyler, Clara. The Jihadist threat in France. Gale Academic OneFile. https://go.gale.com/ps/i.do?id=GALE%7CA348311779&sid=googleScholar&v=2.1&it=r&linkaccess=abs&issn=1940834X&p=AONE&sw=w&userGroupName=anon%7E2813f6b8. Accessed on 20 March 2022.

49 Dutt, Vijay (2006). 'UK terror suspects' faith made in India", Hindustan Times, 19 August 2006.

50 Brown, David. 'Islamic group is linked to London Bridge killer and 7/7 attack,' The Sunday Times, Casablanca, 13 June 2017. https://www.thetimes.co.uk/article/islamic-group-is-linked-to-london-bridge-killer-and-7-7-attack-youssef-zaghba-mohammed-sidique-khan-shehzad-tanweer-richard-reid-abid-naseer-xm0rb8rxw, accessed on 12 June 2020.

51 Ibid.

52 Pandya, Abhinav & Westrop, Sam (2020). 'How did India overlook Tablighi, world's largest radical organization?' The Sunday Guardian Live, 2 May 2020 https://www.sundayguardianlive.com/news/india-overlook-tablighi-worlds-largest-radical-organization, accessed on 7 June 2020.

53 Ibid.

54 Mukhopadhyay, Alok Rashmi. 'Tabligh-e-Jamaat Under the Scanner of German Intelligence.' *Strategic Analysis,* 29(2), Manohar Parrikar Institute for Defence Studies and Analyses, New Delhi, https://idsa.in/strategicanalysis/TablighеJamaatUndertheScannerofGermanIntelligence_armukhopadhyay_0405, accessed on 7 June 2020.

55 Apart from the Nawaz Sharif Family and the former President of Pakistan, even the Former Pakistani intelligence chief (DG-ISI) Lt General Javed Nasir was an active member of Tablighi Jamaat. And he actively supported the radical Islamists in Bosnia and Kashmir. For details See Khaled Ahmed, What did Husain Haqqani write?", The Express Tribune, June 2, 2012, available at: http://tribune.com.pk/story/387841/what-did-husain-haqqani-write/ quoted in (https://cf2r.org/foreign/tablighi-jamaat-and-its-links-with-islamist-terrorism-2/#_ftn16). Accessed on 6 June 2020. Zahid, Farhan. Tablighi Jamaat and Its Links with Islamist Terrorism, Foreign Analysis No. 19 March 2015.

56 "Terrorist Groups: An Overview", *South Asia Terrorism Portal,* Institute for Conflict Management, https://www.satp.org/satporgtp/countries/india/states/jandk/terrorist_outfits/terrorist_groups_j&k.htm accessed on 9 June 2020.

57 Ibid.

58 Earlier it was known as AnjumanSipah-e-Sahaba. SS or SSP was formed by Maulana Haq Nawaz Jhangvi, Maulana Zia-ur-Rehman Farooqi, Maulana Eesar-ul-HaqQasmi and Maulana Azam Tariq in September 1985 in Punjab Province. It is learned that Zia-ulHaq was the mind behind it to defeat the

pro-democracy elements. SSP also receives funds from Saudi Arabia and Wealthy Sunni trusts and individuals in Pakistan including Jamaat-e-Islami. See for details; https://www.satp.org/satporgtp/countries/pakistan/terroristoutfits/Ssp.htm.

59 "Sipah-e-Sahaba Pakistan- Incidents and Statements involving Sipah-e-Sahaba Pakistan: 2017, 2015, 2014, 2013, 1986-2012," *South Asia Terrorism Portal*, Institute for Conflict Management, https://www.satp.org/satporgtp/countries/pakistan/terroristoutfits/Ssp.htm, accessed on 9 June 2020.

60 Maulana Masood Azhar, JeM chief, speaking at a Jehad conference in October 2000 said, "Now we go hand-in-hand, and Sipah-e-Sahaba stands shoulder to shoulder with Jaish-e-Muhammad in Jehad." https://www.satp.org/satporgtp/countries/pakistan/terroristoutfits/Ssp.htm, accessed on 10 June 2020.

61 For details see Raizul Hassan, "An insider's account", View Point Online, available at: http://www.viewpointonline.net/an-insiders-account.html, accessed on 12 June 2020.

62 Elahi, N. (2019). Tehreek-e-Taliban Pakistan (TTP). In Terrorism in Pakistan: The Tehreek-e-Taliban Pakistan (TTP) and the Challenge to Security (pp. 75 – 94). London. New York: I.B. Tauris. Retrieved on 12 June 2020, from http://dx.doi.org/10.5040/9781350988392.ch-005.

63 Rana,Muhammad Amir. "Tablighi Jamaat: Discourse and Challenges", *Conflict and Peace Studies*, April-June 2009, 2(2), Pakistan Institute of Peace Studies, p. 79.

64 Burton, Fred & Stewart, Scott (2008). "Tablighi Jamaat: An Indirect Line to Terrorism" https://worldview.stratfor.com/

article/tablighi-jamaat-indirect-line-terrorism, accessed on 13 June 2020.

65 Raman, B. "Dagestan: Focus on Pakistan's Tablighi Jamaat", *South Asia Terrorism Portal*, Institute for Conflict Management. https://www.satp.org/satporgtp/publication/idr/vol_15(1)/executive_summary_iii.htm, accessed on 14 June 2020.

66 Pandya, Abhinav &Westrop, Sam (2020). "How did India overlook Tablighi, world's largest radical organization"? Sunday Guardian Live, 2 May 2020, https://www.sundayguardianlive.com/news/india-overlook-tablighi-worlds-largest-radical-organization, accessed on 14 June 2020.

67 Ibid.

68 Muhammad Amir Rana (2009). 'Tablighi Jamaat: Discourse and Challenges,' *Conflict and Peace Studies*, April-June 2009, 2(2), Pakistan Institute of Peace Studies, p. 79.

CHAPTER 5

MAPPING ISLAMIC EXTREMISM IN WESTERN DEMOCRACIES

IT IS INDEED very rare to find a country with a predominant Muslim population not having any terrorist organization in the name of Islam.The Islamic terrorist organizations have their own justifications for violence and terrorist activities. Where Islam is a dominant religion or the state religion, Islamists legitimize violence on the ground of absence of practice of what they feel and interpret as true Islam. They stand to oppose both the state institutions and individuals and go after the blood of those who disagree with their version of Islam. The second category belongs to those countries which are not Islamic. In such countries, the Islamic terrorist organizations justify their presence and acts of violence on the ground that Muslims in such countries are subjected to atrocities and non-Islamic practices. And, therefore, a religious war or Jihad is need in both situations. Their line of arguments in support of terrorist activities in France is thus different from the justification of violence in Pakistan or Afghanistan.

Anthony H Cordesman wrote a very comprehensive report on Islamic terrorism and violence between 2011 and 2016 titled 'Islam and the Patterns in Terrorism and Violent Extremism.' He released his working draft in October 2017 wherein he discusses at length how there has been growing Islamophobia and how Christians have been turning to violence against Muslims in the US despite American Muslims standing with the country against terrorism.[1] He concludes that only a small proportion of the Muslim world is engaged in violence, and therefore, the entire faith cannot be held responsible for acts of those few. He argues that terrorists do not represent the core values of Islam. However, he does not reveal how he reached the conclusion without critically examining the key scriptures of Islam. He seems to be limited by the government position and American interests in the Islamic world as he explains that most terrorist activities have occurred in the countries which are partners of the US in different parts of the world.[2]

However, the data which he presents is very interesting and worth noticing. He records that out of the total 70,767 terrorist activities in the world between 2011 and 2016, a total of 60,321 cases were reported from the Islamic States. In other words, 85 per cent of the total terrorist activities took place in the countries where Islam is the dominant or state religion. Most of the countries where Muslims constitute the majority are theocratic Islamic states. That means, only 15 per cent Islamic terrorist activities took place in non-Islamic world.

Further, 51,321 incidents of the total, i.e., 73 per cent were reported from the Islamic states in the Middle East and North Africa (MENA) region.

Another aspect of the report is also startling. It says that seven of the ten countries with the most terrorist attacks in 2016 had vast Muslim majorities, and the death and injuries in the other three involved a large number of Muslim deaths. A total of 83 per cent of the attacks and 90 per cent of the deaths occurred in Islamic countries. The vast majority of suicide and vehicle attacks came from "Islamist" extremist groups that killed Muslims in largely Muslim countries. It goes on to say that "If one looks at the five worst perpetrator movements in the world in 2016, four are 'Islamist' extremist. A total of 88 per cent of 2,916 attacks and 99 per cent of 14,017 deaths that resulted from the top five perpetrators were caused by Islamic extremist groups." And therefore, he concludes that to blame the ideology of Islam behind the violence is erroneous.

One does not quarrel with his facts, but his findings give insight to understand the psychology and drive behind the working of political Islam the world over. It conveys that Islam as a warring religion in its own land as well as in the land of 'others.'[3] Further, this ideology of violence is outcome of both its search and assertion of its uncompromising religious identity. The urge for global Islamic identity is the motive in which there is no place for adjustment or accommodation of others. Where it is dominant it does not accommodate others. And where it is inferior or auxiliary it fails to adjust with others. In countries where followers of Islam constitute significant population but are in minority compared to the other faiths, they fight for equal space in the social, cultural, economic and political domains. The areas which are dominated by them in such countries have either already emerged or are fast emerging as the epicenter of terrorism and terrorist activities. Chechnya in Russia, Jinjiang in China, and Kashmir in India are shining examples of the same. The Islamists are fighting for their separatist agenda. They don't wish to live with the national majority but seek to carve out their own homeland in the name of Islam. The terrorist organizations in these areas work on two aspects; first they attack the state apparatus and second, they engage themselves in ethnic cleansing of non-Muslims. Kashmir is a classic case of Islamic separatism.

There are many countries in Europe where the Tablighis have started asserting their identity as a separate community and using Islam to mobilize co-religionists for doing the same. A closer look at statistics and incidents in some of the European countries in recent decades speak for themselves. Let us look at the situation in France. Both Christians and Muslims there have been living together for several centuries. The Muslim population entered France during Umayyad dynasty when its commander after registering a victory endeavored to capture certain portion of Southern France in 732 AD, exactly 100 years after the death of the Prophet. Though they were defeated in the famous battle of Tours, the forces of Islam kept on attacking France, at times emerging victorious and at times getting defeated. After the fall of the Ottoman Empire in Spain, some Muslims migrated to the southern areas of France. In the 20th century, migration of Muslim labourers (in the 1960s and early 1970s) happened from three states of Africa: Algeria, Morocco, and Tunisia all of which were French colonies. These migrants provided cheap labour to the French industries. This led to rapid increase in Muslim population. The migrant Muslim population from these three countries comprises about 3 million out of 4.2 million Muslims residing in France today. It is now home to the largest Muslim community in Western Europe.[4] These labourers were not deeply entrenched in religious dogmas in the beginning.[5] However, with settlement of Muslims, these North African (Maghreb) countries also started sending preachers to France. And French Muslims gradually started attaching themselves to their religious and ancestral identity.

Conflicts between Christian and Muslim were a rare phenomenon in France in the 1980s and the 1990s. It started changing with the turn of the century. Conflicts between the two were often witnessed in Paris suburbs. After the 9/11 terror attacks in the United States, the relationship between the two communities worsened in France as well. The French Government strongly responded to radicalization of the Muslim community. It sought to discourage the measures that could accentuate the Muslim identity and banned wearing of Burqa in public places.

Islamic groups reacted to this with series of explosions causing huge loss of humans and properties. The government closed down 20 mosques and prayer halls out of the total of 2500 since December 2015 to August 2016 because they were teaching Salafi ideology.[6] The closure triggered several terror attacks by Islamic extremists in the country. Since the Paris attacks in 2015, there have been 22 terror attacks in the country by the radical Islamic forces.[7] It had started with Charlie Hebdo shooting in January 2015 in which the editor was killed by the Islamists for publishing a cartoon of the Prophet Muhammad. However, the Paris attack in November 2015 impacted the Frenchmen the most[8] in which series of bombs were exploded and shooting took place: first at the gate of the National Stadium, Stade De France, where international football match was going on; second, inside the Café house; and third, at Bataclan Theatre. This shook the nation from inside and the State responded to the threat with imposition of three months emergency to deal with Islamic terrorism in which police and armed forces were given free hands to arrest, detain and raid the premises without warrant. The nation was shocked when a Muslim truck-driver killed 86 pedestrian and injured over 400 people by driving his truck into the crowd that was celebrating Bastille Day on the promenade on June 14, 2016. And then came killing of Samuel Paty, a school teacher on October 16, and 'then an attack on a 60-year-old woman and two others in the Notre-Dame cathedral in Nice' two weeks later' shook the conscience of the country.

These incidents were considered barbaric and a challenge to the democratic and secular values of the French nation. The opinion poll after the murder of the teacher showed that 79 per cent of the French considered it a war of Islamism on the country.[9] The French Council of the Muslim Faith (CFCM) sought to distance French Muslims from the radicalized elements but the issue took a new turn when the French president Macron openly criticized the ideology of Islam saying that it divided the world into believer and non-believers and charged the Islamists with trying to shape the future of the nation on those lines.

The Turkish president Tayyip Erdogan, Pakistani Prime Minister Imran Khan and former Malaysian Prime Minister Mahathir Mohamad joined hands to criticize Macron on religious lines. Mahathir went on to justify the violence saying "Muslims have a right to be angry and to kill millions of French people for the massacres of the past."[10] France today has emerged as one of the most vocal critics of radical Islam in the world. In order to demonstrate the solidarity and commitment of the nation to the freedom of press, French President Emmanuel Macron personally visited the office of the Charlie Hebdo and laid a wreath in honour of the killed journalists. His visit also demonstrated the opposition to intolerant idea of Islamists. Further, the government came out with an anti-terror law intended to control 'Radical Islamism.' Muslims criticized it on the ground that it would further stigmatize the Muslims and corner them in the political and social space. The left-liberal intelligentsia also joined the criticism calling it Islamophobic but the people responded positively to the law which increased surveillance on mosques and Islamists organizations.[11] A French man in general has developed the feeling over the years that the threat from radical elements in Islam has increased manyfold in the country.[12]

This phenomenon can be seen in other European countries as well. The United Kingdom is sitting on the crater of a religious volcano. It tasted the fruit of Islamic radicalization for the first time on 7 July 2005 when suicide bombers targeted the three underground trains on different routes and a double decker bus during morning office hours. It killed 52 people and injured another 700.[13] The four bombers also died. It unnerved the policy makers responsible for securing internal security responsible and tackling terrorism in the country. It was a great psychological loss for the British people, and policy makers had no clue on why despite fair principles of democracy in operation and equal opportunity for all, home grown radicalized Islamic citizens chose to kill innocent people. As expected, the British Muslim parliamentarians criticized this. They described the act of bombings a crime against democratic values for the country. But neither radicalization has stopped nor the possibilities of terror threats in the country.

The British try to trace the linkage of their country with the Muslim world to the 8th century AD when the Arabs had established trade link with Spain after its fall during the Umayyad dynasty. However, the first Muslims to reach the shores of England were the North Africans and the Turks in the 16th century Elizabethan times[14] when the Catholic Church had excommunicated Queen Elizabeth in 1570. It was the time when the Queen started building relations with Muslim dynasties and Muslims started coming in and practicing their faith freely in England. The first major groups of Muslims to migrate were the sailors from Bengal in the 18th century. They were working in ships of the East India Company. The first Muslim establishment, therefore, was mainly in port towns such as Cardiff, South Shields and Liverpool. Sheik Dean Mahomet, a Bangladeshi working for the East India Company as Captain, established the first restaurant 'the Hindustani Coffee House' in London in 1810. After some time, the Muslim community established Islamic schools and mosques and also started an Arabic newspaper *Al-Salam* from the Nur ul Islam Mosque in London.

Christians did not have a good impression about Muslims and Islam. They had fought crusades against Islam. Muslims were not enthusiastically accepted or welcomed by the British. However, after the Second World War, Britain desperately needed a labour force to rejuvenate its shattered economy. They invited labourers from undivided India. As a result, there was a huge legitimate migration of Muslims from India; a process that continued even after the Partition. After the Second World War, Muslims from the Arab world and North Africa also started migrating to Britain. The influx was so large that the British Government had to bring in the Commonwealth Immigration Act, 1962, through which it sought to regulate the entry of such migrants.

Islam today is the second largest religion in the United Kingdom and constitutes 5.1 per cent of the country's total population. The largest concentration of Muslim population is found in England followed by Wales and Scotland. Northern Ireland has a scant Muslim population. Bangladeshis, Pakistanis and Indian Muslims constitute the largest single group of

Muslim migrants in the UK. Among these three, Pakistanis are the largest (43 per cent) followed by Bangladeshis (17 per cent) and Indians (9 per cent). Converted Muslims and their children called White Muslims constitute 12 per cent of the total Muslim population. Other Asians and Africans respectively constitute 6 and 7 per cent of the Muslim population in the country. Muslim population in the UK is rising so rapidly that experts have expressed concerns that if the trend continues, London would soon be converted into a Muslim dominated city.[15] There are already some pockets outside London where Muslim constitute more than 50 per cent of the total population. Some pockets in London have majority Muslim population. London has 14.4 per cent Muslim population against 45 per cent Christians followed by 39 per cent Agnostics. In just 200 years, the country has witnessed an increase of 74 per cent in the Muslim population and experts say that soon there would be many pockets in the UK with significant Muslim population. There are 26 parliamentary constituencies where now Muslim population is over 20 per cent.[16]

Thousands of Muslim organizations exist in the United Kingdom. Mosques are mushrooming raising many eyebrows. These have triggered a fresh public discourse where increasing number of British people find such activities a result of deliberate design towards consolidation of religious identity of Muslims. A comparison of the number of churches and mosques in the UK provides interesting analysis. There is a total of 16,000 churches in the country and many are devoid of followers.[17] But there are 1750 mosques for Muslims that comprise just

5 per cent of the population (it was 4.4 per cent according to 2011 Census of UK). In 1961, there were 7 registered mosques in England and Wales catering to a population of 50,000. This kept making a harmonic progression and in 2011, a population of 27.06 lakh Muslims had 1500 registered mosques. The per centage of Muslim population to the total rose from 0.11 in 1961 to 4.4 in 2011. In 1961, there was one mosque for every 7143 Muslims and now it is one mosque for 1900 Muslims. This is phenomenal growth. These mosques are not just prayer centres but also the educational centres where young Muslims are taught in theology and religious practices. The rising population and increasing number of mosques have enhanced the political weight of the community in constituencies of their dominance.

For decades, the United Kingdom experimented with inculcating the liberal democratic traditions among Muslims. It worked on the demand of Muslim Education Trust, an affiliate of the Muslim Council of Britain, for comprehensive reforms in the school education to incorporate Islamic ideas. The government acceded to their demand of putting 'Islamic studies' in school's syllabus at secondary level. It happened in 1993 in respect of state-run schools. The list of demand included 'halal food, appropriate dress for Muslim girls, special dress for sports for Muslim boys and girls, exemption from some aspects of the sex-education, facilities for prayers and inclusion of its approved Islamic books in the libraries of schools.'[18] And the organization succeeded to a great extent. They had complained that the state-run school education wanted to monopolize the minds of the young British through the Judeo-Christian ideology.

In many British Muslim Schools, the book 'Islam: Belief and Teachings' explicitly endorses the ideology of Muslim Brotherhood of Jamaat-e-Islami and establishment of Allah Law in Allah Land.'[19] It was the period of construction of separate identity in the name of religion and the British government acceded to it. The same Muslim organization in the UK then started saying that the Muslim boys and girls should be insulated against secular education! It was a transformation in their thinking. In the 1960s, these Muslim organizations used to say that the British values of tolerance, justice, and equity did not contradict the Islamic values. But now they wanted to secure their children against the same secular values.

The impact of rising power of the British Muslims and their assertiveness veering towards aggression could not be missed by anyone. The Pan-Islamic identity of Muslims had grown so much in size and intensity that the older issue of their marginalization was no longer relevant. The British Muslim Council (BMC) became signatory to the Istanbul declaration of March 2009 which called for Ummah (Muslim Nation) and for Jihad against the occupation of Palestine by Israel. It even justified attacks on Jews all over the world and declared all those who supported Israel to be enemies of Islam. Representative of the BMC, Dr Abdullah, had signed it and the BMC refused to sack him despite warning from the government. This declaration was certainly against the position of the British government on Israel. In August 2006, some British Muslims were arrested for planning explosions in trans-Atlantic flights which were destined for American and Canadian cities. Instead of condemning it and dissociating from such ideas, the BMC lent a tactical support by saying that it all happened because of the anti-Muslim foreign policy of the UK and the US.

Members of the British Muslim Councils are now resisting any kind of change which aims at integrating Muslims with the mainstream British society. Few examples would be important to understand this. In 2008, a Muslim Institute attempted to introduce reforms in the contract of Nikah called Nikah Nama. The intention was to keep the women at par with men in matter of divorce, and also to prevent husband from having two wives. It also permitted even a non-Muslim to be a witness in such a marriage. When this matter became public, all the clerics started denouncing it. Finally, the Muslim Council of Britain (MCB) dubbed it un-Islamic, illegal, misguided and with an aim to 'reinvent' and 'reform' as if our forefathers who practiced it were wrong![20] The Muslim Council of Britain is the main voice of the British Council and also is in government contact. And it openly supports Sharia councils which have developed a huge network over the last few decades.[21]

On 7th March 2015, *The Telegraph* published a report that said that the British Government had decided to go hard on organizations and individuals propagating extremism and it had decided to take measures such as investigating the role of the Sharia Councils and infiltration of such extremist elements in government bodies. Taking reference of the article, the Islamic Human Rights Commission wrote a letter on 11

March 2015 to Deputy Prime Minister Nick Clegg expressing concern that it would lead to further harassment of Muslims in the UK. Be it issues concerning Muslims in Russia or China, India or Palestine or Australia, British Muslims seldom express solidarity with their government and always support the Pan-Islamic cause. This raises a serious concern in all such societies which host Muslim population. They entered these social and territorial space for bread and butter but even after living for decades and centuries attach more loyalty and values for their co-religionists and cultural spectrums of the Arabs and other Muslim world rather than the land of their residence. Burqas were rarely visible on the roads of London earlier or at the markets. But that has changed now in the quest and expression of Islamic identity.

Today, there are several extremist groups in Britain which are working on strengthening Islamic identity of Muslims or building support for the Jihadi organizations outside Britain. Before the advent of Islamic terror, Britain had witnessed extremism that was linked to Northern Ireland. Jihad driven terror attacks have been on an increase. On 22 March 2017, Khalid Masood, an Islamist terrorist motivated by the idea of Jihad, drove a car on the pedestrians outside the Westminster Palace and stabbed a policeman before he was shot down.[22] He wanted to take revenge from British civilians because he was in rage over Western power's military action against Islamic countries in the Middle East. He was not linked to any organization but the rage suggested that he was brainwashed through some radical teachings. On 22 May 2017, a British

Muslim of Libyan ancestry detonated a bomb in Manchester Arena where there was a concert of an American singer. It was a suicide bombing in which 23 people died and 139 got injured. On 3 June 2017, three Islamic terrorists belonging or inspired by the ISIS deliberately mowed down pedestrians by a van they were driving on the London Bridge and then moved towards the nearby borough market and started stabbing whosoever came their way. They killed eight people and wounded over 50 before they were shot down by the police.

Though the British government was very tolerant of these fanatic organizations, their attitude changed after the September attacks in the US. They tracked the organizations that were either promoting or supporting the ideology of Jihad. Actions taken against Al-Muhajiroun is a case in point. This organization follows the Salafi ideology and has been found working in Britain under different names to evade the law. The organization adheres to the principle that the British Muslims are British second and Muslim first. Its followers do not seek their identity in the democratic values but in Islamic heritage which drag them to Arab or Turkish lineage. The United Kingdom is now clueless on how to disengage Muslim youths from the process of radicalization.The secular response has failed indeed, and, therefore, the British society has started responding to the challenges through violence and further isolation of Muslims in the British society. By and large this is the story also of other European countries like Spain, Germany and Italy.

Australia has similar experience of Islam. Muslims reached

Australia as labourers with early European settlements. They were from coastal Africa, Afghanistan and Indonesia. Muslims from Afghanistan were basically cameleers. They settled and married indigenous people in remote areas. Australia is struggling today to strike a balance between the demands of radical Islamists and the secular democratic norms and values which they could develop over the last four centuries. Muslim assertiveness is a recent phenomenon. There is fear of Muslims and Islamic terrorism. What Australians think about the Muslims who live in Sydney suburbs today is very different from what they thought about them two decades back. The Guardian published a survey of Australians in 2019 in which 51 per cent had very negative and 'unfavorable sentiments towards Islam' and 'only 10 per cent looked at the religion positively.'[23] It is all because Muslims which are less than three per cent of the Australian population, often make headlines in the newspapers and televisions for bad reasons.[24] They have come to be identified with violence and fanaticism. Compounded with growing radicalism, the rising population of Muslims in Australia is now a matter of great concern for the native populations.[25]

Muslim organizations publicly endorse radicalism in Islam and refuse to augment any reforms and ideological elasticity. They often accuse the Australian State of demonizing Muslims and their religion. The spokesperson of the controversial organization Hizbut-Tahrir (HuT) said, "Islam is not up for Negotiation or Reform; Islam is what it is."[26] This endorses the inflexibility and inability of the faith to accept new interpretation in the changed circumstances and debunks those premises which emanate from the rational call of modern times. Further, it prepares the psychology among its followers to reject what comes from 'others.' The HuT spokesperson also contended that children of Muslims should not be asked to sing Australian National Anthem in schools.[27] And counter terrorism measures by the police against radicalization was just a design of 'demonizing the faith.' These two sets of arguments can be seen to be advanced by Muslim community members in all parts of the world where they face resistance from other dominant faiths.

The Australian society and its political class have awakened to the challenge of political Islam and citizens and the government have started orienting themselves to counter it before it is too late. Tony Abbott, former Australian Prime Minister, wanted to ban the HuT. The organization asserts that the 'liberal values are imposed through systematic attempts to reform Islam.'[28] It challenged the government by saying that Australia was not doing charity by welcoming immigrants from the Islamic world. They left their world because of economic hardships and conflicts which is all because of the anti-Muslim foreign policy of Western powers to which Australia is a party.[29]

Australia is debating whether or not to abolish the Shariah laws that govern Australian Muslims in personal affairs. Ann Black analyses the whole debate in perspective of how and why it originated in Australia. The government says that everyone is free to exercise his religion but religion will play no role in the structure of law and jurisprudence. This means everyone will have to follow the law of the land enacted by the Australian parliament. The government has rejected the demand of Muslim organizations to be governed by their personal laws. But Black contests the government position on the ground that the Shariah is already in practice among Australian Muslims in matters of marriage, divorce and succession.[30]

The practice of Hudud, Islamic law in matters of criminal jurisprudence, is problematic because the punishment for various crimes includes amputation of limbs, stoning, lashings, death or crucifixion, and lashings, apostasy etc. which are not possible in modern times. Except a few counties like Saudi Arabia and Nigeria, no Muslim country has adopted these punishments. This raises a question that if following the criminal law prescribed by the State does not insult or demean Islam, how can following the civil laws defy the principles of Islam. The Prophet had not said that one can accept criminal laws of the land but not the civil laws.

This also triggers an important debate on whether Muslims are a homogenous entity. Australia is home to immigrant Muslims from about 80 countries. Close to '75 per cent of Muslims come from one region of South Asia (Pakistan, India and Bangladesh).' They come from 50 different ethnicities and cultures and speak different languages.'[31] There is nothing like a homogenous Muslim community but communities.[32] Any attempt to bring them under one Islamic law would aim at consolidation of different Muslim communities into one single identity in a non-Islamic state. Of course, the Quran, the Hadith are common to all Muslims but there is a wide range of diversity across nations in its codification, understanding and interpretations. In India, the Muslim Personal Law was passed and codified by the British government in 1937. It had sought to dissolve the diversity that existed among Muslims across the regions. The Lebanese Muslims are different from Indonesian or Malaysian Muslims in Australia. How can there be one code for all Muslims governing their civil matters? A similar question was raised in the Indian Constituent Assembly debates by Dr BR Ambedkar who destroyed the arguments of Muslim members who were opposing the idea of uniform civil code for all irrespective of religions. The Sharia Code was aimed at producing a homogenized Muslim category by dissolving all the diversities, Dr Ambedkar had charged.

There is no one monolithic Islam in actual existence but demand for a Shariah law suggests the opposite. Further, Islamists don't wish to entertain gender issues particularly raised by women who are opposed to medieval and tyrannical approach on divorce and polygamy. The Champions of Shariah reject the idea of equality for women. As in the case of British Muslims, Australian Muslims argue that "in essence, Australian values and Islamic teachings on the question of freedom are not so vastly different. Both are based on ideas such as human dignity, justice, equity and egalitarianism."[33] In actual practice they are poles apart.

Radicalization of Muslim youths and their recruitment for different organizations such as the ISIS, the Lasker-e-Taiba, the Jemaah Islamiyah, a South East Asian Terrorist Organization and Al Shabaab have already been established by the Australian intelligence security agencies. They confess that these organizations have succeeded in planting home grown sleeper cells which encourage and incite Muslim youths to participate in Jihad against Kafirs and also for supporting Muslims in distant lands such as Syria and Iraq. There have been a series of Islamic terror groups exposed and destroyed by the police and security agencies. And yet they have succeeded in executing attacks on innocent civilians. In July 2005, the Age published a news story in which it said that 'books promoting Islamic holy war and the killing of non-Muslims who insult Prophet Mohammad' were openly being sold in Melbourne book shop.[34] It was an "extreme jihadist material, explicitly calling for violence against non-Muslims" said Ted Lapkin, the director of the Australia-Israel Jewish Affairs Council.[35]

There are several instances of home-grown terror outfits inspired by the ideology of political Islam. In the last one and half decades, Islamist extremists have carried out several terrorists' attacks in different parts of Australia. Holsworthy Barracks terror plot by Al-Shabaab is a case in point. In 2009, Islamic terrorists plotted an attack on the Australian Army Training area in Holsworthy Barracks, a suburb of South West Sydney. The attack was pre-empted and all were arrested before they could execute the plan. On 23 September 2014, an 18-year-old Abdul Numan Haider stabbed two counter-terrorism officers in Endeavour Hills, a suburb of Melbourne, before he was shot dead.[36] In December 2014, an Iranian born Muslim, who claimed himself to be a cleric, held several people hostages in Lindt chocolate café in Central Sydney before he was shot dead after 16 hours of standoff. The 2016 Minto Stabbing Attack, the 2015 Parramatta Shooting, the 2017 Queanbeyan Stabbing Attacks and the 2017 Brighton Siege are other prominent terror attacks that drew national attention in Australia.

Australia is trying to figure out how to stop radicalization. As Lauren Wilson reported for New Corp Australia Networks: "The number of Australians fighting for Islamic State in Iraq and Syria is three times higher than the total number of home-grown Australian radicals who travelled to Afghanistan in the entire twenty-year period between 1990 and 2010."[37] He added further that there is alarming pace at which the ISIS death cult is on an increase in Australia.[38] *The Herald Sun* reported on 10 May 2015 that The Islamic State is expanding its support base in Australia by reaching the national capital Canberra. The Muslim dominated areas are de-facto 'no-go-zones' for non-Muslims for several reasons including lawlessness, insecurity or religious intimidation.[39]

A man known as "Ahmed Y" established a small militant group in Australia in 2001 and advocated the idea of establishing an Islamic State in Australia.[40]This shows how deep radicalization has been affecting Australia which will further intensify with an increase in Muslim population. Rachel Olding wrote in *The Sydney Morning Herald* on 23 August 2014 that there was a well-entrenched terror cell working in Australia which was proved during Operation Pendennis in 2005 wherein the police arrested nine Australians. They were found to be working for 'Jihadi cells' in Melbourne and Sydney 'amassing guns, ammunition and bomb-making equipment for use in terrorist attacks on home soil.' The most important aspect of this article was the revelations that these young men had support of families and relatives for martyrdom for Allah!

An Australian Newspaper reported that a public school in Sydney permitted its Muslim students not to shake hands with female students in the wake of criticism coming from 'senior Islamic figures.' As reported, it was un-Islamic according to the Hadith, the newspaper said.[41] In the 1970s, Muslims in Australia demanded 'Halal' certification for meat claiming that this would boost meat export to the Arab, Middle East and South East Asian countries. The government also saw logic in it and accepted the proposal. At present, there are several Halal certifying institutes and despite protests from certain quarters, the government has no courage to withdraw it because it has come to stay with Islamic identity. These concessions and initiatives of accommodation are not going to change the Muslim mindset that thrives by living in perpetual oasis of victimhood and discrimination in the land of Dar al Harb.

Germany, Spain, Italy, Canada, America and Belgium have witnessed the same pattern in their Islamic population. In Britain, Muslim organizations forced the government to recognize the Sharia Councils which guide Muslims not only on personal matters like marriage and divorce but also on business and finance based on the interpretation of Islamic laws and Shariah. Though the Islamists don't accept that it is a parallel legal system but it is gradually turning out to be so with passage of time. It has increased the role of Maulanas in the spheres of law outside the court. In the Ontario state of Canada, Prime Minister Dalton McGuinty publicly stated on 11 September 2005 that "there will be no Sharia law in Ontario" but subsequently applied it and the superior court endorsed it with gratitude by Justice Jane Ferguson.[42] Women and liberals in Canada described the Shariah courts as regressive and medieval in mindset besides being rooted in patriarchy, but the Islamists had their way and the government was forced to recognize Sharia courts. Surprisingly, Muslim scholars in Canada defended the Shariah court on the ground that it is in consonance with the principles of multiculturalism but failed the push the arguments that why Islamic countries don't recognize the other voices in their systems.

There is a huge Muslim population in Spain, nearly 2 million. The Madrid Rail Bombing in 2004 in which 192 people lost their lives and over 2000 got injured was executed by the Al-Qaeda, a militant extremist organization that follows the Salafi school of Islam founded in 1986. Already facing a separatist violent movement from Basques, Spain made a series of arrests of Jihadi elements following this attack. Since a large part of Spain was in control of the Islamic Caliphate till the 15th century, which they had won in the battles, the Islamists claim that it is the land of their ancestors and it has to be reconquered and liberated from the Spanish Christians.[43]

Belgium finds that the Islam being taught by the clerics do not go with the spirt of the constitution and democratic values of the country. Though Islamic organizations say that they do not preach conservative Islam, the truth is vastly different. They preach hatred according to Belgium officials.[44] The Belgium government apprehends that there are many more things the Grand Mosque of Brussels is hiding. It has apprehension that the mosque built on land leased to the Prince of Saudi Arabia is teaching the Salafi school of Islam practiced in Saudi Arabia. This is not in consonance with the idea of the European Islam, a term Europeans have discovered to distinguish the Islam practiced there from the Asian Islam which they describe as violent. They are either naïve or too clever. Islam is Islam with the same core political and religious ideology everywhere. Had this not been the case, the pattern in all countries would not have been the same. The Shariah and Halal are issues that often-hit headlines in Belgium politics.

Threat of terrorism from radical Islamists is on the rise in Germany which is turning out to be the center for Terrorism in Europe.[45] Germany has not faced any such terror attacks like the ones in Paris or London. The security forces have pre-empted the possible attacks but Islamists have become the biggest threat to the country. It is fast emerging as the epicenter of terrorists related to Al-Qaeda. Several terrorist organizations as well as motivated individuals are engaged in preaching hatred and working towards radicalization of Muslims and throwing them into the orgy of Jihad. Ansar Al Asir, Milli Gurus, The Wolfsburg terrorist cell, The True Religion, Abu Walaa network etc. are operating from different parts of Germany. They engage in recruitment of young boys and even send them to Iraq and Syria to fight for the Islamic cause of the ISIS.[46] According to German Police and the Intelligence Reports, there were 800 potential German Islamic terrorists in the country (which country? Iraq or Syria or Germany) in 2019.[47] Most of them are from the Salafi School of Islam. European intellectuals who used to undermine the challenge of Islamic radicals terming the phenomenon as Islamophobia have started paying serious attention to it. They have been forced to look at it because the hate crimes against Muslims have increased in Britain and other countries.

If one looks at the dynamics of functioning of political and religious Islam, a few patterns emerge. Where Muslims have occupied and ruled for some time, they think it is the land of their ancestors and they must reclaim it. This ruling syndrome guides their psyche even after the rule is over as is the case with Muslims in India. The speech of Sir Syed Ahmad Khan who was the founder of the Aligarh School is worth considering. Sir Syed said: "Our nation is of the blood of those who made not only Arabia, but Asia and Europe, to tremble. It is our nation which conquered with its sword the whole of India, although its people were all of one religion."[48] Muslim leaders wanted that the British should handover power to them after they leave India! A Hindu dominated democratic India was unacceptable to them. Even after the Partition, the Muslim mindset is impacted by this thinking. They continue to harbour the idea that this is the land which was once ruled by their ancestors.

The reaction and response of Muslims to the political questions depend on their numerical strength. If they are in a scant minority, they have no problem with following the laws of the land. But with an increase in population, they start galvanizing around identity issues and use the democratic constitutional structures to achieve them. Countries of Europe provide shining examples of this pattern. Muslims migrated to these countries as labourers, sought several concessions in the beginning including space for prayers and schools. With an increase in population, they demanded inclusion of the Sharia in the system. This intended to distinctively differentiate their identity from the dominant community. This would lead to gradual radicalization and involvement in terrorist activities for their assertion.

References:

1 Lipka, Michael. "Muslims and Islam: Key findings in the U.S. and around the world." Pew Research Centre, 9 August 2017. https://www.pewresearch.org/fact-tank/2017/08/09/muslims-and-islam-key-findings-in-the-u-s-and-around-the-world/. Accessed on 31 December 2022.

2 Cordesman, Anthony H. "Islam and the Patterns in Terrorism and Violent Extremism." Center for Strategic and International Studies (CSIS), 2017. http://www.jstor.org/stable/resrep23296. Accessed on 21 December 2022.

3 'Others' here indicate of the society where Islam is not a dominant religion numerically.

4 https://www.britannica.com/event/Paris-attacks-of-2015, Accessed on 30 December 2021.

5 Beyler, Clara. (January 2006). The Jihadist threat in France Current Trends in Islamist Ideology. Vol. 3. Hudson Institute, Inc. https://go.gale.com/ps/i.do?id=GALE%7CA348311779&sid=googleScholar&v=2.1&it=r&linkaccess=abs&issn=1940834X&p=AONE&sw=w&userGroupName=anon%7E93cb5215. Accessed on 27 December 2022.

6 Serhan, Yasmeen. (August 2016). "France Disappearing Mosques." The Atlantic. https://www.theatlantic.com/news/archive/2016/08/french-mosques-islam/493919/. Accessed on 27 December 2021.

7 Report of the Office of the Director of National Intelligence accessed online https://www.dni.gov/nctc/index.html on 23 January 2022.

8 Ranking of the most significant terrorist acts since 2000 in France 2018
https://www.statista.com/statistics/941657/most-significant-terrorists-acts-since-2000-france/ accessed on 27 December 2015.

9 For French Muslims, every terror attack brings questions about their loyalty to the republic
https://theconversation.com/for-french-muslims-every-terror-attack-brings-questions-about-their-loyalty-to-the-republic-149151. Accessed on 27 December 2022.

10 Ibid.

11 Read the Report Published in The Indian Express; https://indianexpress.com/article/world/french-muslims-say-radical-islamism-law-is-discriminatory-7097795/. Accessed on 21 December 2022.

12 Ibid

13 "Burn injuries from the London suicide bombings: a new classification of blast-related thermal injuries." https://www.ncbi.nlm.nih.gov/pmc/articles/PMC6033474/. Accessed 2 Apr. 2021.

14 Wojtowicz, Anna (2012). "Islamic Radicalization in the

UK: Index of Radicalization", international Institute for Counter terrorism, p.5.https://www.ict.org.il/UserFiles/Islamic%20Radicalization%20in%20UK.pdf. Also See; https://www.bbc.com/news/magazine-35843991.

15 5 facts about the Muslim population in Europe https://www.pewresearch.org/fact-tank/2017/11/29/5-facts-about-the-muslim-population-in-europe/

16 Read the Statistics Given by the Muslim Council of Britain: https://www.mcb.org.uk/wp-content/uploads/2015/02/MCBCensusReport_2015.pdf. Accessed on 31 December 2022.

17 Jenkins, Simon. (October, 2015). "England Churches can survive-But the Religion Will Have to Go." The Guardian.

18 Damon L. Perry. The Global Muslim Brotherhood in Britain: Non-Violent Islamist Extremism and the Battle of Ideas accessed online on 24 May 2020.

19 Ibid.

20 For discussion of Shariah Laws and opposition to the reforms in the Marriages of Muslims see;The independent review intothe application of sharia lawin England and WalesPresented to Parliamentby the Secretary of State for the Home Departmentby Command of Her Majesty, February 2018

21 P Worrall. 'Sharia Law in the UK' (Channel 4, 14 July 2014).https://www.channel4.com/news/factcheck/factcheck-qa-sharia-law-uk> accessed 23 January 2022.

22 https://www.bbc.com/news/uk-39355108, Accessed on 9

March 2021.

23 Australians accepting of migrants but negative towards Islam, poll finds, The Guardian, https://www.theguardian.com/world/2019/may/04/australians-accepting-of-migrants-but-negative-towards-islam-poll-finds, accessed on 25 May 2020.

24 What it means to be a Muslim in modern Australia. https://www.sbs.com.au/guide/article/2018/01/19/what-it-means-be-muslim-modern-australia.

25 In 1981, there were 76,792 Muslims in Australia. In next two decades, there were sharp rise in Muslim population, almost 90 to 92 per cent by 2001 when their population was found to be 2, 81600. But after September 2001 attacks in the USA, one finds a declining trend. Whether it is because of the policy of the government or the anti-Muslim sentiments in Australia, but in 2011, the decadal increase of Muslims fell from 91 per cent to 69 per cent which further was estimated at 27 per cent in 2016.The differential and harsh treatment of Muslims at the airport for Visa and customs check is a reality which is difficult to deny.

26 Howden, Saffron. (November 2015). Muslim children should not be forced to sing national anthem, says Hizbut-Tahrir, The Sunday Morning Herald. https://www.smh.com.au/national/muslim-children-should-not-be-forced-to-sing-national-anthem-says-hizb-uttahrir-20151101-gknwy9.html

27 Muslims opposing Australian National Anthem.

https://tribune.com.pk/story/979232/muslim-students-walk-out-during-australian-national-anthem

28 Uthman Badar, Spokesperson of The organization in The Sydney Morning Herald, 1 November 2015, accessed on 25 May 2020.

29 Ibid

30 Black, A. (2010). Legal recognition of Sharia law: Is this the right direction for Australian family matters? Family Matters, 84, 64-67. Accessed online Version on 25 May 2020.
https://aifs.gov.au/publications/family-matters/issue-84/legal-recognition-sharia-law

31 Ann Black and Kerrie Sadiq: "Good and Bad Shariah; Australia's Mixed Response to Islamic Law." UNSW Law Journal Volume 34(1), p.385.
https://www.unswlawjournal.unsw.edu.au/wp-content/uploads/2017/09/34-1-2.pdf

32 Jamila Hussain, Islam: Its Law and Society (Federation Press, 2nd ed, 2004). P. 202 quoted in Black and Sadiq. Ibid

33 Saeed, A., (2009, 7 August). Muslims must tackle the theology of hate. The Australian quoted in Black, quoted in Black, A (2010). Legal recognition of Sharia law: Is this the right direction for Australian family matters? Family Matters, 84, 64-67. Accessed online Version on 25 May 2020.

34 Row over Melbourne 'holy war' book sales
https://www.theage.com.au/national/row-over-

melbourne-holy-war-book-sales-20050719-ge0jd9.html. Accessed on 25 May 2020.

35 Ibid

36 As Reported in Time Magazine on 21 December 2017.

37 "ISIS: The rise of foreign fighters joining Islamic State - News.com.au." 28 Mar. 2015, https://www.news.com.au/world/middle-east/the-rapid-evolution-of-the-isis-death-cult/news-story/74f78cd251d7d700cfb9645c5b119f3d. Accessed 2 Apr. 2021.

38 Lauren Wilson, (March 2015). The Herald Sun, News Corp Australia Network, 2015. Online access on 26 May 2020.

39 Muslim no go zones. A lesson for Australia. https://morningmail.org/muslim-no-go-zones-lesson-australia/, The Australian Morning Mail.

40 Listed terrorist organizations. https://www.nationalsecurity.gov.au/what-australia-is-doing/terrorist-organisations/listed-terrorist-organisations/islamic-state, Accessed on 28 October 2021.

41 Public School criticized for allowing male students to avoid shaking hands with women https://honey.nine.com.au/latest/muslim-boys-not-shaking-hands-women-hurstville-boys-campus-sydney/1193ecb5-31e4-4639-9cc1-b56830be5612, accessed on 26 May 2020.

42 Tarek Fateh, "Shariah law makes a comeback in Ontario." The Toronto Sun, 11 June 2019. Accessed on 26 May 2020.

43 https://www.counterextremism.com/countries/spain. Also Reported by ABC News and Time Magazine though an ISIS terrorist.

44 Birnbaum, Michael. "The mosque is Belgium's biggest. Officials say it's a hotbed for extremism." The Washington Post, 11 November 2017. https://www.washingtonpost.com/world/europe/the-mosque-is-belgiums-biggest-officials-say-its-a-hotbed-for-extremism/2017/11/10/8a6d7746-b849-11e7-9b93-b97043e57a22_story.html

45 Gohel, Sajjan M. "Germany Increasingly Centre of Terrorism in Europe", August 2011, Vol 4, Issue 8, Combating Terrorism Centre. https://ctc.usma.edu/germany-increasingly-a-center-for-terrorism-in-europe/

46 Mohammad, Jasim. "The Islamist Challenge in Germany", European Eye on Radicalization, 28 August 2019. https://eeradicalization.com/the-islamist-challenge-in-germany/

47 Ibid

48 http://www.columbia.edu/itc/mealac/pritchett/00islamlinks/txt_sir_sayyid_lucknow_1887.html, accessed on 22 November 2020.

CHAPTER 6

ISLAM IN THE WORLD OF ISLAM

WHILE THE FOLLOWERS of radical Islam stand disquiet and disgruntled and are engaged in a state of perpetual fight—both violent and non-violent—for Islamic identity and community interests in countries of Dar al-Harb and Dar al-Sulh, they are also not at ease and harmony in the countries which according to their theological position are lands of Islam (Dar al-Islam or Dar-ul-Islam). A careful analysis of practice of Islam would suggest that Muslims are fighting more with one another than against non-Muslims.[1] Broadly speaking, the entire Muslim population of the world can be placed in two categories; the place where Islam is a predominant religion, and the land where Islam is in minority. The reasons, logic and nature of violence differ from categories to categories.

In countries where Islam is not a dominant religion, the followers fight to be treated equally and fairly in social, cultural, political and economic domains of the country. Their polarizing dissention, cries and calls are intended at just treatment to the Muslims. The predominant nature of complaints of Muslim organizations relate to harassment and discrimination against Muslims in such countries by the state and the majority population. The dominant majority, however, conceives such assertion and identity calls as hostile. Muslims are often depicted and stereotyped as violent, aggressive and intolerant by the dominant community.

The dissentions and conflicts of Muslims in the dominant non-Muslim society have different trajectories, levels and nature. Two categories seem obvious. First, there are countries which have historically remained engaged with Islam such as India, Israel, and Spain. The domains of contest and nature of discord in such societies are different from the countries where Islam arrived long back but where the real numerical strength swelled up only after the Second World War or in early 1970s in wake of greater exchange of trade and people between the Islamic world and these countries. Even in the first category of countries, there is a great deal of variations in terms of reasons, rationale and areas of conflicts. Muslims are in conflict with Israel because Jews nation came up on the land they also consider as their holy land. In case of Spain and India, Muslims consider them to be lands ruled by their ancestors which now have gone respectively into the hands of dominant Christian and Hindu population.

Among all these, India presents a unique case where Muslims ruled the country for centuries but could not convert the entire population into Islam, the way the Prophet and the successive army of Islam converted the entire Arab world using force and violence. They succeeded in carving out a separate homeland for Muslims- Pakistan but a significant proportion of their population stayed back in India. And with the passage of time even in the post-partitioned India, they have exceeded the population of Pakistan as India ranks the second most populated Muslim country in the world. The population of Muslims in undivided India was 23 per cent and the land that Pakistan got was 35 per cent. After the Partition, Muslim population in India declined to 8 per cent which in the last seventy years have risen to 18 per cent.

As Muslims ruled in India for almost a thousand years, the cultural, social icons of Hindus and Muslims evolved and came into conflict with each other. Frenzied Muslims destroyed many temples and erected mosques there upon. While cows were sacred animal for the Hindus, cow killing came to be identified with Muslims. If Akbar and his victories became the points of pride for Muslims, the valour of Maharana Pratap of Mewar became the source of pride for the Hindus.

These were reasons that created and consolidated separate identity of Muslims even when they came from the same racial stocks as the Hindus. This led to radical Islamists belief that they could not live with Hindus and yet maintain their separate identity. As demand for India's independence from the British rule gained ground, they made the demand for a separate nation for the Muslims. Hindus and Muslims were two nations and they could not co-exist was the main assertion of the Muslim League under Mohammad Ali Jinnah. The Indian National Congress, that had become the main vehicle for the fight for Independence, could not give a befitting resistance to this demand for dismemberment of India. Intimidated by largescale violence that happened after Jinnah's Direct-Action Day in 1946, the meek leadership of the Congress acceded to the demand of the Muslim League for creation of Pakistan. But not all Muslims chose to go to Pakistan. The Partition led to largescale riots and massacres of people on both sides of the new countries.

Muslims who stayed in India are doing extremely well and India has the second largest Muslim population in the world after Indonesia. Unfortunately, it seems that the same identity issue that created Pakistan has not settled among Indian Muslims. Competitive politics and appeasement of Muslims for votes has led to further ghettoization of Muslims and consolidation of their separate identity. The same rhetoric that was heard in the 1940s and subsequent years closer to Independence is being heard even today and posing serious challenges to emergence of one national identity.

The second category of the countries with minority Muslim population are those where foot fall of Islam occurred long back but the numerical strength of its followers started increasing when Muslims started migrating to these places after the Second World War. It further swelled up after the 1970s when more and more Muslims and Arab world started migrating and settling in the West in pursuit of education, job and the business. The West appeared to them a better destination for earning and life style. America, Germany, Australia, Norway, Sweden etc. can be put in the second category. Islam reached these countries in the 17th and the 18thcenturies but the real increase in Muslim population can be traced to second half of 20th century.

And, therefore, the countries which we intend to discuss in this chapter are those ones which were crushed by the army of Islam and forced to convert to the new faith. Although Islam has followers in 165 countries of the world, its status as a dominant religion has remained confined to Asia and Africa. It could not acquire an effective numerical strength in North America and South America. Further, except for Spain, it could not penetrate deep into Europe. Australia remained untouched from its grasp till the 16th century. It was the winning religion in physical battles in Asia and Africa. This also brings to our notice that Islam could not reach those lands that were separated by long stretc.h of water mass.

In America, that includes both the North and South, except for Surinam, nowhere else has the Muslim population touched the double digit tally.[2] These countries were not the dens of radicalized Muslims but it would be wrong to propose that there has been no radicalization. In Latin American countries, one finds an important cocktail of drug peddlers, dictators and Islamists which form a part of international criminal network.[3] Nicolás Maduro Moros, a dictator President who ruled Venezuela for almost 20 years had a strong criminal network with drug mafias. He allowed entry of drugs into the system and this was used to corrupt the entire governmental mechanism including the country's highest judiciary. They used American banks in South Florida to mark the money from sources of narco-terrorism. There is a huge Mosque in the middle of the Caracaras, the capital city, but it has less to do with spirituality or religion and more to do with carrying out radicalization programmes. The worst of all, Nicolás Moros, appointed Tareck El Aissami as Vice President. He was a known drug peddler born to a Lebanese-Syrian family attached to a Shia Jehadi group, Hezbollah, in Iraq. Hezbollah, allegedly funded and trained by Iran's Islamic Revolutionary Guard Corps (IRGC), is a Shiite Jehadi Organization that emerged during the Israeli war with Lebanon in the early 1980s. It targeted several Israeli and American establishments in 1980s and 1990s including attacks on the US Marine barracks in Beirut in 1983.[4] The US government finally dragged them in court for misusing the American banking system for Narco-terrorism.[5] The US government has been charging both Iran and Iraq with sending preachers in these countries to convert, indoctrinate the locales into Islam and radicalize them.

The region also saw a unique combination of left revolutionary forces and Islamic organizations. The two notorious left organizations were the Revolutionary Armed Forces of Columbia (FARC) and the National Liberation Army known by its abbreviation ELN. For many years, Cuba with the support of the former Soviet Union kept the Americans tense and threatened. The Barack Obama administration delisted the country from its blacklist in 2015 when the President certified that Cuba was not involved in terrorism and had also assured not to engage in terrorist activities. Cuba was facing the US sanction since 1982 for engagingor sponsoring terrorism. However, Islamic terrorism did not have a strong presence in South and Latin American countries. It was relatively low when compared to other regions.[6]

There are many countries of Africa and Asia which have huge Muslim Population. This includes Egypt whereas of 2021 World Population Review Report Muslim Constitute 92.35 per cent of the total population. In the same way other countries like Algeria had 99 per cent, Morocco-99 per cent, Tunisia - 99.8 per cent, Somalia-99.8 per cent, Mali 95.00 per cent, Chad-58.00 per cent, Burkina Faso- 61.00 per cent, Guinea-89.10 per cent, Niger- 98.3 per cent (it should not be confused with with Nigeria where Muslim population is only 49.60 per cent), Senegal -96.10 per cent, Mauritania-99.9 per cent and Libya 97.00 per cent.[7] Zimbabwe and Ivory Coast have over 25 per cent Muslim population and they significantly influence the country politics. The Muslim population is concentrated mainly in North and North-West Africa. It started immediately after 639 AD and concluded in 647 AD. Islam entered Africa through Egypt which is the closet to Saudi Arabia and gradually spread to different parts of the continent. Egypt that time was under the Roman Empire/Byzantium Empire after defeat of the Persian armies that had occupied it and continued in power for 10 years. By 655 AD, one after another, many lands of North Africa lost their social, cultural and religious demography to Islam. The local chieftains were no match to the army of the Caliphates that succeeded the

Prophet. These countries fell to Islamic expansion one after the other. They also tried to enter Spain and France in Europe also but could not succeed except in Turkey which is treated as a part of both Europe and Asia.

In Asia, particularly in the Arab world and along the Persian Gulf, Islam spread rapidly through conquests by a superior army. However, it had a different trajectory in South East Asia where it spread through traders and got consolidated by the Sufis. These Sufis converted Buddhist and Hindu Monarchs into Islam which later helped it reach the masses. Islamic expansion generally followed the trade route. Hence, Malacca was the first to emerge as Islamic Sultanate after Parameswara Dewa Shah converted to Islam and became Muhammad Iskandar Shah. The Samudera Pasai Sultanate came up on the north coast of Sumatra after Merah Suli was converted to Islam and adopted the name Malik-ul-Salih. Because of different trajectories of expansion, Islam in the Arab world and African countries were of different nature. The aggression found in the earlier is absent in case of Islam in South-East Asia.

When one looks at the World of Islam, a few things appear to be quite apparent. First, close to 70 per cent Muslims belong to the Sunni cult followed by the Shia sect and the Sufi order. Second, while Sunni Muslims generally follow the Hanafi School popular in the Arab countries, the Hanbali[8] school is dominant in Africa. Close to 99 per cent of Islamic population in Indonesia are Sunni Muslims followed by Shias (0.5 per cent) and Ahmadiyas (0.2 per cent). In both Indonesia and Malaysia, Islam has undergone significant changes after the 1990s due to influence of radical interpretation of Islam through Wahhabism, Muslim Brotherhood, Deoband, Jamat-e-Islami of Pakistan and India, and the Tablighis. These schools of thought started influencing Muslims in the name of promoting puritan and true Islam as a complete way of life.[9] Third, there is hardly any theocratic Islamic state which does not have bred international terrorist organizations. For every act of violence, there is a justification by these organizations. When non-Muslims interpret Jihad as violence and war against non-Muslims, they are accused of mis-reading from the *Quran*. They argue that Islam does not sanction war against others. And Jihad means the struggle within the minds and hearts of individuals against the evils for self-purification and righteousness. Many others suggest that Islam favours a defensive Jihad and not offensive Jihad. Defensive Jihad in simple terms is aimed at carrying out religious war only when Islam is under attack. But from the Wahhabis to the Deobandis, they all look at what happened during the times of the Prophet and the four righteous Caliphates. The matter of fact is that the destruction of idols and places of worship of 'others' which happened at the instruction of Muhammad and other Caliphates were not in defence but to eliminate the 'others' faith. These acts of violence were not at all intended at self-purification. And the Islamic scholars have always justified such acts and interpretation of Islamic Jihad.[10] And this interpretation of Islam has historically been in practice throughout the journey of Islam as a religion and political ideology. Wahhabism, Islamic Brotherhood, Deoband and their affiliates have advanced only this further, taking thread from the history of Islam and the theological discourse in its support.

There are four categories of terrorist organizations that work in name of restoring, expanding and reviving Islam across the globe. Falling in the first category are those confined within the territorial boundaries of the countries they operate. Their aim is to achieve certain specific purpose such as the Hamas in Palestine and Israel that seek to liberate the land of Palestine from the Jewish state of Israel. The Hamas is not active in other parts of the world. Similarly, the Hezbollah is working in Venezuela. It is a Jihadi group that seeks to create an Islamic State. It was created during the US' war on Lebanon with the support of Iran but is operational in South America. Second category of terrorist organizations are those that operate in more than one country i.e., who make their presence felt in several non-Islamic states. For example, the Boko Haram in Africa operates in more than one country and try to spread Jihad. Third category of terrorist organizations are those with transnational operations. The ISIS, the Al-Qaeda, the Taliban and the Jaish-e-Mohammed belong to this category. They have the larger goal of spreading the rule of Islam in the world rather than limiting it to a couple of countries.

Most of these Islamic terrorist organizations came up after the 1980s during the Afghan Mujahideen's fight against the Soviet forces and thereafter. The Islamic organizations before the rise of these transnational terrorist organizations were limited by resources, arms and communication networks in executing violence. But these increased phenomenally with flourishing Petro-dollar in the Arab world and enhanced reach of Wahhabism. Muslim fighters from different countries of Arab world had joined the Afghan boys to oppose the Soviet Union's occupation of Afghanistan. They had plenty of money that came from the US and Saudi Arabia. Pakistani regulars provided training and radicalized Islam gave them religious doctrine to sacrifice themselves and take the lives of others. The success in Afghanistan raised their confidence and persuaded them to believe that they could together defeat any power on the planet. Towards the last leg of the Afghan war, these motivated and radicalized Muslims started creating Islamic groups such as Taliban and lending all kinds of support to them in this fight. It was the time when the world saw a sudden spurt in the growth of terrorist organizations pledging commitment and trust to the establishment of puritan Islam.

For example, the first terrorist organization that formally came into existence in Kashmir was Hizb-ul-Mujahideen in 1989, with its headquarters at Muzaffarabad in Pakistan occupied Kashmir (PoK). This organization was developed by the ISI as the armed wing of Pakistan's Jamaat-e-Islami to counter the Jammu and Kashmir Liberation Front (JKLF) which had started advocating an independent Jammu and Kashmir that included even the POK. The JKLF wanted Kashmir to be freed from both India and Pakistan and this was against the ISI gameplan. The Hizb-ul-Mujahideen works for complete Islamization of Kashmir and its full integration with Pakistan.[11] This organization has one of the strongest networks in Kashmir even today with all its five divisions fully functional:

the central division for Srinagar, the northern division for Kupwara-Bandipora-Baramulla, the southern division for Anantnag and Pulwama, the Chenab division for Doda district and Gool in the Udhampur district, and the Pir Panjal division for the Rajouri and Poonch districts."[12]

In fact, formation of terrorist organizations started after the Al-Qaeda came under the leadership of Osama bin-Laden in 1988. In fact, in the war against the Soviet Union in Afghanistan, Palestinian Sheikh 'Abdullah 'Azzam played a crucial role by coordinating and organizing training and deployment of these Islamic warriors. The foundation of the Al-Qaeda was laid down in 1984 when Abdullah Azzam shifted to Peshawar with Osama and started Bayt-al-Ansar (House of Supporter) which was soon renamed as Maktab Khadamat-al-Mujahidin i.e., Office of Services for Mujahidin.[13] He was assisted by Osama bin-Laden who later on emerged as the undisputed leader of all those who had come from different parts of world to contribute to the religious war i.e., Jihad against the Soviet Union.

Osama was essentially anti-West but he also opposed "heretic regimes" in the Islamic world. His purpose was therefore to throw out such regimes and establish the system of Caliphate and government based on the Shariah. And, therefore, he and his organization were also against the American allies in the Gulf and the Arab world such as Saudi Arabia, which was patronizing equally dreadful Salafi schools and extremist organizations inspired by it. The Al-Qaeda, resolves to liberate also Mecca and Medina from the Saudi apart from Jerusalem from the Israeli control.[14] Its purpose is to unite the entire

Muslim world and develop itself as an 'umbrella organization' for all like-minded terrorist organizations wherever they operate in the service of Islam. It works in almost 60 countries today. It also"forges alliance with like-minded terrorist and fundamentalist organizations such as Egypt's Al Jehad, Iran's Hezbollah, Sudan's National Islamic Front, as also terrorist outfits in Yemen, Saudi Arabia, and Somalia."[15] After the killing of Osama bin-Laden by the American SEAL forces in Abbottabad in Pakistan, Al Qaeda's leadership has gone to Ayman Al- Jawahari, former leader of the Al Jehad. It continues to work in almost 60 countries today.[16]

The Al-Qaeda that targeted mainly the Americans and Jewish establishments became the role model for many Islamic terrorist organizations that worked with the same purpose in other parts of the world. From Yamen Hotel Bombings in 1993, where American troops were stationed en-route to Somalia, to the Charlie Hebdo shooting in Paris in 2015, there are hundreds of such terror attacks that were executed by the Al-Qaeda in several cities of the world. The most dreadful of them was the attack on the World Trade Centre and the Pentagon establishment in September 2001. The Taliban in Afghanistan allowed Osama Bin Laden to operate from its areas till the Northern Alliance Forces entered Afghanistan in their war against terror.[17]

And then started surfacing, one after the other, a series of Islamic terrorist organizations in different parts of the world. Their formations, splits and further reassembly under different banners made it difficult for even a brilliant monitor to track the activities and organizational structures of these terror outfits. Islamic terrorism had started from Palestine in 1967, witnessed the second wave after the Afghanistan war came to an end with the Soviet withdrawal, and the third wave captured the attention of the world after 9/11 terror attacks in the USA.

The turning point was in 1967 when Arab nationalism led by the combined forces of Egypt, Syria and Jordan received a crushing defeat and lost their lands to Israel in a six-day war. It was a great loss to Abdul Naseer who had emerged as hero of the Arab world after he nationalized the Suez Canal Company against the wishes of the West. Egypt then was armed by the Soviet Union and championed the cause of Palestine. The combined defeat was a result of the tactical and technical support of the US. And, therefore, the first set of Islamic terrorism emerged with the financial and other kind of support from the Communist regimes of the erstwhile Soviet Union or USSR (Union of Soviet, Socialist Republics). Al Fatah and Popular Front for Liberation of Palestine (PFLP), Popular Front of Liberation of Palestine -General Command (PFLP-GC), far more fundamentalist faction split up from the PFLP, Abu Nidal Organisation (ANO) were the few that started working for the Palestinian cause. They developed international networks leading to terrorist activities in other countries. These organizations carried out several terrorist activities such as bombing, kidnapping and destruction of public properties.

The PFLP operated mainly from Syria. It aligned with the Palestine Liberation Organization (PLO) chief Yasser Arafat but the PFLP-GC advocated and carried out terror attacks in Europe and the Middle East.[18] The PFLP used 'unusual means' such as hot-air balloons and motorized hang gliders for launching cross-border terrorist attacks in Israel and other European countries. Abu Nidal Organization (ANO) that split from the PLO's Fatah faction, carried about several attacks in twenty countries including Israel, America, France and the UK.[19] And these included attacking airports of "Vienna and Rome in 1985, the Neve Shalom synagogue in Istanbul and the Pan Am flight 73 hijacking in Karachi in September 1986, the City of Poros day-excursion ship attack in Greece in July 1988 and killing Jordanian diplomat in Lebanon in 1994."[20] From the late 1980s, its influence started declining and by the turn of the new century it had stopped terrorist activities and shut down many of its operational bases.

The second wave of terrorism started with Islamic revolution in Iran under the leadership of Ayatollah Khomeini in 1979. Before this, Iran was monarchic with Shah Reza Pahlavi at its head. The civil unrest movement which had backing of several Islamic organizations and the left leaning intellectuals forced the Shah to leave Iran on 16 January 1979. Khomeini's armed people captured the loyal forces of Reza Pahlavi and came to power. In subsequent elections, Khomeini was voted to power as the President with a thumping majority. Here was an emergence of a new Hero in the Islamic world which was not liked by many within the Muslim world. Iran declared itself to be a theocratic Islamic State and lent open support to Palestinians including their raids on Israel and American targets.

This was the phase when Iran frequently hit international headlines because of the decisions of President Khomeini who was also a top religious leader.[21] This also brought in a new element to International Islamic terrorism in the form of a Shia terrorist organization, Hezbollah,[22] the party of God, formed by the Lebanese Shia clerics after the Israeli attack on the country in 1982 but fully supported by the Iranian government.[23] The organization operated from Beirut and Al-Beqa in Southern Lebanon and Southern Beirut. Syria also supported it. Hezbollah continued the raids against Israel till the latter withdrew from Lebanon in 2000.[24] Hezbollah established its centres in many countries of Europe, Africa and North and South America. Its primary objective was to throw Israel out from the occupied lands of both Lebanon and Palestine and oppose the Western forces which supported Israel. It also opposed the Arab countries which were allies of the West.

In pursuance of this objective, it attacked the US embassy and its Marine barracks in Beirut in 1983, the Israeli embassy in Argentina in 1992 and the bombing of Israeli Cultural Centre at Buenos Aires. The entire Arab and Muslim world targeted Israel during this period, and all without exception supported various Islamic terrorist organizations directly or indirectly. The rise of Khomeini also triggered a new contest between Iran and Saudi Arabia on issue of leadership of the Muslim world. Secondly, it strengthened the morale of Shias in different countries including Saudi Arabia where they were at the receiving end and faced insults and atrocities.

The late 1970s also witnessed birth of some other terrorist organizations in North Africa. Some of these were Egyptian Islamic Jehad also known as Al Jehad and Tanzim Al Jehad or Jehad group in 1980. It sought to overthrow the Egyptian government and establish an Islamic State in Egypt. Al Jehad assassinated Egyptian President Anwar Sadat in 1981, Interior Minister Hasan Al-Alfi and Prime Minister Atef Sedky in 1993, and bombed the Egyptian embassy in Islamabad in 1995 and the US embassy in Albania in 1998.[25] This terrorist organization from the very beginning had factional conflict and finally the group of Al-Jawahari, who later became the head of the Al-Qaeda after the death of Osama Bin Laden, emerged to be the dominant faction. Al-Jawahari was also instrumental in aligning with terrorist organizations in Afghanistan. The Palestinian Islamic Jehad, the Islamic Resistance Movement which emerged from Muslim Brotherhood of Egypt, also known as the Hamas, were mainly limited in their operations against Israel. They did not attack forces or establishments of the US and the UK directly. Al-Gamaat Al-Islamiyya was another terrorist organization that came up in Egypt with a purpose of throwing out the Egyptian government and replacing it by an Islamic State. It had multinational presence such as in Sudan, the United Kingdom, Afghanistan, Austria, and Yemen.

Apart from Egypt, other countries in North Africa also witnessed mushrooming of Islamic terrorist organizations. These included the Al Ittihad Al Islamiya (Islamic Unity) in Somalia in 1980s which later on merged with the Al-Shabaab; the Ansar-al-Din (Defenders of Faith) in Mali; the Libyan

Islamic Fighting Group (LIFG) which later on attached and finally merged with Al-Qaeda; the Abu Nidal Organisation, the Palestine Islamic Jehad, the Hamas, and the Lebanese Hezbollah in Sudan; the Ansar al- Sharia in Libya; the Al Qaeda in the Islamic Maghreb (AQIM), the Al- Mourabitoun, Jund al- Khilafah and the ISIS in Algeria; the Boko Haram and the Islamic State in West Africa (ISWA); and the Al Qaeda in the Islamic Maghreb (AQIM), the Islamic State in Greater Sahara (ISGS), the Jamaat Nusrat al-Islam wal-Muslimeen (JNIM), the Ansar Dine and the Al-Mourabitoun in Chad. Almost all Muslim dominated countries in Africa or where followers of Islam are numerically dominant have one or multiple Islamic terrorist organizations functioning for the cause of jihad.[26] There is no exception. Some of them which earned the distinction of dreaded notoriety are the Boko Haram and the Al-Shabaab besides the Al-Qaeda which is of Asian origin and which subsequently expanded its operations in many continents either through opening up new chapters or aligning and assisting like-minded terrorist organizations operating from there.

These organizations were born after the Afghan war which marked the fourth wave of Islamic terrorist organizations. The Boko Haram[27] of Nigeria was founded by Ustaz Mohammed Yusuf, who was just a cleric and a graduate equivalent from an Islamic seminary. He founded this organization in 2002 with the official name 'Jama'atu Ahlus-Sunna Lidda'Awati Wal Jihad' which means 'people committed to the propagation of the Prophet's Teachings and Jihad.' However, it is known more as the 'Boko Haram' which in local Hausa language is interpreted as 'Haram' to Western Education.[28] Yusuf held that Western education had corrupted the rulers of the country which was in control of non-believers and it did not matter whether it was Muslim or a non-Muslim at the seat of power. And therefore, it is duty of followers of Islam to establish the 'Pure Islam.'[29] He was highly inspired by Salafi or Wahabi Islam and it is said that he was funded by the Wahabi institutions in Saudi Arabia.[30] He was against Western education even as he was proficient in English as well as modern science. Interestingly, he was not against using modern gadgets and technology pertaining to violence! He opposed the idea that the Earth is spherical as it was against the Islamic belief. However, he could mobilize thousands of Muslims and gave nightmares to Nigeria and other states for years before he was killed by the security forces after his arrest. Due to linguistic (Hausa Language in case of Niger) and ethnic affinity and commonality (Kanuri ethnicity), this Nigerian terrorist organization became known in adjoining parts of Niger, Chad and Cameroon. As a result, all these countries initiated joint operations to combat this organization. The horizontal divide between North and South Nigeria dominated respectively by Muslims and Christians provide the terrain for breeding religious polarization in the name of Islam. The Boko Haram has been targeting the Churches, the armed forces, crowded places like markets, 'soft civilian targets', schools etc. to create terror. It is said that they have mostly resorted to bombing involving even female suicide bombers.

The other terrorist group which unleashed ferocity and violence in Africa was the Al-Shabaab. In fact, the rise of the Al-Shabaab is related to corresponding downfall of the Boko Haram.[31] Its ferocity and striking expanse enhanced geometrically after alliance with the Al-Qaeda. The Chief of Al-Qaeda, Al-Jawahari, and Ahmed Abdi Godane of the Al-Shabaab declared their alliance through a video release in February 2012. In 2016, it was rated as the deadliest in Africa as its strikes killed over 4000 people in that year alone.[32] The Al-Shabaab emerged from the Al-Ittihad Al-Islami (AIAI) which preceded it. In 2003, cracks surfaced in the organization on ideological issues. While the old ranks wanted to try hands in politics, the younger ones (that is why Al-Shabaab nomenclature) were committed to radical violent activities for the goals of Islamic state and Islamic society. They aligned with the Islamic Courts Union (ICU), another organization, and together raided and got control of Mogadishu, capital city of Somalia, in 2006. It was a big development and it led to panic in neighbouring Ethiopia. Ethiopian forces entered Somalia and launched military operations against the radical forces. While the ICU faction fled, the Al-Shabaab faction merely retreated. It later adopted the guerrilla warfare against the Ethiopian forces and forced them to vacate Somalia. It also enhanced its control in Central and Southern Somalia.[33]

Al-Shabaab used the attack by Ethiopia to arouse Somalian pride and used the deep-seated anguish of young Somalians to recruit them in its rank and file.[34] Al-Shabaab used the fragile polity of Somalia that did not witness a stable government since the overthrow of military dictator Mohamed Siad Barre in 1991, and the ethnic divide and poverty in the country to establish itself. It carried out strikes in countries surrounding Somalia and other countries of South Africa and has become a symbol of terror there.

The major upsurge in terrorist activities and organizations took place in Asia with Pakistan emerging as the epicentre of this development. Pakistan that shares borders with Afghanistan provided shelter to Afghan militants and trained and used them for violence in different countries. It was during this time that a dozen of Islamic terrorist organizations sprung up in Kashmir alone. They included "Hizb-ul-Mujahideen (HM), Lashkar-e-Toiba (LeT), Jaish-e-Mohammed (JeM), Al Umar Mujahideen (AuM), Dukhtaran-e-Millat (DeM), Harkat-ul Mujahideen (HuM) previously known as Harkat-ul-Ansar, Harkat-ul-Jihad-al-Islami (HuJI), Jammu and Kashmir Islamic Front (JKIF), Jamait-ul-Mujahideen (JuM), Jamaat-e-Islami (JeI)-Jammu and Kashmir, Jammu and Kashmir Liberation Front–Yasin Malik faction (JKLF-Y), Islamic State/Islamic State of Iraq and the Levant (ISIL) also referred to as the Islamic State of Iraq and Syria (ISIS) or Islamic State."[35] Besides these, there are 19 odds organizations that are inactive. [36]

Neighbouring Bangladesh bred several such Islamic terrorist organizations as documented by South Asia Terrorism Portal which keeps track of the terrorist organizations in South Asia including the Islamists and the Maoists. Its list of proscribed organizations that emerged in Bangladesh in the 1990s and later are "Harkat-ul-Jihad-al-Islami Bangladesh

(HuJI-B), Jagrata Muslim Janata Bangladesh (JMJB), Jamaat-ul-Mujahideen Bangladesh (JMB), Ansarullah Bangla Team (ABT), Ansar al-Islam, Lashkar-e-Toiba (LeT), Islami Chhatra Shibir (ICS), Islamic State/Islamic State of Iraq and Levant / Islamic State of Iraq and Syria/Daish (ISIS)." There are many which are inactive and yet there are four or five which are not banned and active in Bangladesh.[37]

In Afghanistan came the Al-Qaeda, the ISIS and the Laskar-e-Toiba. These organizations are now banned in Afghanistan but not diminished or inactive. Also active are the Talibans that captured power in Afghanistan after the pull out of the US forces in 2021. The Tehreek-e-Taliban Pakistan (TTP) and the Haqqani Networks (HN) are also active in the country. In Sri Lanka, there are over two dozen Tamils extremists' groups as well but they are not in name of religion and not for religion. On the contrary, the ISIS (Islamic State/Islamic State of Iraq and Levant /Islamic State of Iraq and Syria/Daish), the National Thowheeth Jama'ath (NTJ), Jamathei Millathu Ibrahim (JMI) are all motivated by religio-political goals. The ISIS has cells and centres in Maldives.

Pakistan is hotbed of Islamic terrorism. Many terrorist organizations have mushroomed there in the name of religion. The South Asia Terrorism Portal informs that there are over 175 Islamic terrorist organisations in Pakistan spread over all regions-from the illegally occupied territories in Gilgit Baltistan to Khyber Pakhtunkhwa, Sindh, and Punjab and so on.[38] A separate map[39] has been given for the purpose to understand the spread of terrorist bases in Pakistan which has often been described as a nursery and minefield of Islamic terrorism. It has overshadowed the entire Arab world and other Islamic countries in terms of patronizing, sheltering, guiding, training and exporting terror to different countries in the name of Islam. According to Bruce Riedel, a Senior Fellow at the Brookings Institution, Pakistan is today 'home to more terrorist organizations than any other country in the World.'[40] Some of them which have come up as the most dreaded ones are Al-Qaeda, Laskar-i-Toiba or Toyyaba, Jaise-e-Muhammad (Army of Muhammad), Tahrik e-Taliban Pakistan etc. The nomenclatures of these organizations give away their intentions.

The UN banned Lashkar-e-Toiba though Security Council Resolutions forcing Pakistan too to impose the ban. But this organization is still active with the support of Pakistan's intelligence and military establishments.[41] It is this organization that was responsible for the terrorists' attack on Indian Parliament in 2001, the terror attacks in Mumbai in 2008 and the Pulwama incident in February 2019.[42] Lashkar-E-Toiba means 'the Army of the Righteous' or 'The Army of the Pure.' It not only wants to free Kashmir from India but also seeks to Islamize the entire nation and its surrounding states. And therefore, it holds that it is the responsibility of all Muslims to wage a religious war against India i.e., Jihad to restore the rule by Muslims. It considers the US, Israel and India (but not China) as the enemies which are bent on destroying Islam. The LeT was formed by Hafeez Sayeed.

Not very different are the objectives of other organizations such as the Jaise-e-Muhammad (the army of Mohammad) and the Taliban. The JeM was founded by Maulana Masood Azhar who had earlier fought for Harkat-ul-Mujahideen and 'had been linked to the Al-Qaeda.[43] It was the same organization that had hijacked Indian Airlines Flight IC-814 in exchange of which Maulana Masood Azhar was released by Indian authorities. He was working in Kashmir for Harkat-ul-Ansar (HuA) when he was nabbed by the Indian security forces. After the US banned the Harkat-ul-Ansar, it changed its name to Harkat-ul-Mujahideen (HuM). After release, he founded the Jaish-e-Muhammad with the support of Osama Bin Laden and Pakistan's ISI with focus on carrying out Jihad in Kashmir. India had been trying hard to get Masood Azhar to be included in the list of global terrorists. JeM was involved in the attack on Indian Parliament in 2001, Mumbai terror attacks in 2008, Pathankot air base attack in 2016 and the Pulwama attack in February 2019. Masood Azhar is also known to be the man who exported Jihad to Britain. Finally, after a series of international pressure Azhar's name was included in the list of global terrorists on 1 May 2019. China, under the influence of Pakistan, had vetoed earlier attempts to declared Azhar to be an international terrorist.

The Taliban emerged in 1994 from militancy in Afghanistan. It captured roughly one third of Afghanistan by 1996 and declared formation of its own government which was recognized by Pakistan, Saudi Arabia and the United Arab Emirates. It declared Kandahar as the new capital from where it ruled over the territories under its control. It applied Shariah in its worst form such as banning of music, plays, cinema, beauty parlour etc. It not just targeted non-Muslims but also the Shias and other non-Sunni Muslims whom the Taliban considered to be bad Muslims.[44] They banned kite flying, keeping pets at home and used medieval methods of executing human lives. They destroyed 1500-year-old statue of Lord Buddha at Bamiyan. The Taliban was inspired by the Deobandi School of Islam and even Osama Bin Laden fought under its banner in Afghanistan.

The Taliban continued to be in power till 2001 when the US invaded Afghanistan to dismantle Al Qaeda and hunt Osama bin Laden for the dastardly attack in New York in September 2001. The Taliban that was sheltering Osama and supporting the Al Qaeda was dethroned. The arrival of NATO forces in Afghanistan under the leadership of the US broke its backbone. After Osama's death the command structure got weakened but it continued to be a deadly Organization with a capacity to hit target beyond Pakistan, India and Afghanistan. The NATO forces after prolong war in Afghanistan got tired losing lives and this forced the US to come to the negotiating table. When the US forces left Afghanistan, the Taliban captured the country in 2021 and is seeking legitimacy of its government.

Even the countries of the East Asia, where Islam reached through business and trade instead of violence and military triumph, have now come to witness the growth of Islamic terrorist organizations. Jemaah Islamiyah in Malaysia carried out several explosions such as the bombings in Bali in 2002, the bombings at the JW Marriott and Ritz-Carlton hotels in

Jakarta in 2003, the attacks on Australian Embassy in Jakarta in 2004, and Bali in 2005. The organization wants to establish the rule of Islam in the entire South East Asia. Due to its links with the Al-Qaeda and the Taliban and potential threat to the world humanity, it was banned by the USA.[45] The UN, China, Australia, Canada, Japan and the United Kingdom have also declared it to be a terrorist organization.

Indonesia which is known for its tolerance also witnessed the rise of Islamic terrorist organizations in recent years. It is the country which is home to the largest Muslim population in the world comprising close to 13 per cent of the world total. It is a Muslim dominated country with 88 per cent people following Islam. Yet, it is not a theocratic Islamic state and Shariah is not in place for governance. For the last two decades, radical Salafis, Wahabis and Deobandis have been trying their best to alter this. Indonesia loves its cultural past and still cherishes its Hindu ancestry which is evident from the fact that Garuda is the name of its official Airlines and Kuber, a Hindu God of Wealth and Treasury, is the name of its Central Bank. Ram Leela is still played in the country with the same fervour. Ballet from the Ramayan, played on special occasions, enthralls audience with its beauty and rich cultural exposition. The radical Islamists such as the Jemaah Islamiyah (JI) and the ISIS have tried to strengthen their footprints on Indonesian soil and have been trying to destroy the centuries old tradition.

Most of these Islamic terrorist organizations have their formal or informal presence in Gulf countries or the Arab world. But surprisingly, very few of them attack establishments of Saudi Arabia and United Arab and Emirates despite the fact that these are important allies of the United States. The US symbolizes the military, economic and cultural might of the West which these organizations hate. The Islamic State (ISIS) was created in March 2014 and it swamped over a large stretc.h of land in Syria and Iraq both of which share a long border of approximately 599 Km. It thus had both an African and Asian origin. It seeks to mobilize Muslims from all over the globe to create an Islamic State and then restart the system of the Caliphate, the head of the Islamic state. It has developed its own army, legal system, cultural norms and treatments towards the non-Muslims.

Their conducts would put to shame even the primitive animality as they resorted to mass hanging, group shooting, hanging from the trees and so on to perpetrate terror among those who did not toe their ideology. Al-Baghdadi all of a sudden became a name of international infamy with pictures coming from its areas of control where people were being killed in the most heinous and barbaric ways. Although they did not spare even Muslims who rebelled against them, their main targets were the 'ethnic and religious minorities and combat forces working in its areas of control.'[46] They adopted the guerilla warfare against the combat forces in the combat zones and indulged in terrorist activities against opponents in other places. Thousands of Muslims joined the battle in belief that it is a fight for 'Din' (religion) against the infidels, and for the creation of a just Islamic State. They got killed along with the self-appointed Caliphate Al-Baghdadi, and got defeated in

Tamkin i.e., the area of their control. Baghdadi killed himself and his two children by detonating a suicide vest when he faced capture by the US forces in 2019. The ISIS looks scattered now but it does not mean it has been decimated completely.

Conclusion

There is no country with substantial Muslim population that does not have radical Islamists organizations at work. In all the Islamic countries, there are Islamic terrorist organizations without exception. They are not just fighting against the non-Islamic population but also against Muslim sects and the people who in their understanding live as infidels. They are acting against reason and logic and modernity. Industrialization and scientific approach have polluting influence on puritan Islam. They, therefore, make a clarion call to return to the golden age of Islam. Wherever they have come to control the structure of power they have sought to forcefully implement this puritan form through strict dress code, ban on music and recreational activities and so on. They did it in Afghanistan on the portion of the land that they governed. The Boko Haram, the ISIS also have issued instructions to this respect with threat of punishing those who fail to follow the dictates. Needless to say, these terrorist organizations have become a threat to free, liberal and forward-looking democratic societies. Close to 85 per cent victims of Islamic terrorism are Muslims.

The militant fundamentalist nature of Wahhabism is becoming visible to Islamic states too. On 6th May 2021, Saudi Crown Prince Md. Bin Salman called out the Wahhabi religious establishment[47] for ultra conservative interpretation of Islam and faulty interpretation of Islamic scriptures on national television. However, the story doesn't end here. In December of 2021, Saudi Arabia stunned the Islamic world by putting a ban on Tablighi Jamaat and called it "one of the gates of terrorism."[48]

References:

1 Gleditsch, Nils Petterand Rudolfsen, Ida. 'Are Muslim Countries More Violent.' The Washington Post. 16 May, 2016. https://www.washingtonpost.com/news/monkey-cage/wp/2016/05/16/are-muslim-countries-more-violent/. Accessed on 26 December 2021.

2 Mohamed, Basheer (2018). New Estimates Show US Muslim Population continues to Grow, Pew Research Center. https://www.pewresearch.org/fact-tank/2018/01/03/new-estimates-show-u-s-muslim-population-continues-to-grow/. Retrieved on 1 August 2021.

3 Latin America's Socialist Islamist Narco Terrorist Alliance https://www.fdd.org/analysis/2017/09/27/latin-americas-socialist-islamist-narco-terrorist-alliance/. Accessed on 10 June 2020.

4 https://s3.us-east-2.amazonaws.com/defenddemocracy/uploads/documents/CSIF_TFBB_Hezbollah.pdf. Accessed on 10 June 2020. Also see the https://fas.org/sgp/crs/terror/RS21049.pdf.

5 https://www.justice.gov/opa/pr/nicol-s-maduro-moros-and-14-current-and-former-venezuelan-officials-charged-narco-terrorism.

6 See the Congressional Research Service Report by Sullivan, Mark P, Beittel,June S. "Latin America: Terrorism Issues" Published on 15 December 2016. https://fas.org/sgp/crs/terror/RS21049.pdf.

7 Muslim Population bt Country 2022. (n.d.) from https://worldpopoulationreview.com/country-rankings/muslim-population-by-country

8 Hanbali School of Islam is based on the teachings of Aḥmad ibn Ḥanbal (780–855). This School emphasize on the 'Hadith (traditions concerning the Prophet Muhammad's life and utterances) and practice of Islam set by the early generations of Muslims.' See, https://www.britannica.com/topic/Hanabilah, Accessed on 22 January 2022.

9 Azmilk Mohd Tayeb. (2018).*Islamic Education in Indonesia and Malaysia: Shaping Minds, Saving Souls;* Routledge.

10 The destruction of the places of worship of the pagans in Mecca and elsewhere were not in defence.

11 https://www.satp.org/terrorist-profile/india-jammukashmir/hizb-ul-mujahideen-hm. Accessed on 13 June 2020.

12 It soon had developed factions led by Sayed Salahuddin who initially was the patron and Hilal Ahmad Mir who was designated as the Chief (Amir) of the Organisation. Mir was later on killed in 1993 and its Kashmir commander Master Ahsan Dar was also arrested by the security forces. His son Abdul Mazid Dar who succeeded was also killed by an unknown terrorist Organisation 'Save Kashmir Organisation' on the ground that he had started acting as an informant of the Indian government. It is divided in five divisions; "It has

thousands of armed cadres including the women wing Banat-ul-Islam.

13 Maliach, Asaf. "Bin Laden, Palestine and al-Qa'ida's Operational Strategy." Middle Eastern Studies, Vol. 44, No. 3 (May, 2008), Taylor & Francis, Ltd.pp. 353-375. https://www.jstor.org/stable/40262582. Accessed: 12-06-2020. P. 354.

14 https://www.satp.org/terrorist-profile/afghanistan/al-qaeda. Accessed on 13 June 2020.

15 Ibid.

16 It includes Algeria, Egypt, Morocco, Turkey, Jordan, Tajikistan, Uzbekistan, Syria, Xinjiang in China, Pakistan, Bangladesh, Malaysia, Myanmar, Indonesia, Mindanao in the Philippines, Lebanon, Iraq, Saudi Arabia, Kuwait, Bahrain, Yemen, Libya, Tunisia, Bosnia, Kosovo, Chechnya, Dagestan, Jammu and Kashmir, Sudan, Somalia, Kenya, Tanzania, Azerbaijan, Eritrea, Uganda, Ethiopia, as also in parts of the West Bank and Gaza. See for details: https://www.satp.org/terrorist-profile/afghanistan/al-qaeda. Accessed on 13 Jun 2020.

17 Till 1991 Osama Bin Laden was working from Saudi Arabia. However, he was expelled from there the same year. He shifted to Sudan in 1992 but Saudi Arab, Egypt and the USA mounted pressure on the Sudanese government which allowed him to go to the country of his choice. As Taliban had captured a huge portion of Afghanistan, he chose to settle in Jalalabad at Afghanistan where he developed good relation with Mullah Mohammed Omar.

18 Country Reports on Terrorism 2017 - Foreign Terrorist Organizations: Popular Front for the Liberation of Palestine-

General Command. US Department of States, 19 September 2018.https://www.refworld.org/docid/5bcf1f2ec.html. Accessed on 27 December 2021.

19 Ibid. Also see; https://www.pbs.org/wgbh/pages/frontline/shows/target/etc./modern.html. Accessed on 13 June 2020.

20 Ibid

21 Ganji, A. (2013). Who Is Ali Khamenei? The Worldview of Iran's Supreme Leader. Foreign Affairs, 92(5), 24–48. http://www.jstor.org/stable/23527515. Accessed on 22 January 2022. In several terrorist activities outside Iran, Khamenei names were linked with including the infamous 'Mykonos restaurant assassinations'in which several Iranian-Kurdish opposition leaders were assassinated at the Mykonos Greek restaurant in Berlin, on 17 September 1992.

22 Kane, J. R. (2018). A Life Cycle Analysis of Hezbollah: Where the Group Came from and Where It Is Going. American Intelligence Journal, 35(2), 67–73. https://www.jstor.org/stable/26566567

23 Parvaz, D. "Iran 1979: the Islamic revolution that shook the world." Aljazeera, 11 February, 2014, accessed on 14 June 2020.

24 Hezbollah means 'Party of God.' It is a multifaceted organization, a powerful political party in Lebanon. At the same time, it is also a Shia Islam religious and social movement, and a militia group operating from Lebanon and Iran. See; https://www.britannica.com/topic/Hezbollah. Accessed on 14 June 2020. Also See, Levitt, Mathew (2015). HEZBOLLAH: The Global Footprint of Lebanon's Party of

God, Georgetown University Press.

25 https://www.un.org/securitycouncil/sanctions/1267/aq_sanctions_list/summaries/entity/egyptian-islamic-JehadJehadJehad. United Nation Security Council Resolution, 13 of resolution 1822 (2008). Accessed on 14 June 2020.

26 See for Details, the Annexure I

27 In local Hausa language, this means "Western education is forbidden." See https://www.bbc.com/news/world-africa-13809501. Accessed on 12 Jun 2020.

28 Walker, Andrew. "What Is Boko Haram?." US Institute of Peace (2012). https://www.jstor.org/stable/resrep12178. Accessed: 12-06-2020. P.3.

29 Ibid, p.1.

30 Ibid, p. 3.

31 https://www.bbc.com/news/world-africa-15336689. Accessed on 14 June 2020.

32 https://qz.com/africa/995127/al-shabaab-overtook-boko-haram-as-the-most-deadly-terror-group-in-africa-in-2016/. Retrieved on 15 June 2020.

33 https://edition.cnn.com/2015/04/02/world/africa/al-shabaab-explainer/index.html. Accessed on 15 June 2020.

34 Wise, Rob. "Al-Shabaab." Centre for Strategic and International Studies. Case Studies no.2, July 2011. P. 2. http://www.operationspaix.net/DATA/DOCUMENT/4039~v~Al_Shabaab.pdf. Accessed on 15 June 2020.

35 https://www.satp.org/terrorist-groups/india-jammukashmir. South Asia Terrorism Portal accessed on 15 June 2020.

36 Al Jehad, Al Jehad Force (AJF, combines Muslim Janbaz

Force and Kashmir Je, Al Mujahid Force (AMF), Al Mustafa Liberation Fighters (AMLF), Ikhwan-ul-Mujahideen (IuM), Islami Inquilabi Mahaz (IIM), Islami Jamaat-e-Tulba (IJT), Islamic Students League (ISL), Jammu & Kashmir National Liberation Army (JNLA), Jammu & Kashmir Students Liberation Front (JSLF), Kashmir Jehad Force (KJF), Mahaz-e-Azadi, Muslim Janbaz Force (MJF), People's League Tehrik-e-Hurriat-e-Kashmir (TeHK), Tehrik-e-Jehad (TeJ), Tehrik-e-Jehad-e-Islami (TeJI), Jammu and Kashmir Islamic Front (JKIF), Al-Mansoorain etc. For details see https://www.satp.org/terrorist-groups/india-jammukashmir. South Asia Terrorism Portal accessed on 15 June 2020.

37 The Active Islamic Terrorist Organisations include Hizb-ut-Tahrir (HuT), Hizb-ut-Tawhid (HT), Allah'r Dal, Al Qaeda/Al-Qaeda in Indian Sub-continent (AQIS), Al Qaeda/Al-Qaeda in Indian Sub-continent (AQIS).

38 https://www.satp.org/terrorism-assessment/pakistan-pakistanoccupiedkashmir-gilgitbaltistan

39 Map in the Annexure

40 Discussion on the book 'Deadly Embrace: Pakistan, America and the Future of the Global JehadJehadJehad' by Bruce Reidel at The Brooking Institution at Washington DC, January 18, 2011, p.8. Accessed on 15 June 2020.

41 https://www.efsas.org/publications/study-papers/pakistan-army-and-terrorism;-an-unholy-alliance/

42 Jaish chief Masood Azhar, Lashkar's Hafiz Saeed and Dawood Ibrahim designated as terrorists under anti-terror law https://www.hindustantimes.com/india-news/jem-chief-

masood-azhar-lashkar-s-hafiz-saeed-and-dawood-ibrahim-designated-as-terrorists-under-anti-terror-law/story-tr6GOjJYiKxJw0lj6zjHiJ.html

43 Hashim, Asad. "What is Jaish-e-Muhammad?" Aljazeera, 2 May, 2019. https://www.aljazeera.com/news/2019/02/profile-jaish-muhammad-190215061851082.html. accessed on 15 June 2020.

44 Mamdani, M. (2002). Good Muslim, Bad Muslim: A Political Perspective on Culture and Terrorism. American Anthropologist, 104(3), 766-775. Retrieved April 2, 2021, from http://www.jstor.org/stable/3567254

45 https://russiancouncil.ru/en/extremism-asean. Accessed on 15 June 2020.

46 Schweitzer, Yoram. "The Rise and Fall of the Islamic State: A Fifth-Year Assessment." Institute for National Security Studies (2019). https://www.jstor.org/stable/resrep23469. Accessed: 11-06-2020.

47 *Saudi Crown Prince Lambasts His Kingdomâs Wahhabi Establishment.* (n.d.). Wilson Center. https://www.wilsoncenter.org/article/saudi-crown-prince-lambasts-his-kingdoms-wahhabi-establishment

48 https://timesofindia.indiatimes.com/world/middle-east/saudi-arabia-bans-tablighi-jamaat-calls-it-gate-of-terror/articleshow/88234611.cms

CHAPTER 7

ISLAMIC AGENDA AT WORK IN INDIA

Terrorism and Muslim Assertion

INDIA WAS PARTITIONED because the Indian Muslim League asserted that Muslims constitute a separate nation with their distinct culture, civilization and heroes. Even when some of these differences were hostile to the Hindus, Muslims derived inspiration from different sources of history and, therefore, could not live together and needed a separate homeland.[1] Muslims who were reluctant to support the Muslim League till the provincial elections in 1937-38, in which it could amass only 5 per cent of the votes, massively voted in favour of the League in 1946.[2] By introducing 'Direct Action'[3] that led to mass killing of Hindus, Indian Muslim League in fact forced the Partition on the country. About 23 per cent Muslims of British India got about 35 per cent of the land mass of undivided India for creation of Pakistan.

Leaders like Shyama Prasad Mukherjee, Dr BR Ambedkar

and several others advocated exchange of Hindu-Muslim population for lasting peace and a permanent settlement to the issue of Hindu-Muslims divide in India.[4] But the Government in power and the top leadership of the Indian National Congress rejected this saying that this would be validation of the two-nation theory. Accepting the Partition on the basis of two-nation theory and yet trying to reject this in the context of India was the biggest paradox of history. They accepted the premises of Mohammad Ali Jinnah that Hindus and Muslims were two different nations and they could not exist together, but yet they were trying to reject his premises in the case of India. This was an oxymoron and self-consoling argument. The Congress leadership wanted to prove Jinnah wrong and rejected the proposal for exchange of population. They wanted to prove that merely by following a different religion one could not constitute a different nation and hence, Hindus and Muslims should live together peacefully.

For the last seventy-five years, the Indian leadership and the political establishments have been engaged in pursuit of figuring out if the decision of keeping Muslims in India and not accepting the policy of exchange of population at the time of the Partition was right. Over one third of the Muslim population, nearly 35 million, stayed back in India when the Partition happened. The reasons were several including the need to retain property and to maintaining the extended family. The British decision to quit India was postponed by a year and there were millions who did not know which side of the partition line they had fallen into. The leadership and the government on both sides of the divide were assuring the 'other' of security but frenzied mobs on both sides were out to pillage blood on the streets. On the Indian side, there was Gandhi who chose to go to Calcutta (now Kolkata) and then to Patna to stop the carnage of Muslims and Hindus and it worked. Had he not been in Patna only God knows how many Muslims would have survived in the state of Bihar. This was the same Gandhi who was betrayed by Muslims a year ago when they voted for the Muslim League led by Jinnah. On the other hand, in Pakistan, there was no Gandhi, and trains after trains which came from Pakistan were laden with dead bodies of those killed in riots.

When the storm subsided, it was said that the bad Muslims had chosen to go to Pakistan and those who loved India chose to stay back. But everyone knew that it was a flawed premise and a part of the political rhetoric of those that had accepted the Partition. The fact that a predominant majority of Muslims had voted for Pakistan, including those who stayed back later, was ignored. And this was acknowledged by none other than Maulana Abdul Kalam Azad. During a convocation at the Aligarh University in 1949, Azad observed that a typhoon had passed through the land and swept away the dirt but few potholes are still left with dirty water.[5] He was referring to the radical Islamists in India who had voted for Pakistan.

Jawaharlal Nehru, however, tried to wash away the Muslims of their guilt. In one of the debates in the Constituent Assembly, he squarely put the blame of the Partition on the Muslim League and its leader Jinnah.[6] He did not blame the common Muslims.[7] More importantly, he gave legitimacy to the Indian Union Muslim League which had acquired new nomenclature for All India Muslim League by arguing that it was different from the one which inflicted the partition on the country. Surprisingly, there was no change in position of the IUML on the issue of Muslim identity. Nehru was convinced of the secular credentials of the league and subsequently the Congress entered into political alliance with it in Kerala politics.

In partitioned India, the Constitution made provisions to assuage the feelings of the minority. Except for Dr Ambedkar's last speech in the Constituent Assembly and Sardar Patel's blunt talk that 'Muslim cannot ride two horses, and if they like Pakistan they are free to go there', all attempts were made to pamper Muslims in name of minority.[8] It was even argued that those Muslims who had gone over to Pakistan and wanted to come back to India were welcome.[9] Article 26 to 30 of the India constitution provided rights to the minorities which were denied to the majority. They have been given the right to open educational institutions and administer them. In subsequent decades, the Supreme Court went on to say that the State cannot discriminate against such minority institutions in funding and aid.[10] In other words, tax-payers' money (comprising mostly of Hindus) could be paid to the Madrasas that teach lessons in Islamic texts even if these instill elements of exclusivism and intolerance towards other religions. Issues such as the Uniform Civil Code and protection of the cow slaughter were reasons for conflict between Hindus and Muslims even during the time of the freedom movement. Hence, they were kept in part IV of the constitution dealing with the Directive Principles of the State Policy. The Hindu Personal Code was modified to suit the liberal principles of rights of individuals but the Muslim Personal Laws were left untouched. The issue had come up for discussion in the Constituent Assembly but members did not disturb it, despite the fact that the Muslim personal laws that got codified in 1937 had ruined the practice of diverse traditions amongst the Muslims, as Dr. Ambedkar extensively argued.[11]

Vande Mataram lost to Jana Gana Mana as the National Anthem since Muslims opposed it as anti-Islam. During pre-Independence days, the Muslim League said so and opposed its recitation. For Jinnah, it was anti-Muslim.[12] Singing of Vande Mataram at the session of the Indian National Congress used to be regular feature since 1896. BD Paluskar, a legendary classical musician, travelled all the way to render his performance. Opposition to its signing came for the first time in 1908 at the second session of the Muslim League. The president of the organization declared it to be anti-Islamic. It was largely attributed to bitterness that had erupted between Hindu and Muslims after the Partition of Bengal in 1905. But the singing continued. In 1937, the Indian National Congress constituted a committee of three members comprising Rabindranath Tagore, Subhash Chandra Bose and Jawaharlal Nehru. Nehru had adverse comments on the song as he found some of the stanzas and the background of the novel as possible 'irritants for Muslims.'[13] Tagore was not that harsh but he was also not very forthcoming in support. It was only Subhas Chandra Bose who said that undermining 'Vande Mataram' would send out a wrong message to the people of Bengal and, therefore, it was decided that it would be sung but the last three stanzas were dispensed with.[14] After the Partition, the matter again came up for discussion in the Constituent Assembly and keeping in mind the Muslim sensitivities 'Vande Mataram' lost to the 'Jana Gana Mana.' Dr Rajendra Prasad tilted the decision in favour of 'Jana Gana Mana.' Furthermore, Urdu was given a due place with other Indian languages despite the fact that Urdu had come to be identified with the image and identity of Islam and Pakistan had declared it as the national language. The Hindus and Muslims had polarized on the issue of Urdu in pre-Partition times. Urdu with Arabic script which also was the script of the Quran, and Hindi with Devanagari script in which religious texts of Hindus are written respectively became the identity of Muslims and Hindus and they fought against each other on these lines.[15]

The Partition certainly brought joy to Hindus but it baffled a large section of them who could not swallow the mutilation of undivided India. Their motherland was divided just because a section of Hindus had converted to Islam and instead of deciding to live together forced the Partition. They were happy since because for the first time after centuries of servitude under Medieval Muslim rulers, the Mughals and the British, they had their own government elected by their votes to shape the destiny of the country. There was no more fear of forced conversion, destruction of their temples and being treated as inferior by the white people.

In these thousand years, the Hindus felt that they had lost not just their lands and estates to Muslim but also the cultural artefacts. Thousands of their temples had been desecrated or demolished by Islamic invaders and converted into mosques or left devastated. Millions of people were forced to change their faith under the threat of swords and manipulations. The language of the court, administration and education was first replaced by Persian and Urdu and then by English under the British rule. Sanskrit was reduced to the language of Ashrams and Hindu Mathas. The native education system was in complete disarray as India lost its indigenous system of imparting knowledge.

The political leadership had no preparation or blueprint for all these issues. They had no vision to nurture and develop new India on the basis of its core cultural values called Bharatiyata. Mahatma Gandhi had articulated his thoughts on this in his book *The Hind Swaraj* in 1909 but he was silenced by the British who banned the book as being seditious. His idea of village republic, protection of cows, defending Hinduism and Hindi language, the idea of Swadeshi and the critique of Western industrial civilization which he had espoused in *The Hind Swaraj* had no respect in the eyes of his protégé, Jawaharlal Nehru. India started as a modern republican nation with constitutionalism and liberal democracy as its hallmark.

There was no harm in this but it left many questions unanswered including the one that asked what was Indian or Bharatiya in the new political system. A large section of the society felt cheated and betrayed as this did not reflect the civilizational and cultural identity of India. The Saffron flag, which emblemed India's civilisational identity, was denied the status of becoming the country's national flag. Green was included in the national flag allegedly to assuage the feelings of Muslims. The Government did not muster even the courage to state that temples demolished by the invaders would be restored to their pristine glory. Somnath was an exception but it happened because Sardar Patel had put all his political and organisational weight behind its restoration and rejuvenation. And he was supported by the then President of India, Dr Rajendra Prasad, despite strong reservations of Nehru. The only thing that turned partly to their expectation was acceptance of Hindi as an official language of India for communication. But this too was adjoined by English which was to continue initial for 15 years but has now become a permanent marker of the constitution. Now none talks of completely doing away with English.

From the perspective of Indian Muslims, their demands for reservation in the legislature were denied. Patel categorically said that they cannot ride two horses and that they were free to go to Pakistan if they continued with this kind of demands in the post-divided India. Similarly, Hindustani, a mix of Urdu and Hindi, as desired by the Muslim representative in the Constituent Assembly, was not accepted as the language for communication for the Republic of India. Abdul Kalam Azad was not happy with this decision and he chose to stay away from the Committee which was to take a decision on this. Further, in 1951, the Aligarh Muslim University was duly acknowledged as a Central University by the Act of the Parliament and the minority status of the university was not disturbed.

The Partition, however, left a deep scar and trust deficit between the two communities as it witnessed cross migration from one border to the other and killing of millions on both sides of the border. Muslims across the country had overwhelmingly voted in favour of Pakistan and, therefore, there was a palpable hatred in Hindus against Muslims in general. People had gradually started responding to the calls of Hindu nationalists and the organizations that derived inspiration from India's glorious past. However, the murder of Mahatma Gandhi by a fanatic Hindu changed the whole discourse. It was not just the murder of an individual but a man who had come to be identified with the nationalist struggle and birth of India as a sovereign nation.

Since, Hindu nationalists were dead opposed to Gandhi's appeasement of Muslims, Hindu nationalists of all shades dubbed 'right-wing' became villain overnight. Nehru used this opportunity to silence the right-wing leaders within the Congress and also the organizations that championed the ideology that derived inspiration from India's cultural past. The image of powerful socio-cultural forces like the Rashtriya Swayamsewak Sangh (RSS), which could have challenged Nehru, ideologically and politically, was tarnished after the assassination of the Mahatma. There was no direct or indirect relationship of the RSS behind the murder of the Mahatma, a fact established at the end of a long drawn legal battle on the issue. But Nehru banned it without any delay and projected it as a conservative, regressive and reactionary force that was an obstacle in nation building and in developing India as a modern nation.

Instead of restoring Bharat to its fundamentals, secularism became a far more marked discourse because Pakistan had chosen to be a theocratic Islamic state. And then came the big narrative that majority communalism is far more dangerous than minority communalism.[16] This Nehruvian view was just the opposite of Patel's who castigated this minority-majority syndrome by arguing that a minority which forced the Partition on the country cannot be said to be weak and deprived ones.[17] All this made Nehru a great saviour of the Muslim identity and the Muslim cause after the death of Gandhi. The anger that had erupted against Muslims got diverted towards the right-wing social and cultural organizations. The Indian Muslim League, a reincarnation of the Muslim League, survived but the RSS and the Hindu Mahasabha were banned. Indian Muslims became a major vote-bank for the Congress and they continued to be so till the Emergency was imposed in 1975 and the campaign of forced sterilization during the period was seen by Muslims as an attempt by the Congress to limit the growth of their population in India.

The guilt of the Partition among Indian Muslims continued almost for a decade and they did not raise any major identity related issues that had happened before the Partition. The Partition had created such a situation where any talk of their identity and greater say in the system was seen with suspicion and responded with hostility. This was a period of accommodation for the Muslims who were in the process of coping with the new reality of their weakened numerical, economic and social strength.

While this may appear to be a period of relative peace, it was not without conflicts. Wherever the numerical strength of Muslims was higher than Hindus, the nature of social tensions and hostility continued as usual. Muslim dominated areas continued to be administratively sensitive. Aligarh that housed Aligarh Muslim University that spearheaded the idea of Pakistan for Muslims, continued to be the stronghold of Muslims in areas divided by the railway line. In 1950, riots broke out in the city when a Hindu boy threw colour on a Muslim boy. Minor scuffle soon turned into inter-community conflicts. Again in 1956, riots broke out because Muslims resented a publication by the Bhartiya Vidya Bhawan which allegedly depicted the Prophet in bad light. The city also witnessed riots in 1961 which inflamed even Meerut since the student killed in Aligarh was a resident of Meerut city. These riots were minor in scale. The major one broke out in 1961 in Jabalpur when a Hindu girl committed suicide after she was raped by two Muslim boys.[18] The same year, riots also broke out in Aligarh and Meerut. In brief, by the beginning of the 1960s, riots had returned as a renewed reality in the national life of India.

Even after the death of Nehru in 1964, appeasement of Muslims continued as before since they had turned into a major vote bank for the ruling Congress. Lal Bahadur Shastri's ascendency to power had perplexed Muslims as the former had cosy relations with the RSS and other such organizations that prided on India's past. Further, Shastri was rooted in indigenous culture and did not believe in Hindu bashing. But Shastri's tenure ended shortly with his sudden death in 1966 and Mrs. Indira Gandhi, who became the Prime Minister after him, carried forward the appeasement policy of her father. She projected herself as a champion of Muslims and the minority cause particularly after the split of the Congress in 1969 though she also sought to project herself as true Hindu leader after she became the Prime Minister in 1966.[19] She did not accord Minority status to the Aligarh Muslim University despite the fact that there was a persistent demand from the Muslim community. In 1966, the Central Government introduced some changes in the Aligarh Muslim University Act of 1920 to make it more secular.[20] This was not liked by Muslims who challenged the decision on the ground that it was a minority institution and therefore, the government interference was unconstitutional. The Supreme Court however decided against the University in the famous case of Azeez Basha. It justified the position of the Central Government that it became a central university only through the Act of the Parliament.[21] This became a point of contention between the Congress and Muslim leaders who asked the government to declare the AMU as a minority institution. The Emergency brought in a fresh rapture in the relation between the two when Muslims became victims of the forced sterilization. Although all sections of the society were targeted, Muslims interpreted this to be aiming at restricting the numerical growth of Muslim population in India.

The ascendency of Muslims in Indian politics had started showing signs after late 1960s when the Indian Union Muslim League (IUML) deserted the Indian National Congress and joined hands with the Communist Party of India- Marxist (CPM) in government formation in Kerala. The IUML which remained with the CPM from 1967-69 extracted the pound of flesh by forcing the government to succumb to its demand of carving out a Muslim majority district as Malappuram after redrawing the boundaries of Kazhikode and Palghat districts. This was resented by the Bharatiya Jan Sangh (BJS) and the Indian National Congress. This was communalism at its worst in India post-Independence, where a separate district was created on the basis of religion.

The increasing numerical strength emboldened the Muslim leadership. The 1971 data revealed that the Muslim population had swelled up to 11.2 per cent from 9.6 in 1951. On the other hand, the Hindu population had come down from 84.6 per cent in 1951 to 82.73 per cent in 1971.[22] The increasing rate of population of Muslims became a subject matter of debate and nationalist political, social and cultural organizations started sensing a renewed threat of Islam in India. The Muslim leadership on the other hand sought to test their increasing numerical clout by hitting the streets in Aligarh demanding that Aligarh Muslim University be declared a minority institution. It led to riots in the city in 1972. The rioters attacked the police force resulting into firing that led to several casualties.[23]

It would be important also to note here that India's intervention in the East Pakistan crisis was not liked by Muslims of India in general. Though Muslims did not express their displeasure on the streets, the reactions of the Urdu press and their editorial explained the Muslim mindset. *Jamiat Times* published from Delhi even refused to criticize the Pakistani military actions and atrocities on Bengalis in East Pakistan.[24] Maulana Minnatullah Rahmani of Monghyr (Bihar) refused to sign a paper circulated by Lok Nayak Jayaprakash Narayan which condemned the role of Pakistan in Bangladesh. The Maulana rather condemned India for the communal riots.[25] Most of the Urdu press were not liking interest the government of India evinced in the crisis. They were suggesting that India should take a balanced position and not interfere in the crisis. Mrs. Gandhi was aware of the Muslim mindset and, therefore, her government placed restrictions on the publication of *Nasheman* (Bangalore), the only Urdu political weekly with a nationwide circulation in November 1971.[26] Later on, after the war started in December, the editors of *Nasheman* (Bangalore), *Da'wat* (Delhi), *Radiance* (Delhi), *Sangam* (Patna), and *The Jamiat Times* (Delhi) were taken into custody under the Internal Security Act.[27] The comprehensive defeat of the Pakistani military and liberation of Bangladesh as an independent nation was seen in Pakistan as a defeat of Muslim forces by the Hindu.[28] The same sentiments were also witnessed in some sections of Muslims in India. The national Emergency gave them the reason to articulate the anger.

During the Emergency, forced sterilization became the

gravitating point for Muslims. Though the programmes were aimed at population control, Muslims took it as a considered attempt on part of the Congress government to control their population. The sterilization policy was started as a part of family planning programme of the Government of India which was part of a 20-Points programme. Sterilisation was done at settlement of Bangladeshi refugee camps in India.[29] The opposition parties, including the BJS, opposed this policy. Post-emergency, Indian Muslims for the first time came out openly against the Congress in North India. The newly formed Janata Party appealed to Muslims to vote for it. Several Muslim leaders came out to extend support to the Janata Party. The Shahi Imam of Jama Masjid, Delhi, openly appealed to Muslims to vote for the Janata Party.[30] The Janata Party found Sheikh Abdullah as its new ally in Kashmir. The Sheikh had been kept out of Kashmir politics for long by the Congress. The Janata party also promised to improve relations with Pakistan which it did after coming to power. The Indian Prime Minister Morarji Ranchhodji Desai was conferred upon the highest civilian award of Nishan-e-Pakistan, a decision taken by Gen Zia ul Haq but was given by his successor in 1990.

The Muslim politics had gradually changed track from accommodation to assertion and was slowly returning to the crude Islamic agenda after the Bangladesh war. The Jamaat-e-Islami-Hind (JIH)'s student wing the Students Islamic Movement of India (SIMI) was founded on 25 April 1977 by a professor of Journalism and Public Relations, Mohammad Ahmadullah, who taught at Western Illinois University,

Macomb, Illinois. The objective of the SIMI was and is to wage Jihad in India and convert the country into Dar-ul-Islam (land of Islam) by converting the entire Hindu population by use of violence.[31] The SIMI approves the interpretation of Islam as explained by the founder of Jamaat-e-Islami Pakistan, Sayed Abul A'la Maududi. It endorsed the kind of Jihad undertaken by Osama Bin Laden.[32] The SIMI which is also depicted as Indian Mujahideen is known to have links with global Islamic terrorist organizations such as the Harkat -ul-Jihad-Islami (HUJI), the Hizbul Mujahideen and the Lashkar-e-Toiba. The Jamaat-e-Islami Hind severed its relations with the Jamaat in 1981 when the SIMI took stand against Yasser Arafat of Palestine.[33] Surprisingly, the Janata Party government did not act against the SIMI. In the 1980 general elections Mrs Indira Gandhi returned to power at the Centre. This time she was careful about the Muslim sensitivity. Here a new appeasement started both at the level of Central Government and the Government in the States ruled by the Congress.

In 1981, the Congress government at the Centre acceded to the demands of the Muslim organizations to declare Aligarh Muslim University a minority institution. The Congress Government in Bihar under Dr Jagannath Mishra declared Urdu as the second official language of the state. This was followed by the state of Uttar Pradesh where the decision was challenged in the Supreme Court which upheld the decision of the state government. The 1981 census further gave impetus to Muslim politics. The decadal growth of the Muslim population was 7 per cent higher than the national growth rate. It was

30.78 per cent compared to the national average at 24.07 per cent. The Muslim population by then had increased from 35.4 million in 1951 to 80.3 million in 1981.

The increased population was also due to the high degree of influx of population from Bangladesh. It had changed the religious demography of Assam. The people of Assam wanted to identify the infiltrators and deport them. But the Congress government could not muster the courage to do so. Even the admission of presence of the Bangladeshis in the state was resented by Muslim organizations in the state. They threatened to pull down the state government. The Congress government at the Centre could not muster the courage to come out with a law to tackle the issue of infiltration from Bangladesh.[34] It brought in the Illegal Migrants (Determination by Tribunals) (IMDT) Act but as the Supreme Court of India observed it was more to protect the illegal infiltrators than detecting and deporting the infiltrators back to Bangladesh.[35]

The Bangladeshi population in India has now changed the religious demography of many Indian states, the worst victim being Assam, West Bengal, Bihar, Uttar Pradesh, Delhi etc. Muslims in Assam floated a terrorist organization called the Muslim United Liberation Tigers of Assam (MULTA) with the help of Bangladeshis as well as Assamese Muslims.[36] By then the appeasement of Muslims had already become a buzzword in Indian politics and the Bharatiya Janata Party (BJP) had come out with a slogan of 'Justice to all and appeasement of None.' The Minority Commission of India by then appeared to have turned into a Commission for Muslims and the term minority for all practical purposes had got reduced to refer to the Muslim community. This became evident from the list of the Chairman of the Minority Commission till then. Other minorities were not given their due representation.

Muslim politics further tested its strength on the streets during the regime of late Rajiv Gandhi. The issue was compensation to Shah Bano, a 62-year-old Muslim woman divorced by Muhammad Ahmad Khan. She had three sons and two daughters in the marriage that lasted for 43 years. The Supreme Court rejected the basis of Shariat to decide the amount of compensation and the husband was directed to pay the compensation as decided by the court.[37] This was appreciated as a progressive judgment by a cross section of society but opposed bitterly by the fanatics and the radicals among Muslims. The Muslim clerics and the Muslim Personal Law Board (MPLB) threatened to launch a nationwide movement claiming the judgment to be interference in their personal laws.

Then Prime Minister Rajiv Gandhi appeared to be appreciative of the judgment as evidenced through a powerful speech by his young minister Arif Mohammad Khan in parliament. However, he was unable to withstand the pressure from conservative Muslims and retreated from his grandstanding on the issue. His government used the brute majority of the Congress and passed the Muslim Women Act (Protection of Rights on Divorce), 1986, to assuage those who had felt hurt by the Apex Court decision. The act overturned the judgment of the Supreme Court. This was a blatant surrender of the State before the medieval mindset of some sections of the Muslim community. The communal face of the Congress was exposed even to those who were reluctant to accuse the Congress party of promoting, defending and sheltering the radical elements within the Muslim community. Sadly, this was done by a person who was dubbed in the media as modern, liberal and guided by rational values. Political expediency had overtaken the better of him.

Nationalists and Hindu organizations reacted sharply to this communal surrender. Rajiv Gandhi had sensed this and perhaps to atone for his sin or to strike a balance between the Hindus and Muslims, he facilitated the opening of the lock of the gate of Shri Ram Temple at Ayodhya which was closed after the dispute arose in 1949. Muslims had considered the disputed structure as Babri Masjid and protested against the Court's decision on opening of the lock. The pace at which the date was fixed for hearing of the case which was biting dust for four decades and the way the order of the Court was implemented within a few hours of judgment speak volumes of the forces at work behind it. It was largely attributed to the role played by the Congress in expediting the judgement.

Wazahat Habibullah who had worked at the PMO with Rajiv Gandhi has claimed in his recent book *My Years with Rajiv* that Rajiv Gandhi was not behind opening of the locks. But Pranab Mukherjee who was always close to the Gandhi establishment and became the President of India has squarely blamed Rajiv Gandhi for the opening of the lock. In his book *The Turbulent Years: 1980-96,* he termed it an "error of judgment" and an act of "absolute perfidy."[38]

Rajiv Gandhi government's surrender before radical Islamists was a turning point in Indian politics. It fuelled a new Hindu movement and a new Hindu renaissance which was never seen before. Opening of the lock of the Ram temple gave the opportunity to the Vishwa Hindu Parishad to mobilise Hindu saints of all shades and sects. It launched a series of programmes and movements for building a grand temple at the disputed site.

Sensing the sentiments of Hindus, the Bharatiya Janata Party also took a formal stand to support the cause in its national executive meeting at Palampur in 1989.[39] And finally, Lal Krishna Advani rode the Chariot to start the Ram Rath Yatra to educate the people on the importance of Ram Janmabhoomi in India's cultural life. This was also one of the largest mass mobilization programmes in the history of modern India after Independence. Advani made a distinction between genuine secularism and wrong use of the term by Leftists and others to attack the BJP and other nationalist forces. He called it 'pseudo-secularism'- a term that became very popular in political and academic discussions.

Advani debunked the framework of Nehruvian secularism and succeeded in communicating the message to people that secularism practiced so far was nothing but Hindu bashing on the one hand and appeasement of Muslims on the other. The Ram temple movement aroused a new Hindu consciousness which also reflected in the electoral space. The support base of the Indian National Congress eroded drastically and was replaced by the BJP in assembly elections of various states as well during parliamentary elections.

The Hindu mobilization finally culminated into demolition of the disputed structure at Ayodhya by a frenzied mob. This led to a bitter polarization between the Hindus and the Muslims. Bombay (now Mumbai) witnessed a series of bomb blasts which was retaliated fiercely by the Hindus. The decade of 1990s had already seen Kashmir on the boil with the start of Islamic terrorism in its worst form. Nearly 3.5 lakh Hindus were forced to leave the Kashmir valley in midst of killings and threats on a daily basis. The Students Islamic Movement of India which had taken birth in Uttar Pradesh had by now strengthened its roots in Kerala and Tamil Nadu. The organization was engaged in bomb explosions and violence targeting the Hindus.[40] It tried to kill BJP leader LK Advani in Karnataka,[41] attacked an RSS office in Bangalore and so on. Finally, the BJP government had to ban the SIMI in 2001.

Islamic terrorism had taken firm roots in India towards the end of the 1990s as several modules were identified and unearthed across the country. One after another, series of bomb explosions took place. In 1999, the Indian Airlines plane was hijacked to Kandahar and the passengers were released only after release of five dreaded terrorists including Maulana Masood Azhar. In 2000, the Red Fort in Delhi was attacked by terrorists belonging to Lashkar-e-Toiba. In December 2001, Indian Parliament was attacked. In 2002, 58 Hindu Kar Sevaks returning from Ayodhya were charred to death by Islamic radicals who burnt the two coaches of the Ahmedabad bound Sabarmati Express in broad day light. This resulted into massive retaliation from the Hindus in Gujarat leading to killing of over thousands of Muslims. The opposition parties that were silent after killing of innocent women and children at Godhra fumed at the riots and its aftermaths. This double standard exposed their hypocrisy and helped people realize that these politicians had different yardsticks to react on deaths of Hindus and Muslims. Finally, the army had to be called in to quell violence in the State. In September 2002, two Islamic terrorists attacked the Swaminarayan Akshardham complex at Gandhinagar in which 30 innocent people were killed and several others injured.

The BJP government at the Centre responded to the rising Islamic threat by introducing the Prevention of Terrorism Act, 2002 (POTA) after the terrorist attack on parliament. This was resisted by Muslim leaders. Since all terrorist attacks were executed by Muslims, they were the ones who were arrested and put behind the bar. Undoubtedly, several innocent Muslims youths also might have been victims of state's drive against terrorism. But Muslim leaders and clerics propagated this as a deliberate attempt to defame Islam and harass Muslims. The Congress that was opposed to the BJP sided with these clerics in campaigns against the POTA. They described it anti-Muslims and anti-minorities.[42] When the Congress formed the coalition government at the Centre in 2004, the repeal of POTA which had become a part of the Common Minimum Programme was implemented. The repeal came despite the fact that similar Act in name of Maharashtra Control of Organized Crime Act,

1999 (MCOCA) was at work in Maharashtra.[43] The POTA was projected as a draconian law whereas the fact was that the opposition was merely responding to the calls of Muslims and the price was to be paid when it came to power.

Later on, India witnessed several such bombings such as Ahmedabad Bombings in July 2008, Mumbai attacks in 2008, series of Bomb blasts in Patna in September 2013, Mumbai train bombings in 2006, Hyderabad bombings in August 2007, serial blasts in Lucknow, Varanasi and Faizabad Courts in 2007, Bangalore Chinnaswamy Stadium bombings in 2010 and nine synchronized bomb blasts in Jaipur in May 2008. There were several others which can be listed to demonstrate the kind of bomb explosions which were gradually becoming the order of the day. People were scared to move out in crowded places for the fear of terror attacks. Interestingly, the people who were arrested during the UPA government at the Centre were also from the Muslim community. However, there was one exception to it. Now there was a role division within the Congress party by which the government killed or arrested terrorists and the party condemned the police actions for targeting Muslims.[44] It was like hunting with the hound and running with the hare. Muslim organizations questioned many encounters and the Congress preferred to play to the gallery even at the cost of governance. The Batla house encounter in which three terrorists were killed became the centre of such controversy. While Congress leader Digvijay Singh openly dubbed the encounter as fake and travelled down to meet the family of the killed terrorists in Azamgarh, Union Home minister P Chidambaram conveyed to parliament that it was a genuine encounter.[45] Digvijay Singh even went to the extent of asking for a judicial enquiry into the matter.[46] Senior Congress leader Salman Khurshid quoted Sonia Gandhi as 'crying and feeling sleepless during nights' over killing of these young men (terrorists).

Secondly, two new revelations hogged the headlines of national television news channels and newspapers when the agencies investigating into Samjhauta Express blasts and Malegaon blasts claimed that these were executed by Hindu radical organizations. Earlier these agencies had found the blasts to be handiwork of Islamic terrorist organizations. A new term 'Saffron terror' or 'Hindu terror' started doing the rounds in public and political discourse. It suited the defenders of Islamists who now forcefully advanced the arguments that terrorism has nothing to do with religion. Now they quoted Colonel Purohit and Sadhvi Pragya Thakur who were put behind the bars by the Special Task Force to buttress their arguments. The political fabrication behind the 'Hindu Terror' or the 'Saffron Terror' came to light when a senior official in the office of Home Ministry revealed in details in his book how the whole notion was manufactured under duress to malign the right-wing cultural and social organizations.[47] Thus, while the state and the government acted against Islamic radicals, the Congress kept itself busy in assuaging the feelings of Muslims by questioning the encounter on one hand and creating the bogey of Hindu terror on the other. The Hindu Terror narrative has now fallen flat and Sadhvi Pragya Thakur is a member of

Lok Sabha from Bhopal.

These aforesaid blasts were the ones that took place outside Kashmir. In Kashmir, Islamic terrorism raised its head post-1987 elections. It had started with demonstrations, threat calls and targeted murder of Kashmiri Pandits. In 1989, prominent Kashmiri Pandits were served notice by the extremists to leave Kashmir. They were worried that in case they fail to follow the instructions, their children will pay the price. Further, they declared that Kashmir is a land of Allah and there is no place for Hindus.[48] These threats were soon executed into reality with a series of killings of Kashmiri Hindus. On 14 September 1989, a prominent lawyer and BJP leader Pandit Tika Lal Taploo was killed in broad daylight when he was heading to the High court. In December 1989, Justice Neelkanth Ganjoo was gunned down. He was the one who had given death sentence to Maqbool Batt, a dreaded terrorist of Jammu and Kashmir Liberation Front (JKLP) who was involved in killing of CID officer Amir Chand.

ML Bhan, a government employee was killed on 15 January 1990 in Srinagar. Baldev Raj Dutta was kidnapped from Lal Chowk and torturously killed on 19 January 1990 at Nai Sarak, Srinagar. These are just a few names and incidents to quote for the purpose of understanding the reign of terror that had engulfed the valley. Panun Kashmir, the organization of the displaced Kashmiri migrants, later on submitted a list of 1341 pandits killed in the valley and in other parts of the state.[49]

Radical Islamists used fiery anti-Hindu, anti-India

slogans, posters, advertisements in newspapers, press releases, loudspeakers on mosques to threaten the Pandits.[50] They communicated in clear terms that Kashmir is a land of Islam and Kafirs (Hindus and Sikhs in particular) have no place in it. Hindus must convert to Islam.[51] This land will be governed by Nizam-e-Mustafa i.e., Shariat. Secondly, if they do not convert to Islam, they must leave the valley. With this they also added that Pandits must leave behind their wives and daughters. "Kashmir banawon Pakistan, Bataw varaie, Batneiw saan" (We will turn Kashmir into Pakistan along with Kashmiri Pandit women but without their men folk).Thirdly, if they do not follow either they will be killed. It was declaration of Jihad against the Kafirs. This was expressed clearly through the slogan: "Islam hamara maqsad hai, Quran hamara dastur hai, Jihad hamara Rasta hai" (Islam is our objective, Quran is our constitution and Jihad is our path to achieve that). Thousands of Kashmiri Muslims joined the militants and extremists on the streets when such slogans rent the air. It created fear and terror through the nerves of every Kashmiri Pandit. All of them passed every night in silence till they were able to escape from the land of their ancestors.[52]

This outbreak of Islamic terrorism was a result of several factors, both internal and external. However, Pakistan had an important role in training, arming, funding and exporting the terror modules to India. Americans were supplying resources to Pakistani President General Zia-ul-Haq to fight the Soviet Union in Afghanistan. Pakistan diverted the funds to export terrorism to India. This effort got multiplied after the Soviets accepted defeat and decided to withdraw. The extremists who were fighting Jihad in Afghanistan turned towards Kashmir in India. The political and military establishment in Pakistan was working under the plan 'Operation Topac' that was based on the theory of inflicting thousand cuts to India using non State actors. It had begun with crossing over of Muslims from Kashmir to Pakistan, particularly members of the United Muslim Front (UMF) who had participated in the much-discussed assembly elections of Kashmir in 1987. The mass scale riggings in the elections had frustrated the young Islamists who could not win the elections and crossed over the border to receive arms training to avenge their loss.[53] The officers of Pakistan's Inter-Services Intelligence (ISI) took this as an opportunity to brainwash these youths for launching Jihad.

However, they were caught by the Border Security Forces (BSF) when they tried to enter back into India and were handed over to the police. Chief Minister of Jammu and Kashmir, Farooq Abdullah, released them from jail in July 1989 in name of good gesture from the administration. Those released included Hamid Sheikh, Ashfaq Wani, Javed Mir and Yasin Malik who had clear links with Pakistani establishments. The government of Jammu and Kashmir then had argued that such gestures would help neutralize violence in the valley. But what followed was contrary to what was expected. Extremists got emboldened by the knee-jerk and softer response by the government. The weak coalition government at the centre added to the problems. Extremists kidnapped Rubaiya Sayeed, the daughter of the then Union Home Minister Mufti

Muhammad Sayeed in the VP Singh government and got some of the dreaded terrorists released in exchange. The absence of stern action by the Indian state encouraged the terrorists further. They hijacked the Indian Airlines aircraft flying from Nepal, took it to Kandhar and finally got dreaded terrorists released.

Even after the exodus of Kashmiri Pandits from the valley, these terrorists continued to eliminate the left-over Hindus. On 25 January 1998, 23 Hindus were killed in the Wandhama Massacre; On 17 April 1998, 26 Hindus were killed in the Prankote Massacre; on 19 June 1988, 25 Hindus were killed in the Chanpari attack, and 30 and 19 Hindus were killed in the Amarnath and Kishtwar attacks respectively in August 2000 and 2001.

Three decades down the line, Kashmir continues to suffer from terrorism. So far, more than three dozen radical Islamist organizations have sprung up in the state. Some of them have been proscribed, whereas some of them become inactive with time. There are close to a dozen that are still active. Some of them that hit the headlines for their violent activities are Hizb-ul-Mujahideen (HM), Lashkar-e-Toiba (LeT), Jaish-e-Mohammed (JeM), Harkat-ul Mujahideen (HuM) previously known as Harkat-ul-Ansar, Al Barq, Al Badr, All Parties Hurriyat Conference (APHC), Jammu & Kashmir Liberation Front (JKLF), Lashkar-e-Jabbar (LeJ) etc. They are the ones to have been involved in attacks on civilians, government establishments and armed forces' establishments. Though India's political establishment and parties do not use the term

Jihad in public to refer to ongoing violence by the radical Islamists in the state, they privately admit that the activities are carried out in the name of Jihad.

The important point to note is that the Muslims in the country came out openly in support of Rohingya refugees but they never took to the street to condemn and criticize Kashmiri separatists. They limited themselves to paying lip services on Television debates and in newspaper stories. In the last one decade, terrorists have launched several attacks on the armed forces including the Uri attacks in 2016 and the Pulwama attacks in 2019. The Indian Government came out with strong response. It conducted surgical strikes within nine days of Uri and the Balakot air strikes within 11 days of the Pulwama attacks. This indicated the change Indian mood and the fact that India could not be taken as a soft state that would not retaliate. Helplessness seen in earlier times was replaced with strong action.

After returning to power in 2019, the Narendra Modi government annulled Article 370 and Article 35A of the Indian constitution on 5 August 2019. According to Article 35A, which was inserted through the presidential 1954 rather than constitutional amendment, the state government was within the right to decide the state subject including permanent residents. This was used to deny citizenship rights to the Hindus in particular who had migrated to the state from Pakistan or Punjab during and after partition. Further, while the people from the state could buy property in any of the states in India no one out of Kashmir could buy land in the state. This was done to ensure that outsiders do not migrate and settle in the state and change the religious demography.

Now the state has been divided into two Union Territories; the Jammu and Kashmir and Ladakh. The Central Government has also now facilitated for buying of immovable property in the state. The Security forces continue to embattle with the terrorists in encounter and search operations. The Indian State has clarified by its action that it would do everything to end terrorism. It has been trying to engage youths in political and non-political activities.

In the last two decades, the virus of Islamic terrorism has engulfed several other parts of India. After 2001, when the SIMI was banned, its office bearers and cadres switched over to the Popular Front of India (PFI). This is evident from the fact that most of the key leaders of the SIMI became officer bearers of the organization.[54] The PFI came to limelight in July 2010 when its members chopped off the hand of Professor TJ Joseph in Kerala for putting a question on the Prophet since radical Islamists considered it blasphemy. In 2015, all the persons involved in this crime were convicted by the court and all of them belonged to the Popular Front of India (PFI).[55] Today, the PFI has presence in 23 Indian states and its members have been arrested for political killings, religious conversion and radicalization of young Muslims besides sending them to Syria and Iraq to fight for the cause of Islam in support of the ISIS.[56] PFI members have been arrested from Uttar Pradesh, Karnataka and Assam for their involvement in terror attacks and violence. They also have been at the thick of the controversy over 'Love

Jihad' in Kerala and elsewhere for increasing the numerical strength of the Muslims.

With the ascendency of the BJP government at the Centre, the trend of Muslim appeasement has taken a break. As the BJP has always been a vocal critic of appeasement politics, it has sought to avoid any such activities which could invite similar criticism from its political opponents. Further, the BJP took the revolutionary step of empowering Muslim women by bringing a law to ban instant Triple Talaq. The government side gave powerful arguments to defend the individual rights of suffering Muslim women. The opposition parties failed to counter it. Muslim organizations threatened the government to launch a movement to oppose the law but the government did not buckle under the pressure.

However, the most daring among all of them was the decision to repeal Article 370 and 35A which the party always considered to be the source of separatism in the valley. This has now facilitated the path to downsize the numerical strength of Muslims in the valley by giving the right to outsiders to purchase land and settle in the State. The BJP government further took the bold decision of passing the Citizenship Amendment Act 2020 (CAA) to grant citizenship to persecuted religious minorities in Afghanistan, Pakistan and Bangladesh. Obviously, it was against the influx of the Muslims from these countries and to give protection to those non-Muslims from these countries who came to India when faced with persecution.

With Union Home Minister Amir Shah spoke in Parliament about the need for a National Register of Citizens

(NRC), many Muslim organizations lapped it up as an issue on which they could oppose the government. They realized that this would lead to detection of Bangladeshi Muslims and termination of their citizenship. They hit the streets to oppose the move. The opponents of the BJP sensed a political opportunity. They clubbed the NRC and the CAA together and raised the constitutionality of the issue of giving protection to non-Muslims coming from outside but not doing the same for Muslims. A movement was launched from Shaheen Bagh at Delhi but it soon became a nation-wide protest. In substance, it was a protest by Muslims for protecting the Muslims from Bangladesh, Afghanistan and Pakistan who had illegally entered India. All the radical Islamists organizations of the country took part in it and supported the protest. This included the PFI, the Deoband and the Tablighis.

Most Hindus were agitated over the Shaheen Bagh protest and wanted the road blocked by the protesters to be cleared for traffic. Polarization and counter polarization finally led to massive riots in Delhi in March 2020. The charge-sheet filed by Delhi Police in the court and also reports of independent enquiry suggest that it was a pre-mediated riot for which radical elements in the Muslim community were preparing since long. This was corroborated by confiscation of massive arms and ammunitions, inflammable liquid and bomb making items in search operation from Aam Admi Party (AAP) Counsillor Tahir Hussain.[57] The slogans at Shaheen Bagh and elsewhere were not just against the Indian state; they were also in name of Islam and occasionally against Hindus. A video of a child which went viral was seen to be proudly saying that he would love to kill Home Minister Amit Shah. This produced counter polarization in Hindus.

Needless to say, the debate on increasing assertion of Muslims along their identity question has once again come at the centre stage of public discourse. An increase in numerical strength of Muslims in different parts of the country has sent alarming signals to those who wish India to survive as a secular democracy. There is a genuine fear that if their numbers reach a certain proportion of the population, India may not be able to guard its civilizational values of Sarva Dharm Sambhav. History and experience of other countries show that the followers of Islam do not have conviction and commitment to constitutional democracy and secular values. They talk of all these only till the time they are in a minority. Where ever they reach numerical majority they would impose their religious agenda and make it difficult for others to live peacefully. An instance of their arbitrariness in Muslim dominated expanse is visible through the example of district Jamtara in state of Jharkhand, where instead of Sunday (a public holiday followed by entire nation), Friday was declared as a holiday in Urdu school on the pretext of Jumma[58]. Another 2 instances which corroborate this argument emerge from the of Bihar in Madhubani district. A report by Tv9 Bharatvarsh unveiled the real intentions of Madarasas which was to propagate Urdu and Islam in the garb of teaching modern subjects. This reflects Madarasas intention to impart extremist values of the Islam which echoes in their primary assertion of Muslim identity above all and assist them in imposing their religious agenda wherever they reach numerical majority[59].Their understanding has source in the doctrine of Islam which makes a distinction between believer and non-believer and gives a clarion call to convert the non-believers into believers.

Massive increase in Muslim population in West Bengal, Bihar and Uttar Pradesh has already become a cause of concern. The increasing numerical strength of Muslims in the country would be detrimental to India because it would lose its civilizational and cultural narrative to Islam in times to come. The Hindu side cite the examples of violence in Malda and Basirhat where Muslim mobs burnt down the homes and properties of Hindus and the state police failed to provide adequate response because the police was not empowered to handle them with a tough hard.[60] This is precisely the reason that the BJP could convince people about the rising threat of radical Islamists in West Bengal. This was evident from the fact that nearly 57 per cent Hindus voted for the party in the last parliamentary elections.[61] It is no wonder that the BJP has become the largest opposition in the West Bengal assembly even as it failed to dethrone Ms Mamata Banerjee from power in the state in 2021.

Terrorist modules are gradually spreading their tentacles in different parts of the country. Islamic terrorism is no more a talk in respect of bombings and killings in Kashmir. It has reached Bengal, Maharashtra, Karnataka, Kerala, Andhra Pradesh, Haryana and Uttar Pradesh. Muslim dominated areas are fast increasing with each new census.[62] And Muslim dominated areas continue to be the sensitive areas often termed proverbially as 'mini-Pakistan' by non-Muslims. Muslim organizations also have returned to the key issues of more representation of the community in government and legislatures. They have been pressuring the political parties to make reservations for Muslims in government. The Deoband issued a Fatwa few years back in 30th general session of Jamiat that Muslims should not sing 'Vande Mataram' as it is anti-Islam.[63] And it was done in the presence of 10,000 clerics. They also cautioned the government against any reforms in Madrasa education. It was the UPA government at the Centre at that time. And they are determined not to allow the government to identify Bangladeshi infiltrators and deport them back. They know how to react to and defend the Rohingya settlements in India but do not take position for the Kashmiri pandits' return to the Kashmir valley. In terms of Hindu-Muslim divide, the country is facing the same situation that it witnessed during the Partition.

References:

1 The Presidential Speech of Jinnah in the Annual Session of the Muslim League in 1940 in which he argued that Muslims are not minority but a separate nation in all sense of terms. http://www.columbia.edu/itc/mealac/pritchett/00islamlinks/txt_jinnah_lahore_1940.html, accessed on 7 December 2020.

2 In 1946 elections the Muslim League had contested elections on the issue of Pakistan and the Muslims throughout the country voted for the League in Muslim dominated areas.

3 The Direct Action started after the Muslim League refused to accept the terms of the Cabinet Mission and instead of joining the government at the centre announced the Direct-Action Day. This led to 'The great Calcutta Killings in August 1946 and then in October in Noakhali which was a predominantly Muslim area with 82 per cent Muslims. Hindus were butchered like animals and the state which was under the control of the Muslim League allowed this to happen. For details See; Ghosh, B. (2011). Religion and Politics in Bengal: The Noakhali Carnage 1946-47. Proceedings of the Indian History Congress, 72, 936-946. Retrieved December 7, 2020, from http://www.jstor.org/stable/44146785.

4 Tejani, S. (2013). The Necessary Conditions for Democracy:

B R Ambedkar on Nationalism, Minorities and Pakistan. Economic and Political Weekly, 48(50), 111-119. Retrieved December 7, 2020, from http://duelibrary.informaticsglobal.com:2065/stable/24479052. P.111. Even Jinnah was in favour of it. But Nehru and many other did not approve of it. Members admitted this in the Constituent Assembly Debates also. See;https://indiankanoon.org/doc/215406/. Accessed on December 8, 2020

5 Maulana Abul Kalam Azad made this observation before the students of the Aligarh Muslim University Convocation Ceremony in 1949. https://documents.pub/document/maulana-azads-convocation-address-at-aligarh-muslim-university-20-02-1949.html

6 Constituent Assembly Debates On 16 December, 1946." https://indiankanoon.org/doc/1082532/. Accessed 5 Apr. 2021

7 Nehru in the Constituent Assembly Debates said so. https://indiankanoon.org/doc/548244/

8 In the Constituent Assembly some Muslim members such as Muhammad Ismail raised the demand for separate electorates for Muslims to ensure proper representation of the community. But this was contested by many including the members from other minority communities. https://indiankanoon.org/doc/1663158/. Accessed on 8 December 2020, The Constituent Assembly Debates on 26 May 1949, Part I.

9 Sardar Bhupinder Singh Man had objected to the cut-off date of 19 July 1948 for those who returned to India by this date. See; https://indiankanoon.org/doc/215406/. Accessed on 7 December, 2020

10 Kumar, V. (2003). Minorities Right to Run Educational Institutions: TMA Pai Foundations in Perspective. *Journal of the Indian Law Institute, 45*(2), pp.200-238. Retrieved April 5, 2021, from http://www.jstor.org/stable/43953411.

11 Ambedkar on Uniform Civil Code in the Constituent Assembly Debates
https://indiankanoon.org/doc/870715/

12 Iyengar, Radhika. A history of the origins of the Vande-Mataram and its journey thereafter, The Indian Express, 27 July 2017. https://indianexpress.com/article/research/a-history-of-the-origins-of-the-vande-mataram-and-its-journey-thereafter/

13 Ibid

14 Ibid

15 Ahmad, R. (2011). Urdu in Devanagari: Shifting orthographic practices and Muslim identity in Delhi. Language in Society, 40(3), 259-284. Retrieved December 8, 2020, from http://duelibrary.informaticsglobal.com:2065/stable/23011824, p.261

16 All India Congress Committee Meeting (AICC) 11 May 1958. https://inc.in/brief-history-of-congress/1955-1965

17 Sardar Patel in Constituent Assembly Debates held on 26 May 1949 while participating in debates on minority rights. On 25 May 1949 Muslim members had argued that by not giving reservation to the Muslims while continuing the reservation for the Scheduled Castes it amounted that Hindus continued to have suspicion about Muslims.
https://indiankanoon.org/doc/1663158/

18 See for Details Justice Shiv Dayal Srivastava Commission of

Inquiry report. https://www.outlookindia.com/website/story/disturbing-trends-police-system/218047

19 Noorani, A. (1990). Indira Gandhi and Indian Muslims. Economic and Political Weekly, 25(44), 2417-2420. Retrieved November 29, 2020, from http://www.jstor.org/stable/4396930)

20 The first Amendment in the Aligarh Muslim University Act of 1920 was made in 1951 in which the provision of the 'compulsory religious education' was done away with to bring the Act in consonance with Article 28(3) of the constitution. In the 1965 Amendment the power of the Court which happened to be supreme was reduced to only advisory functions. It also reduced the internal reservation of Muslims from 75 to 50 per cent. This was treated as interference in the minority status of the institution and therefore taken to the court where the court justified the decision of the Parliament.

21 S. Azeez Basha And Anr vs Union of India on 20 October, 1967. The central argument is that if the academic institution is not established by the minority, it has no right to be described as Minority Institution. https://indiankanoon.org/doc/1801897/, accessed on 22 January 2022

22 Population Trends for Major Religious Groups in India from 1951-2011. Table 1.1.22. Socio-Economic and Caste Census, 2011. https://censusindia.gov.in/2011-prov-results/data_files/india/final_ppt_2011_chapter3.pdf

23 "Hindu-Muslim Communal Riots in India II (1986-2011)" 20 Aug. 2013, https://www.sciencespo.fr/mass-violence-war-

massacre-resistance/en/document/hindu-muslim-communal-riots-india-ii-1986-2011.html. Accessed 5 April 2021

24 http://www.columbia.edu/itc/mealacritchett/00litlinks/naim/ambiguities/14muslimpress.html#n02. Accessed on 8 December 2020

25 Ibid,it was reported in the Jamiat Times of 11 June 1971.

26 Ibid

27 Ibid

28 Ibid

29 Brown, C. (1984). The Forced Sterilization Program under the Indian Emergency: Results in One Settlement. Human Organization, 43(1), 49-54. Retrieved December 8, 2020, from http://www.jstor.org/stable/44125646

30 Shahi Imam of Delhi Jama Masjid for the first time made appeals to the Muslims to vote for the Janata Party in the 1977 elections. However, in 1980 he again changed his stand and appealed to the Muslims to vote for the Congress. He also once supported Mulayam Singh Yadav (2012) and the BJP (2004).

31 SIMI wants to convert India into a Shariate based Islamic state. It is against anything and all things which are against the Islamic culture. This includes even opposition to the Idol worshiping. https://www.satp.org/satporgtp/countries/india/terroristoutfits/simi.htm. Accessed on 22 January 2022

32 Fair, C. (2010). Students Islamic Movement of India and the Indian Mujahideen: An Assessment. *Asia Policy,* (9), 101-120. Retrieved April 5, 2021, from http://www.jstor.org/stable/24904973

33 "A breach of trust - Frontline - The Hindu" 17 December

2004, https://frontline.thehindu.com/world-affairs/article30225764.ece. Accessed 5 April 2021

34 A tale of two demands - The Hindu." 20 Dec. 2019, https://www.thehindu.com/opinion/op-ed/a-tale-of-two-demands/article30351525.ece, Accessed 5 April 2021

35 Sarbananda Sonowal vs Union Of India & Anr on 12 July, 2005
https://indiankanoon.org/doc/907725/. Accessed on 8 December 2020

36 Ragi, S. (2013). Price of the IMDT Act : Migrants and Ethnic Politics in Assam. *The Indian Journal of Political Science, 74*(3), 545-556. Retrieved April 5, 2021, from http://www.jstor.org/stable/24701064

37 Mody, N. (1987). The Press in India: The Shah Bano Judgment and Its Aftermath. Asian Survey, 27(8), 935-953. doi:10.2307/2644865

38 Mukherjee, Pranav (2016). The Turbulent Years: 1980-96. Rupa Publications India, New Delhi.

39 Ram temple row: Apex body of Hindu saints says BJP-VHP 'no longer trustworthy' 24 Jan. 2017, https://www.hindustantimes.com/india-news/ram-temple-row-apex-body-of-hindu-saints-says-bjp-vhp-no-longer-trustworthy/story-R0QwQFb5QJ2aE0nkVp2v9L.html. Accessed 5 April 2021

40 Hindu-Muslim Communal Riots in India II (1986-2011) 20 Aug. 2013, https://www.sciencespo.fr/mass-violence-war-massacre-resistance/en/document/hindu-muslim-communal-riots-india-ii-1986-2011.html. Accessed 5 Apr. 2021

41 "SIMI men targeted Advani, Modi: Police." Anubhuti Vishnoi,

Mar 31 2008.
http://archive.indianexpress.com/news/SIMI-men-targeted-Advani-Modi-Police/290542/

42 https://timesofindia.indiatimes.com/india/Lalu-attacks-Paswan-and-Nitish-on-POTA/articleshow/1283192. The times of India, PIT, 2 November 2005.

43 Ujjwal Kumar Singh. (2004). Repeal of POTA: What about Other Draconian Acts? Economic and Political Weekly, 39(33), 3677-3680. Retrieved December 8, 2020, from http://www.jstor.org/stable/4415404

44 Batla House Shootout 'Fake': Digvijay Singh - Outlook India." 12 Jan. 2012, https://www.outlookindia.com/newswire/story/batla-house-shootout-fake-digvijay-singh/747494Accessed 5 Apr. 2021

45 Ibid

46 Digvijaya Singh seeks judicial probe into fake Batla House encounter." 24 May. 2016, https://m.economictimes.com/news/politics-and-nation/digvijaya-singh-seeks-judicial-probe-into-fake-batla-house-encounter/articleshow/52422720.cms. Accessed 5 April 2021

47 Mani, RVS (2018). The Myth of Hindu Terror: Insider account of Ministry of Home Affairs 2006-2010, Vitasta Publishing, New Delhi.

48 Former Director General M MKhajooria quoted by Tikoo, Tej Kumar, http://www.indiandefencereview.com/news/kashmiri-pandits-offered-three-choices-by-radical-islamists/
accessed on 2 December 2020.

49 https://www.efsas.org/publications/study-papers/the-exodus-of-

kashmiri-pandits/.

50 Zalimo, O Kafiro, Kashmir hamara chod do." (O! Merciless, O! Kafirs leave our Kashmir), "Kashmir mein agar rehnahai, Allah-ho-Akbar kahnahoga"(Anyone wanting to live in Kashmir will have to convert to Islam)La Sharqia la gharbia, Islamia! Islamia! (From East to West, there will be only Islam), "Musalmanojago, Kafirobhago", (O! Muslims, Arise, O! Kafirs, scoot)"Islam hamaramaqsadhai, Quran hamaradasturhai, jehad hamara Rasta hai" (Islam is our objective, Q'uran is our constitution, Jehad is our way of our life)"Kashmir banega Pakistan" (Kashmir will become Pakistan), "Kashirbanawon Pakistan, Batawvaraie, Batneiwsaan"(We will turn Kashmir into Pakistan alongwith Kashmiri Pandit women, but without their men folk), "Pakistan se kyaRishta? La Ilah-e- Illalah" (Islam defines our relationship with Pakistan), Dilmeinrakho Allah ka khauf; Hath mein rakho Kalashnikov. (With fear of Allah ruling your hearts, wield a Kalashnikov)Dil Mein Rakho Allah ka khauf; Hath mein rakho Kalashnikov. (With fear of Allah ruling your hearts, wield a Kalashnikov), "Yahan Kya Chalega, Nizam-e- Mustafa" (We want to be ruled under Sharia), "People's League ka paigam, Fateh, Azadi aurIslam" What is the message of People's League? Victory, Freedom and Islam.

51 Kashmiri Pandits offered three choices by Radical Islamists http://www.indiandefencereview.com/news/kashmiri-pandits-offered-three-choices-by-radical-islamists/. Accessed 5 April 2021

52 Tikoo, Colonel Tej K (2012). Kashmir: Its Aborigines and Their Exodus. Lancer Publishers LLC, New Delhi.

53 Chowdhary, Rekha (2016). Jammu and Kashmir: Politics of Identity and Separatism. Routledge, New Delhi. Also, Zutshi, Chitralekha (2018). Kashmir: History, Politics, Representation, Cambridge University Press, p.103.

54 "Is PFI the new SIMI? ED raids offices, netas across 9 states." The Times of India Dec 4, 2020. http://timesofindia.indiatimes.com/articleshow/79556959.cms?utm_source=contentofinterest&utm_medium=text&utm_campaign=cppst. Accessed on 21 January 2022

55 https://www.thenewsminute.com/article/2010-kerala-professor-hand-chopping-case-nia-finally-arrests-accused-pfi-member-66322. Accessed on 9 December 2020

56 The Print, https://theprint.in/india/popular-front-of-india-radical-outfit-with-simi-links-now-under-caa-protests-scanner/340196/ accessed on 5/12/2020

57 "Delhi riots: Petrol bombs found on AAP corporator's rooftop; Tahir Hussain claims rioters took over his home" 27 Feb. 2020, https://www.timesnownews.com/delhi/article/delhi-riots-petrol-bombs-found-on-aap-corporators-rooftop-tahir-hussain-claims-rioters-took-over-his-home/558320. Accessed 5 Apr. 2021

58 Zee news Desk, (2022, July 11) Jamtara School News: जामताड़ा के स्कूलों में संडे के बजाय जुमे के दनि छुट्टी पर बवाल, सरकार ने मांगा जवाब https://zeenews.india.com/hindi/india/jamtara-schools-muslim-dominated-areas-changed-weekly-off-from-sunday-to-friday-jharkhand-govt-ordered-inquiry/1252557

59 Bihar के मदरसों में चल रहा था ये काम, TV9 भारतवर्ष का

वस्फिोटक खुलासा | Madrasas Survey | Live #TV9D Video, Youtube https://www.youtube.com/watch?v=TQiUNRNbyL0

60 Banerjee, Rabi. "Rioting on the wall." The Week, July 23, 2017.

61 News 18 Analysis on Bengal Parliamentary Elections 2019 https://www.news18.com/news/ivideos/news18-analysis-why-bengal-could-become-the-gateway-to-delhi-in-2019-elections-2027633.html

62 Census Report of 2011 suggests that there has been significant rise in Muslim dominated districts and constituencies in India. https://pib.gov.in/newsite/printrelease.aspx?relid=126326

63 "Jamiat issues fatwa against singing Vande Mataram." Headlines today. https://www.indiatoday.in/latest-headlines/story/jamiat-issues-fatwa-against-singing-vande-mataram-59917-2009-11-03. Accessed on 22 December 2021.

CHAPTER 8

POLITICAL IN PURITAN ISLAM

The Basis of Hate Against Non-Mulims

ISLAM IS AT war with every other religion in the world. Followers of Islam are also at war with themselves. The war against non-Muslims is premised on the ground that these people do not follow the Quran, the Hadith and the Sharia, and express no allegiance to the Allah and Muhammad Saheb as the Prophet. The proponents of such ideas hold the view that the non-Muslims follow and practice false paths and false Gods. They also advance the arguments that it is mandate of the Islam to Islamize the world and, therefore, justify the war against non-Muslims. Their fight against the co-religionists is directed against those who, in their eyes, are not following the true or puritan Islam and are conditioned by their past or socio-cultural context.

Thus, there are Muslims who openly express their firm faith in Islam but they become the targets of the Islamists on the ground that they do not follow the right course and contents of Islam. For these extremists, they are the enemies of Islam or bad Muslims or heretics or apostates. Some theologians have even depicted and equated them with the pagans.[1] The bad Muslims and heretics are those who have allowed the elements of other religions and values of the modern West to make inroads into the Islamic practices and are responsible for dilution of pure Islam.[2] They claim, therefore, that their war is for a greater and a nobler cause which is restoration of puritan Islam and bringing the entire world to the fold of true Islam i.e., Islamization of the world. That is what makes them, as they claim, stand against the infidels as well as the bad Muslims.

The Islamists have a justification for every fight. When they attack Israel, their argument is Israel has occupied Muslim land. Similarly, when they attack the Americans, their argument is the US continues to damage Muslim countries. The United Kingdom, France and other European nations are on their target because the foreign policies of these countries are perceived to be anti-Muslims and the fact that they always side with the US. The terror attacks in India are justified on the ground that Muslims are gradually being side-lined and coerced in the existing political system. Terrorism in Egypt, Sudan and Syria is justified on the ground that the fight is against the heretics and the apostates. Every act of terrorism has a reason based on a lot of thinking. When the Taliban destroyed the statue of Lord Buddha, many even in Pakistan and other Muslim dominated countries criticized this dastardly act. But the Taliban silenced the believers with an audio message that it was not a crime to destroy the God in the figurine of non-believers. And then there were many in Pakistan who came out openly to defend the act of the Taliban.

Whenever there is terror strike by any Islamic outfit, it upsets the ignorant moderate Muslims as their faith faces the brunt of the attack and the entire community is shown in bad light. The Maulanas would issue statement of condemnation and reject such acts as against the spirit of Islam. They further add that the people engaged in the violence are bringing Islam into disrepute. They reiterating that Islam is a religion of peace and that true Islam stands for equality, justice, harmony and brotherhood among human beings.[3] Therefore, those who are engaged in all such activities such as kidnapping or brutal murder in name of Islam are actually deviants.

Interestingly, such reactions are the stereo-types applicable in non-Islamic democratic countries such as India, the US, the UK and France where Muslims are in a minority. This principle is not adopted for countries where Muslims are in a dominant majority. Secondly, all such condemnation is almost followed by a rider that Islam should not be vilified for acts of misguided individuals and the government and society should look into the reasons for such occurrence. In other words, instead of looking into the proactive and inflammatory theological position of the religion, they attribute it to factors outside the religion. In an attempt to answer why such incidents, the apologists for Islam invariably talk of persecution of Muslims.

When 9/11 happened in America, there were many who condemned it but there were many others who rejoiced and appreciated the bravery of the terrorists who, in their eyes, had taught a well deserving lesson to the US.[4] Many who justified it saw in it a demonstration of Islamic masculinity which could hit even a mighty power like the US. American Muslim organizations by and large condemned this act, but thousands of Muslims gathered in North London at the Finsbury Park Mosque to celebrate the 'bombing of the World Trade Centre.' For them, it was a 'towering day in the history of Islam.'[5] London was not the only place where gleeful and elated eyes demonstrated an overwhelming proportion of contentment and pleasure on what the terrorists had done to the US. It was not a 'wedge-driving rumour' as Robert H Knapp argues, which might be true in few cases but a reality in many.[6] This was the discourse followed by Republican presidential candidate in 2015 who said that he was witness to such celebrations in the New Jersey city and he refused to take back the words and the charges. Besides the common Muslims, the left-liberals who are critique of market and Americans peddled the theory of retribution. They also saw in it an American conspiracy to accelerate further attacks on Muslim population. In India too, the left -liberal Hindus, and some Muslim scholars by and large touted the same arguments to explain the reasons behind the attack.[7]

Amidst all these, a very important question that gets unanswered is why Muslims use terror as a weapon to avenge discrimination by the political and social system they live in. In other words, why dissatisfaction by Muslims alone breeds terrorism? After all, Hindus also live in the US, the UK, France, Germany and many other countries in both the Northern and Southern hemisphere but not a single Hindu terrorist organization exists and operates anywhere. Should it be concluded from this pattern that only Muslims are victimized and discriminated against, and Hindus are not victimized by political and governing systems of these countries? Should it be accepted that laws in Britain favour Hindus and discriminate against Muslims? And, therefore, the most pertinent question that emerge is does Islam have something within its theology that turn Muslims into suicide bombers to kill non-Muslims or does it emanate from the wrong teaching or fallacious interpretations of the Quran?

One more question which is often ignored in the intellectual discourse is why Muslims talk about inclusivity only in land where they have thin or minority presence? How does Islam look at the non-believers theologically and in practice? If Islam suggests exclusivity and war against infidels and Muslims do not contest it because that carries the weight of the Quranic injunctions, is it fair on the part of Muslims living as minority in different cultural and political space to have the moral right to demand equal space in the cultural and political domains of other religious settings? Making it a little simpler, if Islamic societies do not allow equal space to other religious denominations in their cultural, religious and social settings how can they demand fair and equal rights in other societies? This is not a question to justify the retributive theory of treatment but to expose the moral yardstick which is used and invoked by Muslims to demand fairness. But this question remains nuanced why there is no demonstration against human rights abuses of non-Muslims in Muslim dominated countries? How many times Muslims have raised their voice against the Islamic theocratic states that do not allow even practice of other religions in public space?

The terrorists, however, partly disagree with such explanations partly. Their battle or war is not just for fair treatment of Muslims in the land of Dar-ul-Harb but also to fulfil the unfinished agenda of Islam i.e., to Islamize the societies and establish Islamic State with the system of Caliphate that was practiced when Islam was founded. And they use the phrase of returning to puritan Islam as their ultimate mission. Take a look at all the terrorist organizations which have global operation such as the Al-Qaeda, the Boko Haram, the ISIS, the Taliban and the Al-Shabaab, and identify what they ultimately wish to achieve. Their one answer is they are in the service of Islam. They want the Islam that was practiced in the times of the Prophet and the four Caliphates who followed him.. Their understanding of Islam thus stands in sharp contrast to those who argue that Islam does not believe in violence. Then, should it be treated that the understanding by such terrorist organizations is motivated by selfish reasons and hence they should not be treated as the representative interpretation of Islam? One may agree to this proposition that majority of Muslims do not think the way the terrorists interpret but this leads to another issue that all the terrorists are product of one or the other school of Islam where they are taught theology and its interpretations and the motivation to think and work for a divine Islamic society.

This brings the whole issue of 'puritan and true Islam' to the centre of discourse. Are terrorists doing something which is banned in Islam or something which does not have a place in Islam? Is there any consensus on what constitutes true Islam or puritan Islam? Should a distinction be made between the true Islam and the puritan Islam? Whether a good Muslim means a puritan Muslim or vice versa? Is pure and puritan Islam more dangerous than the mixed or syncretic Islam? More importantly, what constitutes true, pure or puritan Islam? Whether the great values and universal doctrines of perennialism and eternity constitutes the essence of true Islam? Or, is it the dress code or the length of the beard or the size of the upper and lower garments that make true Islam? If true or puritan Islam is all about peace, spirituality, brotherhood and harmony, what makes Islam distinctive since other religions talk of same values? All these questions are interlinked and have layers of complexity and therefore a serious examination of the concept of puritan Islam becomes important.

Broadly speaking there are two sects in Islam: the Shias and the Sunnis. Other cults arise from the interpretation of the texts in new ways and laying down some new elements and ways which were not essentially against but different from the traditional practitioners. After the fourth Caliphate, the Islamic world witnessed different interpretations of *The Quran*. New elements and forms of were introduced besides the traditional practices. The emergence of the Ahmadis and the Vohra Muslims endorse this point. The Sufi tradition which is mainly linked with the Sunni cult is also treated as an order within Islam but not a different sect.[8] The divide between the Shias and the Sunnis goes back to the times of death of Prophet Muhammad. An ailing Prophet died without deciding his successor. Opinion was divided on who should succeed him. A powerful section close to the Prophet wanted to follow the Sunnah i.e., the tradition which suggested electing the successor by a few who were close to the Prophet. This was the group that was loyal to Abu Bakr, the father-in-law of the Prophet. The second group of Muslims favoured Ali, the cousin and son-in-law of the Prophet, to be named the successor. They argued that Ali had all along lived with the Prophet and was the first Muslim after the Prophet and hence was entitled to succeed him. As discussed earlier, Abu Bakr was elected as the successor without even informing Ali who was busy in organizing the last rites of the Prophet. Ali had to wait till the third Caliphate was assassinated. Ali was assassinated too, and in the battle of Karbala his children and many close relatives of the prophet also lost their lives as they were enslaved by the chief of the Umayyad dynasty. Since Ali was denied what was due to him and later on, killed by the Sunni Umayyad, the day is remembered as the day of martyrdom in the Shia calendar.

In the eyes of the Sunnis, the Shias do not practice pure Islam. The Shias do not accept this charge. The Sunnis and their organizations, therefore, often attack the Shia mosques in Pakistan and elsewhere. In India too, we have seen how the Shias have been attacked in Lucknow on occasions of Muharram.[9] Similarly, the Sunnis do not recognize the Ahmadis and the Vohras as Muslims and often oppose and attack them. The

Vohras trace their ancestors and live in Patan areas of Gujarat. They were mainly Shias but in the 15th century, a divide took place in their ranks and almost a dominant majority, nearly 80 per cent of them converted to Sunni Vohras who now live near Karachi in Pakistan.[10] The Vohras are well to do families both in Pakistan and India and mostly engaged in trade and businesses.

The Ahmadis are a persecuted minority which claims to be Muslims but neither the Shias nor the Sunnis in either Pakistan or India accept them as such. Though it was not possible to do so in India because of the supremacy of the constitution, Pakistan passed a constitutional amendment law in 1974 in which the Ahmadis have been defined as non-Muslims.[11] Subsequently, an ordinance was issued during General Zia-ul-Haq's regime debarring them from propagating themselves as Muslims. They were also debarred from worshipping in mosques of other sects. Nor could they refer to their prayer centres as mosques! The fault of the Ahmadis lies in belief that Mirza Ghulam Ahmad, the founder of this cult, is the messiah or Mahdi who will reappear few years before the Judgment Day and will rid the world of evils. The Sunnis consider this claim blasphemous as it rejects the core premise that the Prophet was the last messenger. The Ahmadis, therefore, are heretics in the eyes of both Sunni and Shia Muslims.[12]

This does not end here. Radical Sunnis do not consider the Sufis as true and puritan Muslims. And therefore, both the Deobandi and the Salafi schools have been found attacking the Sufi cult despite the fact that the founders of the Deoband came from the Sufi (Tariqa) order. There are many who do not consider Sufism as 'authentic Islam' despite the fact that the Sufis practice all those five things which every Deobandi is prescribed to do. The conservative Deobandis and Salafists think that saint-based devotion or shrine-based worship is proscribed in Islam, as this is expressive of veneration of someone other than Allah.[13] Thus, this is one kind of idolatry and, therefore, reprehensible and a punishable offence.

This brings us to focus on the moot questions: What is Islam and what does it mean when somebody makes a call for puritan Islam? Puritan Islam has become a contestable concept since every second organization including those espousing terrorism tries to explain in its own way and seeks to realize it. Islam is a religion propounded by Prophet Mohammad who claimed to have divine message from the angel Gabriel, a messenger of Allah. These divine messages were uttered by the Prophet from time to time which were partly noted down and partly treasured in the memories of his companions which were put together after death of the Prophet. Thus, *The Quran* was not produced during the lifetime of the Prophet but coded and compiled after his death and was based on mix of memory and the written manuscripts.[14]

Apart from *The Quran*, the other two elements which every Muslim adheres to are the Hadith and the Shariah. The Hadith comprises talks and preaching of the Prophet in his lifetime. And the Shariah, which according to the followers of Islam, are divine and it has four sources; *The Quran*, the Sunna (the words and deeds of the Prophet which is compiled in Hadith), the Qiyas (analogical reasoning)[15] and the Ijma (Juridical Consensus). All the sects and orders of Islam commit to the trinity. However, the last two leave a greater scope for interpretations because they involve human interventions based on intellectual interpretations (fiqh), though the fundamentalists within the Muslim community do consider that Qiyas and the Ijma are not in category of fiqh.

The idea of puritan Islam underscores that Muslims should essentially follow *The Quran*, the Hadith and the Shariah. But here lies the problem. What is the true interpretation of *The Quran*, the Hadith and most importantly the Shariah. The Shariah deals with details on methods of worship, ways of conducting life activities by Muslims, the dos and don'ts, methods and means of punishments etc. Needless to say, the Shariah deals with the life of a Muslim as an individual as well as a community encompassing civil, religious, cultural and criminal components. And it was not codified at the time of the Prophet. It has largely been in the hands of the Caliphates, the Imams and the Ulemas to interpret and give injunctions on situations arising from time to time. And therefore, different schools of Jurisprudence have come up in Islam even within each sect.

These schools are not the product of *The Quran* or the Hadith but the interpretations which are different from each other. Sunni sects have four schools within; Hanafi, Maliki, Shafi'i, and Hanbali. The Shias have Jafari or Imami schools which is further sub-divided into the *Usuli* and the *Akhbari* schools. Usuli draws inference from ijtihad whereas Akhbari

School draws on the wisdom of Imams. All these go to suggest that there is no universally accepted document like the Shariah. It has been documented as per the schools of jurisprudence within Islam and there are a lot of variations in it. Describing the Shariah as a divine code is not true. Rather the Shariah is made from deductions drawn from *The Quran* and the Hadith based on schools founded by several tall religious personalities in Islam who interpreted these texts by applying their own wisdom. Hence, it is a secondary document. And the existence of different schools suggests that there is no consensus among the scholars of Islam on the Shariah.

Interestingly, all terrorist organizations and their ideological mentors like the Deoband and Wahhabism talk about following puritan Islam i.e., the Islam followed during the life of the Prophet and the four righteous Caliphates after him. The important points are: Are terrorists wrong when they talk of establishing the Islamic state and Islamic society? Are they wrong when they use force and violence against Kafirs? Is the interpretation of the concept Kafir manipulated and interpreted wrongly by the terrorists? Is the concept of 'Jihad against non-Muslims' talked about and practised by terrorists misplaced and misinterpreted? Does it have a theological sanction? Does forceful implementation of the Shariah codes in the form of banning music and dance and implementing a certain dress code have any theological sanction? And most importantly, did all these not happen at the time of the Prophet or the four righteous Caliphates? These issues require serious examination.

Let us explore what Islamic terrorist organizations have to

say about Islam. From Al Qaeda to Boko Haram and from Taliban to ISIS-- they all subscribe to the ideology of global Jihad which in simpler terms refers to establishment of Islamic states and Islamic society. In other words, they want to Islamize the entire world and establish one global Islamic state. This was what the Prophet had aspired for and worked during his lifetime which was subsequently carried out by their righteous Caliphates. Therefore, what these organizations aspire for cannot be said to be against the inherent mission of Islam. These organizations work on the premise that global Islam is possible only when Islamic countries practice true Islam or puritan Islam and they become bases from where the mission could be taken to other parts of the world. The process would go on till the whole world comes under the umbrella of Islam.

This is not possible suddenly where Muslims are numerically weak or where the Islamic state is not powerful enough to inflict military victory on enemy countries and force people to convert to Islam. In such a scenario they have to wait till the right opportunity comes and the target country should be treated as the land of Dar-ul-Sulah. Wahhabism explains it when it divides the world between Dar-ul-Harb and Dar-ul-Islam. Dar-ul-Harb is land of Muslims where Muslims or Islam dominates and Dar-ul-Harb is the land that is dominated by non-believers. This land has to be converted into Dar-ul-Islam and the Muslims should fight for this. India too has been declared to be Dar-ul-Harb. But there are countries such as the United States and Australia where Islam is in minority and its followers cannot fight or wage a war against the dominant majority. They have no option but to peacefully coexist and promote Islam in such countries.

For these terrorist organizations, the rulers of Muslim dominated states have lost the paths of the Prophet and true Islam and turned themselves as apostates and heretics. They collaborate with the anti-Islamic forces and hence need to be overthrown.[16] Since the elements of apostasy have been significantly compounded by the intervention, occupation and exploitation of Muslims by the West, particularly the United States, these countries should be treated as enemies of Islam. They deserve violent attacks so that they could be evicted from Muslims' lands. That is why these terrorist organisations target the US and the West in different parts of the world- from Syria to Lebanon and Afghanistan to Iraq. They, then justify all their terrorist activities on the ground that they are doing these for the sake of restoring the power of Islam which had lost its might and ancient glory. In pursuit of accomplishing these objectives, these terrorist organizations have no hesitation in forcing others to accept Islam or inflicting death on those who refuse to convert.

No one can question *The Quran* or the Prophet in the land of Islam and examples are numerous to suggest that people have been put to death on account of blasphemy. Several others continue to be hounded like animals be it Tarek Fatah, Taslima Nasrin or Salman Rushdie. There are also examples of hands being chopped off as happened in Kerala or violent demonstrations if anybody makes a critical assessment of *The Quran*. The important question that needs to be examined is whether the actions of these terrorist organizations have a theological sanction. That brings us to closely examine what *The Quran* has to say on it and what the Prophet and the four rightly guided Caliphates practiced in their times.

The Quran makes a clear distinction between believers and non-believers i.e., Muslims and Non-Muslims. A believer is one "who have faith in Allah, and His Messenger and have never since doubted, and who fight for his cause with their wealth and possessions." (Surah 49, Ayat 15). And then goes to instruct Muslims not just to reject all the religions which their forefathers practiced but also instill an element of animosity. Surah 7, Ayat 173 makes it clear that Muslims must understand that their forefathers 'followed falsehood.' Therefore, they should not be followed. And don't love them even if he is father or your brother, son or the nearest relatives if he does not believe in three things- Allah, his Apostle i.e., the Prophet (because rest of their predecessors were practicing falsehood) and the last day i.e., the day of the judgement. (Surah 58, Ayat 22). And then goes on to say that the believers should not befriend even his father or brother if they choose 'unbelief over faith.' Those who do it are wrong doers. (Surah 9, Ayat 23). In other words, if a Muslim befriends a non-believer, they should forget any mercy from Allah. (Surah 3, Ayat 28, also Surah 4, Ayat 144). Those who don't believe (in Allah) they are the worst beast in the eyes of Allah. (Surah 8, Ayat 55). Then the text further stokes fear in the minds that only those will be finding a place in the paradise who worship Allah. Rest will face the fire of hell. (Surah 5, Ayat 72). Because unbelievers who worship idols are God's enemy.

(Surah 25, Ayat 55). They must 'mend their ways.' And if they do, their past will be forgiven. (Surah 8, Ayat 38).

So, what is the mandate of *The Quran* against the unbelievers or infidels or Kafirs? It directs the Prophet with these words "O Prophet! Exhort the believers to fight." (Surah 8, Ayat 65). Whom to fight? Surah 9, Ayat 29 instructs: "Fight against those who believe not in Allah, nor the last day, nor hold that forbidden by Allah and His Messenger, Nor Acknowledge the religion of Truth, from among the people of book, until they pay the Jizya with willing admission, and feel themselves subdued." Make a war on unbelievers till the 'Allah religion reigns supreme.' (Surah 8, Ayat 39).

The Quran assures three things; first, Allah has already provisioned the worst for the unbelievers in hell. Surah 22 and Ayat from 19-21 unravels that the unbelievers in hell will face the fire. For them "will be cut out a garment of fire, over their heads will be poured out boiling water, melting their skins. And, that which is in their bellies. They shall be lashed with red iron." This is prepared only for those who do not believe in faith i.e., Islam. (Surah 2, Ayat 191). One after another, there are several verses in which the hell has been marked out as a permanent place of abode for the unbelievers where they will be punished in multiple ways. Therefore, Allah calls upon the believers that they should wage a war against the unbelievers. (Surah 25, Ayat 52, also see Surat 9, Ayat 123). 'Fight and slay the pagan' and Arrest, besiege and punish them is the mandate that comes from *The Quran*. (See Surah 2, Ayat 191. Also, Surah 4 Ayat 91). And then comes the message: "I shall cast terror into the hearts of the infidels; strike off their heads, maim them in every limb." (Surah 8, Ayat 12).

The Book assures the believers that Allah will certainly ensure victory for them in their fight against the infidels. It will be Swords in their hands but that will have the blessings of Allah. *The Quran* says; "Allah will chastise them at your hands", he will "lay them low" and will "give you victory over them" and "heal the breast of the believers." (Surah 9, Ayat 14). It further motivates the believer that "twenty steadfast will be able to 'vanquish two hundred and a hundred will be able to' vanquish a thousand unbelievers. (Surah 8, Ayat 65). It goes on to assure the believers that if they lose their lives in the war against the infidels yet they are alive. (Surah 2, Ayat 154). It is actually not he who is slaying but Allah is slaying the infidels for him. (Surah 8, Ayat 17). It is actually Allah who will smite the unbelievers.

Therefore, they should not worry about their lives in battle against the Kafirs or unbelievers. Then he is hard on the believers and instructs them that it is obligatory on their part to take on unbelievers even if they do not like it at the personal level. (Surah 2, Ayat 216). Thus, *The Quran* makes it mandatory for Muslims to fight for the cause of Islam and fight against the infidels and polytheist even if the believers do not like. All this is to be directed only against the unbelievers. The Muslims are not supposed to kill any Muslim, as per *The Quran*. It directs the believers to be 'merciful to one another.' (Surah 48, Ayat 29) and "never should a believer kill a believer except by mistake" and whoever does it in case by mistake, he should free a believer slave.

If all these quotes are put together in a sequence of order it appears like this: A believer is one who believes in Allah, the Prophet and the Judgement Day. Those who do not believe in these are practicing falsehood and committing sin. The believers must wage war on the unbelievers till the latter accept the Supremacy of the religion of the believers. Allah is with the believers. Unbelievers are sure to find a place in hell where they will be put to severe punishments. It is mandatory on part of believers to wage a war against the infidels, even if they do not like it personally. Even if they receive death, they are alive in the eyes of Allah. Needless to say, *The Quran* prescribes a violent war against non-Muslims. It prescribes death for the unbelievers. And this is what produces incentives for the Muslims to be suicide bombers against the infidels or Kafirs because such acts find sanction in *The Quran* which is a divine text coming right from the mouth of Allah through his messenger.

These provisions of *The Quran* and their further accentuation by Islamic clerics make Muslims intolerant towards other faiths. They develop a psychology of fear in their minds that befriending the unbelievers would be sin and make Allah angry. A separate identity formation for Muslims and the fight for it is enshrined in *The Quran*. Islam insulates Muslims against any possible influence from outside and that is what makes it so deadly and destructive towards multiculturalism. Look at the mandate of *The Quran* on inter-religious marriage. It says "Don't marry pagan women unless they embrace Islam.

A slave woman who believes is better than pagan women, even though she attracts you. Nor marry your girls to pagans unless they embrace Islam. A slave who believes is better than an unbeliever, even though he attracts you." (Surah 2, Ayat 221). A true believer in Islam will not marry an infidel girl or boy until she or he embraces Islam. This gives a perspective of how to create Islamic identity and be intolerant towards other faiths.

All these elements of violence and intolerance that flow from *The Quran* is countered by Islamist scholars as several verses of Quran suggest that Allah is the most gracious and the most merciful (Surah 1 and Ayat 1, 2, 3) and he does not ask everyone to essentially follow Islam. Some of the Ayats certainly indicate this. For example, Surah Al-Kafirun says as follows: "I do not worship what you worship, nor do you worship what I worship, I will never worship what you worship, nor will you ever worship what I worship, for you is your religion, and for me is mine." (Surah 109, Ayats 2-6). *The Quran* also says: "Don't revile those who worship other Gods, lest in their ignorance they revile your God. Each person adheres to their beliefs, they act as they please. But in the end, all shall return to their Lord and will be told of the wrongs they did." (Surah 6, Ayat 108). These verses definitely are conciliatory and accommodative in nature and provide space for co-existence of other religions. But the important point is do these verses undo the verses which prescribe war against the infidels? *The Quran* does not answer this.

In light of the two sets of injunctions in *The Quran* for the believers and about the Allah, the questions that arise are how did scholars interpret *The Quran* and how the text has been used by the followers of Islam? This requires examinations of interpretations of the Islamic scholars, particularly in the land of Islam, for in the land of non-Islam, interpreters are most likely to adjust the textual interpretation to suit the situations and time. For example, in India itself, the interpretations and practice of Islamic tenets of today are different from what was practiced during the Islamic rule, during the Sultanate period and the Mughals. Similarly, the interpretation of *The Quran* and the relations of Muslims with Non-Muslim by the Deoband in Pakistan are different from the Deoband in India despite the fact that they both adhere to the same syllabus. So, is the case of the organizations based on Islamic theology in Pakistan and India.

The most important, however, in this context is the practice of Islam by the Prophet and his successors. Were they tolerant to and merciful to the people who practiced other faiths? Did Islam allow other faiths to exist side by side or coerced them to forgo their ancestral religions? Did the Prophet and his successors and followers practice conduct of love and harmony towards people of other faiths? Do we have evidence to support that the Prophet and his followers respected the places of worship belonging to other faiths during their expeditions? Do we have evidence to support that the Prophet was gracious and generous to people of other faiths? I find that the journey of Islam unfortunately does not support the claim of being 'generous and gracious towards other belief systems. A little dive into the early and formative phase of Islam, therefore, needs to be examined.

The Prophet had attacked Mecca in 629 AD with nearly 10,000 armed Muslim warriors. While most of them were from Medina, some others had joined him on the way. The Prophet decided to do it after the victory at the Battle of Badr in Saudi Arabia in March 624 AD. He raided the Meccan caravan coming from Syria and destined for Mecca. Despite being less in number, Muslims under the leadership of the Prophet defeated the Meccans despite the support that came to the caravan from the Meccan army. The victory was divinized by the Prophet who stated that it was Allah and the Angels who fought for Islam.[17] The defeat of the Meccan enhanced Prophet's prestige in Medina and enabled him to mobilize a far greater number of forces for attacking Mecca. The Prophet who had returned with plundered wealth in the Battle of Badr now mobilized Muslims to attack Mecca where his army decisively defeated Abu Sufyan, the Chief of the Quraish tribe. Abu Sufyan surrendered and accepted Islam finding it to be the only way to escape death. He took this defeat as the defeat of the Meccan God who was proven weaker compared to Allah. Later on, he became the military commander of the Prophet in attacks on other tribal lands in the Arab world.

The defendants of the Prophet justify the attack on the ground that it was the Meccan who had violated the Treaty of Hudaybiyyah reached between the Prophet on behalf of the city of Medina and Quraishi tribe of Mecca in January 629.[18] However, they do not answer why did Mohammad and his followers and companions demolish the statutes and shrines which the pagans used to worship in Mecca before Islam spread its wings? There were the Jews and the Christians and tribal gods and ancestral figurines which Meccan used to follow. It is said that nearly 360 idols around Kaaba were demolished overnight.[19] And none other than the Prophet guided, instructed and supervised the destructions. Al-Uzza, Al-Lat and Manat were the three pre-Islamic Gods worshipped by Arabian people. There was a sacred stone at Nakhala near Mecca and Quraish people used to invoke this Goddess in war. The shrine dedicated to this Goddess and the statue was demolished by Khalid Ibn Al Walid at instructions of the Prophet.[20] Apart from demolishing the temples at Kaaba, his followers destroyed other places of worship in entire Eastern Arabia.[21] The pre-Islamic Arabia since the days of Adams had customs of idols craved on stones which they used to worship. They also used to worship the figurines of their ancestors as well at place of their burial.[22]

The Prophet after military victory over Mecca ensured that there was no trace of idol worship. The Meccans accepted Islam not because they had faith in Islam or *The Quran*, as *The Quran* was not at all in existence during that time. The military defeat was interpreted as defeat of an inferior or weaker God against a powerful God of Islam. The Prophet also did not give them choice and they had no option but to accept Islam to save their lives. Needless to say, the demolition of the places of worship by the Prophet became an ideal reference for his successors and followers to practice the same.

Muslims take inspiration from the acts and examples set by

the Prophet who demolished the Meccan gods on the pretext that they and their ancestors were following falsehoods. The territorial march of Islam and Islamization of the lands in Asia and Africa suggest that the tribal chiefs in those days were subjected to military conquest and they were left with only two options: accept Islam or face the swords of Islam. Yamen, Egypt, Iraq, Iran, Oman--all fell to Islam through military conquests and they all lost their ancestral Gods buried under mounds of sands. Yemen faced attacks during the times of the Prophet. Al Aswad Al Ansi belonged to the Banu Ans tribe of Yemen who after defeating Shahr, the ruler of Sana (the largest city in Yemen), declared himself to be the Prophet. This was not liked by Muslims who declared him apostate and killed him in the battle. This way Yemen came under the rule of the Caliphates. Egypt witnessed conquest by Muslims from 639 to 646 AD. The order to attack Egypt and bring it under the rule of the Caliphate was done by Omar, the second Caliphate. He sent only 4000 warriors with a competent commander 'Amr ibn al-'As. Though the Caliphate messaged to him to return, given the military might of Egypt under the Roman Byzantine rule, the Muslim army kept registering victory one after the other. The famous Roman general Aretion was asked by Amr-Ibn-al-As to either accept Islam or pay Jaziya or fight. This is what we find in the Quranic injunctions against infidels. The former chose to fight and was defeated comprehensively. This opened the gate for Islamization of Egypt.

The conquest of the Arab by the Islamic forces and subsequent demolition of the existing abodes of God indicate that iconoclasm was followed by righteous Caliphates as well during their military conquests. Afghanistan and India are the shining examples of it. Muslim invaders who raided India not just plundered the wealth but admonished the religion and destroyed the places of worship of indigenous Hindus. Afghanistan once was a great Buddhist centre with places of worship all around. But they all lost their structures to iconoclastic hysteria of Islam. In India, Islamic invaders demolished temples everywhere they went and every path they passed through. The Ram Temple at Ayodhya, The Kashi Vishwanath Temple at Varanasi, the Shiva Temple at Somnath, the Krishna Temple at Mathura and thousands such small and big temples in the country witnessed the sordid tales of Islamic iconoclasm in India.

Sita Ram Goel in his comprehensive research published in a book titled "Hindu Temples: What Happened to them" has demonstrated with proof how over 2000 temples were demolished by Islamist iconoclasts and Mosques constructed over them. And no historian so far has disputed his research findings. The number may have been at dispute but no historian worth his salt has ever denied the demolition of temples and Buddhist structures by Muslim invaders and rulers in the country.[23] The arguments by secularists that they were demolished for the sake of wealth that these temples possessed are untenable since historians who accompanied these invaders have clearly stated that these demolitions took place after invoking Islamic religious scriptures. The matter of fact is that Islam has a definite 'undeniable iconoclastic ethos' and it was just the continuity of the Abrahamic tradition in a far more aggressive way.[24] Even the Sufis of India had appreciated the destruction of temple at Somnath and elsewhere and some of them like Nizam al-Mulk Tusi, Sanai and Atar compared them with destruction of idols of the Arabs by the Prophet.[25] Muhammad Iqbal goes on to proclaim the entire world in some way or other belongs to Muslims.[26]

When the Taliban under the leadership of Mullah Umar started demolishing the figurines or statutes in Afghanistan under its control, it shocked civilized societies across the world. The demolition created international news when the thousand-year-old statue of Lord Buddha at Bamiyan was destroyed by the Taliban militia. In light of the criticism, Mullah had put the question before the Muslims of the World: Whether they would 'rather be the smashers of idols or the sellers of idols?'[27] Interestingly, several religious and Islamic cultural organizations found this question relevant and sided with Mullah Umar. Besides Afghanistan, a lot many people rallied behind Mullah Umar such as Jamat-e ittihad-e 'Ulama (an organization supported by the JUI) - Jamaat-e-Islam etc.'[28] The organization openly sided with Mullah by declaring that 'selling idols was wrong' and congratulated the Taliban for reviving the 'Tradition of Abraham.' The head of the organization and then leader of Pakistan's opposition, Maulana Fazlur Rahman, also applauded the Taliban and congratulated them for having fulfilled the "Prophetic Tradition."[29] Thus, what the Taliban does or the Islamic zealots did to the non-Muslim religious icons and temples were perfectly the model that the Prophet had followed at Kaaba.[30]

The territorial and numerical expansion of Islam involved war, violence, assassinations, forced conversions, destruction of places of worship of other religions and idols and all other means to achieve the mission of political dominance. And for every criticism they took refuge in the acts of the Prophet and his successor Caliphates. Richard Gabriel depicts the military raids of the Prophet as a new Guerrilla style of war unheard and unseen so far in the Arab world as it had combined violence with religious ideology.[31] From Mecca to other parts of the Arab, the early Islamic conquests were military conquests followed by religious conquests. Islam spread through a military conquest in which the option available for the unbeliever was to make a choice between conversion to Islam or fight till defeat or death. It happened in times of the Prophet and the same tradition was followed by the four righteous and other Umayyad Caliphates.

The ideology of puritan Islam thus unravelled itself as a mission based on the central premise of converting unbelievers into believers in order to accomplish the mission of global Islamic society and Islamic state under the system of the Caliphate. It seeks to punish those who do not believe in Islam. It endorses demolition of faiths of others. It is not that the liberal version of Islam or reformists movement did not take place to rationalize the tenets of Islam but they always lost the ground to the radicals who interpreted other faiths and their followers as enemies of Islam. And such interpretations have come not only from the Sunni theologians but also the Shias and the Sufis, considered moderates voices within Islam.

A careful scrutiny of the writings of some of the key scholars of Islam and those of predominant schools and seminaries in the last three centuries becomes imperative to understand the Islamic mind and its mission. This provides also insights into understanding the ideas on Puritan or true Islam. The discussion on the three representative scholars coming from three territorial and geographical locations can throw light on this. These three streams are Wahhabism from the land of Islam, the Deoband from Pakistan and India, and the Sufi thinkers from India. Since Wahhabism has already been discussed in detail in this book, let us focus on others.

Though Deoband originated in India, it would be better to rely on the interpretation of Deoband in Pakistan on Islam. The Deoband in India has its own limitation of speaking the truth since it operates in space where Hindus are in a majority. Also, it is important to rely more on the interpretations of Islam prior to the British ascendency to power since post-Mughals and post-British interpretations have chances of getting influenced by power and social settings. Therefore, I have chosen Shah Waliullah in India who wrote towards the twilight of the Mughal Empire and is known as one of the towering theologists on Islam. Similarly, the founder of Jamaat-e-Islami of Pakistan, Abul-Ala-Maududi is often depicted as Karl Marx of contemporary Islam who not just influenced the politics of Islam in Pakistan but also Syria, Egypt and many other Muslim dominated countries.

Shah Waliullah and Abul-Ala-Maududi are considered to be one of the greatest commentators of Islam for all times. Waliullah is often equated with Al-Ghazali and Razi. Al-

Ghazali was a medieval Persian polymath, a great theologians and mystic who profoundly contributed to the interpretation of Islam. Al-Razi is acclaimed as one of the greatest physicians in the Islamic traditions. Both are very consoling names in the Islamic world. Some even think that Shah overshadowed both of them. Even Allama Iqbal, himself a great scholar of Islam, considered Shah Waliullah one of the greatest theologians on Islam. For him, he was 'the last great theologian of Islam.'[32] Waliullah was a gifted writer and orator who inspired all schools of Islam in South Asia. Muslim scholars often rally behind him, but for non-believers what is most important is not what he spoke on scholarly interpretations on Shia-Sunni conflict and interpretations on the Hadith but how he interpreted Islam with respect to other religions. It is also important because he claimed himself to be a Sufi which for many does not represent the exclusivist and intolerant ideology of Islamists.

But ideas of Shah Waliullah would disappoint the moderates and liberals since he whole heartedly supported the idea of intolerant Islam in India. This is evident from the fact that the Mahmud of Ghazni, Mughal emperor Aurangzeb and Ahmed Shah Abdali were icons of Islam in his eyes.[33] Needless to highlight that Hindus consider these rulers as infamous invaders who indulged in inhuman acts of violence, murder, assassinations, plundering of wealth, destruction of temples, forced conversion and hatred towards the Indic religionists of India. Waliullah considered the rise of the Marathas, the Jats and the British as threat to Islam in India.[34] For him, they all represented infidels. And therefore, they needed to be countered. The Muslims in India were left with no power to do it and, therefore, he wrote a letter to Ahmad Shah Abdali, a notorious invader who had not spared even Muslims, to come and attack India to emancipate Muslims from possible seizure of powers by infidel Hindus.

In other words, Shah Waliullah accepted that the power of Islam essentially depended not on its spiritual ingredients but political power and territorial occupation. The second element he focused was segregation of Muslims from non-Muslims which the Tablighis also followed later on. This was nothing but application of the Quranic injunctions in which Allah proscribes the practices of non-Muslims. This had elements of formation of separate identity from the Hindus on the one hand and alignment of Indian Muslims with larger community of Islamic societies which lay outside the territorial boundaries of India. It essentially carried the element of Pan-Islam. The Indian Muslims, he said, must look towards the Muslim nations and communities beyond the Indian territories and always sync with the larger Islamic world.[35]

Needless to say, the proposition of Islam that comes from the writings and interpretation of the faith by Shah Waliullah makes it clear that non-Muslims are Kafirs. The letter written to Ahmad Shah Abdali confirms this as he wanted Abdali to attack India just because the country was most likely to slip into the hands of the Hindus. His father, Shah Abdur Rahim, also defined Jihad in the same sense i.e., a war against the infidels rather than war against the evils within an individual self.[36] Further, one should also not ignore the fact that his son was the one who had declared India as the land of Dar-ul-Harb.

Shah Waliullah was not just a theologian. He claimed to have been receiving divine messages during meditation.[37] He projected himself as a divine entity that had the blessings of the Prophet. This, he claimed, during his visit to Mecca where he had spent about a month and 'prayed in the sacred mosque.' This was akin to the claims of Baqi Billah and Ahmad Sirhindi who said the Prophet appeared to them in their dreams or in state of trance during meditation.[38] Both Waliullah and Sirhindi represented the Sufi traditions in Islam but they had hatred towards the Hindus. The concept of infidels and Kafirs and the treatment to them was not very different in their scheme of thought and interpretation of Islam. The Hindus were infidels for them and deserved punishment including death.[39] These reputed scholars of Islam do not project Islam as a tolerant religion at all.

Similarly, the writings and speeches of Abul Ala Maududi who inspired numerous political and terrorist organizations in Pakistan and elsewhere are big names in Islamic scholarship. He influenced various Islamic political outfits in countries such as Egypt, Indonesia, Syria and Malaysia, and it is often said that Maududi is to 'Political Islam' what Karl Marx is to Communism.[40] His idea of Islamic revolution set forth the arguments in favour of Islamization of politics and economy before complete Islamization of the country. His ideas inspired terrorist organizations like Muslim Brotherhood of Egypt and its ideologue Sayyid Qutb[41] and even Osama Bin Laden of the Taliban and Al-Qaeda.

Maududi was associated with Indian Deobandi and the Jamaat-e-Hind but decided to leave India and settle in Pakistan. But he was not happy with the notional declaration of Pakistan as a theocratic Islamic state. For him, even the Muslim League was the party of pagans because the league had no blueprint for a Sharia State.[42] He wanted much more than that including complete Islamization of all gamut of Pakistani State and Pakistani society. He wanted a complete Islamic revolution and, therefore, could never digest the liberal parliamentary politics in Pakistan. Maududi is known for interpretation of holy Islamic texts in light of political framework. He concluded that 'the decline set in because Muslim rulers had abandoned 'pure Islam', *Asali* Islam.[43] Whether it was the Mughals or the Nizam, they declined because they spent their force in winning territories rather than applying the Sharia. He was thus critical of Akbar's generous approach towards the Hindus.

Maudadi propounded that the state was central to Islam and thus advanced the arguments in favour of an Islamic state. Allah for him was the one who governed the metaphysical as well as the political world. Allah must, therefore, be the ruler of the political realm. This is possible only when the political power applies the rules of Allah just as an executor. In other words, only the State which was based on the Sharia and applied the Islamic injunctions was the right State. This obviously excludes the democratic principles of modern state and argues for a theocratic Islamic state in which non-Islamic would have to conform to Islamic rules. Non-Muslims such as the Hindus and the Christians were infidels or Kafirs for him and they did not deserve equal power with the Muslims. This unravels how poisonous and exclusivist his thoughts were as far as non-believers are concerned. And this is coming from one who is treated as all-time great theologian of Islam! The Deoband in India criticized him for making a politically motivated interpretation of Islam but similar accusations were returned from Pakistan against the Indian Deoband charging the latter of diluting Islam.

Both Maududi and Shah Waliullah present a case of Islam which is not very different from what the terrorists talk about as far as treatment with other faith systems and establishment of Islamic state at global level is concerned. This throws challenge for the societies where followers of Islam are significant in number. They have a problem of co-existence and intermingling in the non-Muslim societies. Islam is a religion which presents a strong case of political dominance and, therefore, it is a Statist religion that seeks a conformist religious subject. The words of the Koran are divine and unalterable and hence cannot be challenged. There were many in India who propounded that Islam directs its followers to be loyal to the land in which they are born and live in. This theory was advanced for the first time by Maulana Abul Kalam Azad and later on by Maulana Wahiduddin Khan.[44] But there are very few takers of this interpretation outside India or Pakistan or for that matter in the Arab world from where Islam originated and spread out to the different parts of the world. The matter of fact is that *The Quran* makes a clear distinction between believer and non-believer and passes cruel injunctions against unbeliever/ Kafir.

Modern scholars of Islam find it really difficult to justify the tenets of Kafir and treatment to the Kafirs and Jihad. Ashgar Ali Engineer argues that the violence in the journey of *The Quran* occurred because Islam was facing hostile societies around with which its followers had to handle and, therefore, they resorted to violence. In other words, violence is not the doctrinal element of *The Quran* but empirical requirement.[45] Rafiq Zakaria also has tried to reject the interpretations that it is *The Quran* which is the source of violence against people of other faiths. He rejects the entire range of atrocities that were perpetrated by Muslim rulers in India and were justified by the Islamic jurists of the time. He termed it to be a result of wrong interpretations of Islam. Thus the actions of Muslim rulers such as destructions of Hindu temples, forced conversions of Hindus into Islam and forcing them to pay religious taxes were all ill-conceived and misinterpreted. Hindu for him is also not Kafir because they also are the people of the book. They too have religious books like *The Vedas* which guide them into spirituality. If we further believe him, Jihad also have been misused for the lust of power as it is religious deed to purify oneself against the evils and its violent form is justified only when there is a deliberate attempt to obstruct the believers from practicing their faith.[46]

This argument looks very impressive but this interpretation is hardly acceptable to Islamic scholars in the Arabic and Muslim world. The Islamic jurisprudence prescribes death for the Kufr and those who are apostates. Dr Mohammad Israr Madani, a Deobandi scholar in Pakistan holds that defending Islam and honour and dignity of the Prophet is the religious obligation of all Muslims. And apostasy for him is when somebody is "abandoning or forsaking Islam; repudiating any of Islam's basic and principal tenets; reverting to the former state of falsehood from the absolute Truth of Islam or converting to any other religion …proclaiming Prophethood for oneself or believing in an impostor as a Prophet after the last Prophet of Allah, and indulging in any deeds or uttering something that leads to kufr (disbelief)."[47] Polytheist, atheists are all Kafirs and the penalty for the Kafir is death or paying taxes for their survival.

Needless to say, the idea of pure Islam proves to be a dangerous concept because it takes the followers of Islam to the age of origin and formative phase of Islam which under the tutelage of the Prophet and four righteous Caliphates proved very harsh to those who did resisted. A puritan Islam makes instructions very clear for Muslims to wage a war against the infidels. The injunctions are not about a fight between good and bad but between believers and non-believers. This injunction is what militates against the harmonious living of humans with different religious paths. And that is what makes puritan Islam so dangerous and so difficult to handle.

References:

1 Maududi called even the members of Indian Muslim League as Pagans because they believed in Western Parliamentary democracy and speak of secularism.

2 Look at the writings of Shah Waliullah, one of the most revered theologians amongst the Muslims. He articulated that the Muslim rulers were not the true Islamists as they got engaged in territorial expansion and ignored application of sharia which resulted into decline of Muslim power in India.

3 True Islam is for brotherhood and harmony.

4 Examples of bravery of terrorists who destroyed the Twin tower https://www.history.com/topics/21st-century/9-11-attacks

5 Dhondy, Farrukh. "London Muslims "Celebrate" 9/11." https://www.city-journal.org/html/london-muslims-%E2%80%9Ccelebrate%E2%80%9D-911-12387.html. Accessed on 29 June 2020

6 Robert H Knapp quoted in K Langlois, J. (2005). "Celebrating Arabs": Tracing Legend and Rumor Labyrinths in Post-9/11 Detroit. The Journal of American Folklore, 118(468), 219-236. Retrieved June 29, 2020, from www.jstor.org/stable/4137703. Accessed on 29 June 2020

7 Some of them argued that American government deliberately did so in order to attack Afghanistan. "US Professors Claim

9/11 an Inside." The Times of India, New Delhi, 7 September 2006.

8 Sufism is not a Sect but an order within the Sunni sect. The term was first used by a German Professor, F A J Tholuck. The word Sufi is equated with Saint or Yogi who either has realised the God or is on path of seeking the truth. See; Anjum, T. (2006). Sufism in History and its Relationship with Power. Islamic Studies, 45(2), 221–268. http://www.jstor.org/stable/20839016

9 There has been a history of conflicts between Shias and Sunnis in Lucknow on occasion of Muharram. With first major riots starting between the two communities in 1908 it continued till recent years. "Muharram Clash in Lucknow." The Telegraph Online published on 28 April 1999.

10 Engineer, A. A. (1994). Human Rights and Dawoodi Bohras. Economic and Political Weekly, 29(31), 1998–2001. http://www.jstor.org/stable/4401548.

11 Pakistan through its 2nd Constitution Amendment declared Ahamadias as non-Muslims. There are many Islamic countries where they are not allowed to declare even their faith publicly. They are subject to both Islamic and state suppression. See the United States Commission on International Religious Freedom Reports 2021 on Ahmadias. https://www.uscirf.gov/sites/default/files/2021-10/2021%20Ahmadiyya%20Persecution%20Factsheet.pdf, Accessed on 22 January 2022

12 Ahmadias are called heretics by Shias and Sunnis because to them Ahmadias challenge Prophet Muhammad as the last divine. Indian Government however treat them as one of the

sects within Islam. See; Shaikh,Zeeshan. "Ahmadiyyas find place as Islam sect in census." The Indian Express, 4 August 2016, Mumbai.

13 Anti-Saint or Anti-Shrine? tracing deoband'sdiSdain for the Sufi in Pakistan https://www.baylorisr.org/wp-content/uploads/2019/11/Deoband-Anti-Sufi-1-1.pdf. P.106.

14 It also needs to be taken into account that there was another Quran which was drafted by a cousin of the Prophet, Ali. This was however rejected by the nobles of Medina led by Abu Bakr.

15 There is a school within the Shia sect that is very large in number in Iran that does not recognize Fiqh but relies on Akl(wisdom). This school is called Twelver.

16 Lia, B. (2008). Al-Qaida's Appeal: Understanding its Unique Selling Points. Perspectives on Terrorism, 2(8), 3-10. Retrieved June 18, 2020, from www.jstor.org/stable/26298362. Accessed on 18 June 2020

17 The Battle of Uhud was also led by Muhammad and Quraish army had defeated them. Even the Prophet had received injuries. This goes to say that victory and defeat had nothing to do with God.

18 The treaty was an understanding between Muhammad on behalf of the state of Medina and Meccan that neither side attack each other and the Meccan would allow the people of Medina to visit Mecca on pilgrims. This was concluded when the Prophet was en-route to Mecca on Pilgrimage.

19 KIRKBRIDE, D. (1969). Ancient Arabian Ancestor Idols. Archaeology, 22(2), 116-121. Retrieved June 26, 2020, from

www.jstor.org/stable/41667956. Accessed on 26 June 2020. p. 117

20 Elias, J. (2007). (Un) making Idolatry: From Mecca to Bamiyan. Future Anterior: Journal of Historic Preservation, History, Theory, and Criticism, 4(2), 12-29. Retrieved June 26, 2020, from www.jstor.org/stable/25835009. p. 16

21 Ibid.

22 Kirkbride, D. (1969). Ancient Arabian Ancestor Idols. Archaeology, 22(2), 116-121. Retrieved June 26, 2020, from www.jstor.org/stable/41667956. Accessed on 26 June 2020. P. 117-121.

23 Even Yogender Sikand And Richard Eaton have accepted the demolition. And they have tried to conceal the number. Eaton, Richard. Essays on Islam and Indian History (OUP Delhi 2000).

24 Elias, J. (2007). (Un) making Idolatry: From Mecca to Bamiyan. Future Anterior: Journal of Historic Preservation, History, Theory, and Criticism, 4(2), 12-29. Retrieved June 26, 2020, from www.jstor.org/stable/25835009

25 Ahmed, Azaz (1964). Studies in Islamic culture in Indian Environment, Oxford University Press, Oxford, p. 79.

26 "इक़बाल का मुस्लिम हैं हम वतन है सारा जहाँ हमारा" 9 Nov. 2017, https://www.bbc.com/hindi/india-41925447. Accessed 5 Apr. 2021.

27 Mullah Umar had justified it on the ground that it was in consonance with the Islamic dictums. However, later on when the government by Taliban in Afghanistan faced internal criticism its representatives in the West and the USA tried

to rationalise it on the ground that it was done out of rage as money was being spent on maintenance of the statue while children were dying of hunger. See, Crossette, Barbara. "Taliban Explains Buddha Demolition." The New York Times, March 19, 2001. Also See Fernando, Benita. "The legacy and return of the Bamiyan Buddhas." The Indian Express, Mumbai, 12 March 2021 online. https://indianexpress.com/article/explained/bamiyan-buddhas-3d-projection-taliban-7223686/ Accessed on 22 January 2022. However, the theory of intense rage does not fit into as the destruction continued for weeks and finally dynamite was used against the same.

28 Ibid

29 Elias, Jamal J. (2013). 'The Taliban, Bamiyan, and Revisionist Iconoclasm," in Leslie Brubaker and Richard Clay (Edit). Striking Images: Iconoclasms Past and Present, Ashgate, London. Pp.145-163

30 Elst, Koenraad. "Vandalism Sanctified by Scripture." The Outlook, 31 August 2001.

31 Riaz, R. (2016). Comparative Analysis of Gulzar Ahmed and Richard Gabriel on the Military History of the Prophet (peace be on him). Islamic Studies, 55(1/2), 131–147. http://www.jstor.org/stable/44739737. Accessed on 27 December 2021. P. 134

32 Banerjee, Anil Chandra (1980). Two Nations: The Philosophy of Muslim Nationalism, Concept Publishing Company, New Delhi, p.44

33 Shah Waliullah had great appreciation for Aurangzeb.

He wanted restoration of Islamic political Supremacy in India which was on decline after death of Aurangzeb. See Sahasrabudhe, Rohit. "261 Years Since Panipat: How A Sufi Preacher Reached Out to Abdali and Asked Him to Restore Islamic Supremacy In India." Jan 14, 2022. https://swarajyamag.com/culture/panipat-a-failed-attempt-to-revive-islamic-supremacy-in-india. Accessed on 22 January 2022

34 This is evident from his letter written to Ahmad Shah Abdali.

35 Banerjee, Anil Chandra (1980), p.45.

36 Shah Abdur Rahim was the founder of the Madrasah-I Rahimiyah. He was also a member of the committee appointed by Aurangzeb for compilation of the code of law, Fatwa-e-Alamgiri.

37 This he himself acknowledged in his work Fuyûdal-Haramayn which he wrote after returning India in 1732.

38 This he reiterated in his letter to Najibuddaulah also wherein he reiterated that Ruhelas would occupy the Jat Fortes and this had already been decided in the most secret world.

39 For Shah Walliullah the infidels deserved punishment including death.

40 Paracha, Nadeem F. "Abul Ala Maududi: An existentialist history", The Dawn, Updated January 01, 2015 , accessed on 28 June 2020.

41 Ahmad, I. (2009). Genealogy of the Islamic State: Reflections on Maududi's Political Thought and Islamism. The Journal of the Royal Anthropological Institute, 15, S145-S162. Retrieved June 28, 2020, fromwww.jstor.org/stable/20527694). Accessed on 28 June 2020

42 Maududi was critical of Muslim League and found that it did not represent true Islam. He wanted establishment of a far more radical Islamic rule to be established in Pakistan.

43 Maududi quoted in Ahmad, I. (2009). Genealogy of the Islamic State: Reflections on Maududi's Political Thought and Islamism. The Journal of the Royal Anthropological Institute, 15, S145-S162. Retrieved June 28, 2020, from www.jstor.org/stable/20527694). Accessed on 28 June 2020

44 Wahiudddin Khan was given Padma Vibhushan by the Government of India in 2020. He wrote column for organizer and Panchajanya, closely linked to the RSS. Asgar Ali Engineer has also argued that Maulana Azad opposed partition on theological grounds. See; Engineer, A. A. (1988). Maulana Azad and the Freedom Struggle. Economic and Political Weekly, 23(50), 2633–2635. http://www.jstor.org/stable/4394113. Accessed on 21 January 2022. Also see, Douglas, I. H. (1972). "Abul Kalam Azad and Pakistan" A Post-Bangladesh Reconsideration of an Indian Muslim's Opposition to Partition. Journal of the American Academy of Religion, 40(4), 458–479. http://www.jstor.org/stable/1460895

45 Engineer, Asghar Ali (1995). The Quran and the Concept of Kafir. P.1. However for contested arguments read; Ghosh, A (1983). The Quran and the Kafir. The University of Michigan, USA

46 Zakaria, Rafiq (1995). The Widening Divide: An Insight into Hindu-Muslim Relations. Penguin Books

47 Madani,Muhammad Mohammad Asrar (1994). Verdict on Blasphemy and Apostasy. Idara-e-Islamiat, Lahore, p. 129

CHAPTER 9

DIFFERING RESPONSES TO TACKLE THE RADICAL ISLAM

DEMOCRACY HAS ITS limitations when it comes to handling conflicts and dissent. The State cannot use brute power to suppress dissent as they have to work within the framework of democratic and constitutional values. The democratic framework accords sanction to the individual freedom and rights at the centre of discourse and discounts all such attempts that could sabotage these values. It plays a remarkable role to balance individual and community interests and identity. The state and its administrative agencies, accordingly, cannot put the entire community under surveillance for a crime committed by one or more of its members. A corollary to that is the entire community cannot be blamed or punished for a crime committed by one of its members.

And this is where the dilemma and the trouble arise when a community gets associated with violent activities. There is no doubt that all Muslims are not involved in terrorist activities. But equally true is the fact that a predominant majority of the terrorists pledge their adherence to Islam. It has produced a unique kind of challenge for the democratic societies which have to walk a tight rope. Democracies have to use force to tackle violence but it has to ensure at the same time that the community as such does not become the target of societal reactions and state responses. This is not what Totalitarian states have to negotiate with. Democracies, however, cannot afford to ignore them.

The Challenge of Islamic terrorism is a worldwide phenomenon irrespective of the nature of political systems and the territorial boundaries. Its activities are visible as much in India as in Spain, Germany or the United Kingdom. And every country now has been trying to give an adequate response to the menace of radicalism and terrorism. Engaging with Islam, accordingly, unravels different patterns in different countries depending on the nature of the political system, the territorial concentration, overall numerical presence of Muslim population, ideological and religious orientation of that population and the nature of Islamic challenges itself.

The challenge from Islam in India is different than the challenges it poses in countries like the United States, the UK, Germany or China. Accordingly, the nature of responses of the states to the challenges of Islamic terrorism is also different in different countries. This differential response varies from democratic to non-democratic states. This is contingent on how the states evaluate the nature and magnitude of the threats and the challenges which Islamic population throws in a particular social and cultural setting. Thus, we have different models depending upon the nature of the challenges.

Let us try to analyze the situation in Communist China. The overall population of Muslims in China is very small, approximately 1.8 per cent of the total population, but their concentration is very high in the Xinjiang province adjoining the Tibetan region of China. Though there are 10 separate Muslim sub-categories, the one which has a larger population in Xinjiang is the Uyghur Muslims. The Uyghurs belong predominantly to the Sunni sect. A few of them also practice the Sufi traditions. They want to secede from China and establish a separate homeland. The Uyghurs have formed the East Turkestan Islamic Movement (ETIM) to accomplish their goals. The terrorist outfit of this organization is the Turkestan Islamic Movement (TIM) which is alleged to have links with the Taliban and the Al-Qaeda. Members of the TIM fought in Syria along with the ISIS to further the Islamic agenda. The global connections of the Uyghurs accelerated the militant activities in the Xinjiang province, particularly after 2009 but it also allowed China the ground for launching a 'war on terror' campaign that was used by the US and the Western forces in Afghanistan.

China has been ruthless towards Uyghur Muslims and their separatist tendencies. The Chinese state agencies work with the basic postulates that all liberties are applicable till they do not challenge the ideology, territorial sovereignty and integrity of the Chinese state. In other words, one cannot challenge the Communist ideology which allows the state to exercise disproportionate power against any voice of dissent and difference. One is free to exercise his freedom only to the extent he does not challenge the ideology and structure of the state. Accordingly, China has attempted to introduce two-pronged strategies; repressing extremist Islam on the one hand, and developing an indigenous version of Chinese Islam different from Arab Islam or Indian Islam.

China has strictly applied the one-child policy and Uyghur women are subjected to forced abortion to keep the numerical strength of the community under check. Urban Muslim women are often harassed and sometimes even forced to marry non-Muslim Chinese. Members of Chinese police are also deployed in Muslim homes as 'guests' under "pair up and become family" programme in nearly one million Uyghurs homes. The policy and its practices violate the private space of the individual family but the Uyghur Muslims are coerced to follow it. The Chinese state tracks "every face, every family and every movement of Muslim Uyghurs in Xinjiang."[1] Further, there is a high degree of policing and surveillance over Uyghur Muslims through 'use of sensors, facial recognition scans, bio-metrics,' besides monitoring the social media platforms, mobile messages and other data sources. An Uyghur Muslim may be arrested on the ground of growing long beard, "wearing veils, calling family members abroad, applying for a passport and having 'too many' children." Even a phone call overseas is monitored reflecting policing on Uyghur Muslim.

Further, China also works on the schemes and programmes intended to disconnect Chinese Muslims from the Arab world and other Pan-Islamic attachments. The male members are sent to the concentration camps which they call vocational education training camps or re-educating schools. But fortifications all-around such camps reveal that these camps are more than that. People coerced in these camps are monitored round the clock by the Chinese state system. Stories leaked out from such camps suggest that they are taught and trained in Islam by state appointed Maulanas who interprete Islam in such a way that it produces ideological coherence with the Chinese Communist party and the Chinese state. They are educated in *The Quran* but the interpretations are made by officials of the Chinese state.[2] China has banned foreign Islamic organizations and their activities which could possibly pollute their mind. And accordingly, the Tabhlighi Jamaat is not welcome in China.

In brief, the Chinese model of containing Islamic extremism is based on four factors: dilute the extremism that exists in interpretation of Islamic ideology through state appointed theologians; comprehensive monitoring of Uyghur Muslims with the help of technology including forced stay of Chinese police in the family for months under family programme; containing their population using all means including forced abortion of Uyghur Muslim women; and finally, using brute power against the terrorist violence. This brute power has no limitations since there is no independent judiciary or other such agencies to monitor human rights abuses where the state itself is involved. Western liberal democracies and human rights agencies have expressed their concern on human rights violations, but the Chinese state has ignored them. This is a model of 'Repressive Non-democratic state model' which works toward annihilation of distinct identity and forcible assimilation of the dissenting identity.

In Russia, Islam is the second most widely professed religion after Christianity. Muslims comprise nearly 20 million which is about 10 per cent of the total population.[3] During the Communist regime, the Soviet Union tried to suppress the religious identities and religious theologians including the Islamic ones and replace them with the Communist world view. They directed all their power—legal, economic, political, cultural, administrative—to achieve this end.[4] But once the pressure was out under perestroika and glasnost, Islamic identities re-emerged more vigorously. Many parts of Russia which had their Islamic elements returned to their roots such as Uzbekistan, Tajikistan, Armenia, Azerbaijan, Turkmenistan, Kyrgyzstan and Kazakhstan. Nearly 65 million Muslims split from the Soviet Union, except for Kazakhstan, and became members of the International Islamic Organization. However, Nine Muslim republics continued to be a part of Russia. This includes Tatarstan, Bashkortostan, Dagestan, Adygea, Ingushetia, Northern Ossetia, Kabardino-Balkaria, Karachayevo-Cherkessia and Chechnya.

Islam in Russia is not homogenous but ethnically heterogenous. There are minimum 21 Muslim nationalities such as Adygei, Avars, Azeris, Balkars, Bashkirs, Chechens, Cherkess, Dargins, Ingush, Kabards, Karachai, Kazakhs, Kumuks, Laks, Lezgins, Tabasarans, Tajiks, Tatars, Turkmen, Turks and Uzbeks. However, there are two sets of Islam which are often talked about in Russia; one which is widely accepted as the 'Tatar Model' which refers to Muslim majority province of Tatarstan. This is also called Secular and pacifist model because its members are loyal to the Russian state and are not exclusivist in outlook.[5] Contrary to this, there are the Chechen Muslims who are continuously engaged in crimes, violence and terrorist activities. It is the Chechen Muslims who have emerged as a nuisance for Russia.

Chechnya became part of the Soviet Union in 1921 when Joseph Stalin persuaded it to join the federation and promised to give it the requisite autonomy. But it never remained peaceful. Widespread protests were witnessed since 1924. Chechnya has a large Muslim presence. In light of protests and rebellion, nearly half a million Muslims were forcibly deported to different locations or regions of Central Asia in 1940-41 on the suspicion that they had sided with Germany during the war.

They were allowed to return only in 1957. However, Chechnya always remained a difficult region to govern. When the Soviet Union started disintegrating, Chechnya declared independence in 1991. The Russian Army entered Chechnya but returned in 1993 after an accord. From 1993, for technical purposes, Chechnya enjoyed independence till it was brought under the direct control of Russia in 2000. And since then, conflict has been going on. Like Xinjiang, Palestine and Kashmir, Chechnya has also become a target of Global Islamic Jihad. The way Muslims from several countries participated in Jihad in Syria, several of them also participated in Chechnya's fight against Russia. Similarly, there are also several home-grown Islamic terrorist groups which fought against the Bashar-Al-Assad government in Syria backed by Russia.[6] In the last few years, several terrorist groups have emerged with the mission of carrying out Jihad against Russia and they are loosely 'allied with Al-Qaeda's global Jihad.'[7]

Russia has worked on two pronged strategies. First is to segregate the traditional Russian Islam from the Salafists and the Wahhabis who could possibly poison the pacifist elements within the Muslim community. Russia consciously makes a difference between traditional Islam and modern Islam to communicate to its people that it is not against the religion per se but certainly against the Salafi cult of the faith. It is the foreign connection of Islam which Russia fears. And therefore, it has been sponsoring international conferences to promote spiritual Islam. However, series of terrorist attacks and violence such as the Moscow theatre hostage crises in 2002 and the Beslan siege in 2004 made Russia realize that Islamic fundamentalism is a trans-national phenomenon with the potential to seriously threaten the country's unity. Therefore, it has demonstrated commitment to fight against the Islamic terrorism and fine-tuned laws to deal with the menace. In 2016, the Russian government came out with 'Yarovaya Package' which made it mandatory for the telecom companies and internet service providers to keep the data and voice messages for 30 days so that terrorist activities could be tracked in case something goes wrong. This, however, does not apply on Twitter, Facebook, WhatsApp etc. President Putin has demonstrated being tough against terrorism and never hesitated from using raw force to suppress terror. However, Russia is tilted towards the statist approach to handle Islamic terrorism.

Israel has been a target of the entire Muslim world ever since the Jewish state came into existence in 1948. The country came into existence from the UN-peddled partition plan of 1947 in which the Jewish state and the state of Palestine for Arabs were created. This was a plan that was actually piloted by the UK which was in possession of the land as per the mandate of the League of Nations. The British had committed a homeland for the Jewish people. It resulted in the influx of Jewish people to their ancestral land from different parts of the world but at the same time it also invigorated Arab nationalism as this land was part of the Ottoman Empire. While the Jews accepted it, the Arabs rejected it on the ground that the land in question had been the land in possession of their ancestors for centuries. This resulted in the Arab-Israel war in 1948 in which nearly half million Arabs were forced to flee their villages and urban settlements to the adjoining states of Syria, Jordan, Egypt and Arab dominated Palestine region. The Palestinian based Arabs have been fighting against this, as they argue that Israel itself is a result of illegal occupation of Muslim land by the Jews. In 1967, a combined force of Syria, Jordan, Lebanon and Egypt attacked Israel. The war continued for six days and Israel not only defeated the combined forces but also occupied their territories like the Golan Heights from Syria and Jordan and the Gaza strip from Egypt. This was a major defeat of the Arab-Muslim forces, including the Egyptian President Abdul Naseer who had emerged as a hero after forcing the combined attack of France, UK and Israel to back out on the issue of the Suez Canal. It was this new earned heroic image that had propelled the President to lead the attack on Israel.

Israel continues to be the target of all Islamic terrorist organizations. Muslim countries in general rejected the very existence of Israel and had pledged to destroy it. In 1964, the Palestinian Liberation Organization (PLO) was formed with the sole intent of launching an armed struggle against Israel. This was designated as a terrorist organization by both the USA and Israel. However, it emerged as a sole voice of Palestine after the same was recognized by the Seventh Arab Summit in Rabat in 1974. The PLO remained engaged in violent activities but after the Madrid Conference in 1991 it showed inclinations for a political settlement. This conference was sponsored both by the Soviet Union and the USA to facilitate the peace process between Israel and Palestine. Several attempts from the Camp David in 1978 to the Oslo Peace Process in 1993 and 1995 were made in which both the PLO led by Yasser Arafat and Israel acknowledged each other's role in the peace process. The former accepted the existence of Israel and the latter recognized the PLO as the representative of the people of Palestine and, thereby, having the authority to negotiate on their behalf. However, they could not make much headway. This was also not liked by the Hamas.

In the late 1980s, particularly after 1987, the Hamas

emerged as a very powerful Islamic group operating from Palestine controlled Israel. Suicide bombings and rocket attacks became the order of the day. The Hamas was both a political organization and a militant group. Its charters clearly stated its aim was to destroy the Jewish State and replace it with an Islamic Palestinian State. The Israeli state has retaliated strongly every time they have been attacked and they have inflicted casualties double than the ones caused by the Hamas. Initially, it was suspected that the Hamas was a creation of the PLO but it was founded by Ahmed Yassin who had worked with the Muslim Brotherhood in Egypt.

Israel has resorted purely to masculine power to tackle political Islam in its territory. The use of force has pushed Muslim population to the Arab concentrated areas of the country and the core territorial area of Israel now has a predominant Jews majority. The terrorist and Islamic organizations fighting for Palestine have become weaker over time.. Muslim countries also have come to realize that they cannot now undo the existence of Israel and one after another most of them have reconciled to this reality and have established diplomatic relationships with it. The weakening of the Soviet Union also dented the capacity of the PLO, which became a divided house after the death of Yasser Arafat, to do much against Israel. And, even the Hamas has realized that destruction of Israel is impossible and, therefore, amended its charter that does not seek destruction of Israel but establishment of a Palestinian State in the West Bank and the Gaza Strip which have over 95 per cent Muslim population. Israel is a multi-party democracy but it has political consensus over the existence of the Jewish state of Israel and policy towards Islamic extremism. That is why there is no discussion on the secularization of the Muslim mind or appeasement policies towards the Arab or Muslim population within Israel.

But the same cannot be said about the US, European countries and India. These countries also have different challenges and different trajectories of engaging with religious and political Islam. Islam was not a ruling denomination in Europe and America. Except for achieving limited gains in Southern Spain which Islam ruled for quite a few decades, it could not get wide reach in Europe. Though all these countries claim to have encountered Islam several centuries back, in reality it emerged as a serious political actor only after the Second World War.

India, in that sense, is a completely different story from Europe. The US. Islamic invaders raided India at different times, plundered wealth and launched barbaric attack on indigenous culture and civilization. Muslim rulers wielded influence in the country for almost eight hundred years till the arrival of the British rule. They waged wars and killed and converted millions into Islamic faith. They won battles and did all that could be done to denigrate and demolish the indigenous pride. They demolished temples, broke idols, ridiculed native religions, and tried to alter the language and culture of the natives. This was the strength of the Sanatan Dharma that India could not be converted completely into Islamic society. And finally, when the British Empire in India crumbled, Hindus were still in majority and dominant population.

It was a unique case in history where Islam had failed to homogenize the population. As a result, Hindus and the converted Muslims entered into a wide area of contest in history, historical icons, language, cultural and religious symbols, and political and administrative control. India was finally partitioned on religious grounds but instead of an exchange of population, India rejected the two-nation theory that claimed that Hindus and Muslims were two nations and hence could not live together. Pakistan, a separate State for Muslims was created but India welcomed those Muslims who stayed back. After lull of a full decade the country was faced with the same issues that were raised during the Partition. These issues were the status of Urdu language, reservation on the ground of religion in government services, cow slaughter, religious conversion, national song Vande Mataram, status of Sanskrit language and so on.

Decades after Independence these issues have not been buried. India has become a breeding ground of Islamic terrorism. Besides Kashmir, which is home to more than five dozen radical Islamist groups, other parts of the country are also coming gradually under the grip of radical Islamists. The Muslim dominated areas and States are turning into hotbeds of radicalization. Kerala contributed nearly 60 per cent of the Indians who joined the ISIS to fight in Syria.[8] Increasing radicalization of Muslims across the globe has also paced the radicalization of Indian Muslims. The internet highways and social media network[9] have enabled the youths to connect with several sites wherefrom they download the chemical of Islam which poison the minds and take them to the battlefield where they are ready to fight for Islam irrespective of the borders. There are several radical Islamist groups that have shot into limelight including the banned Students Islamic Movement of India (SIMI), Karnataka Forum for Dignity,[10] Islamic Sevak Sangh,[11] and the National Democratic Front[12] of Kerala which was later on succeeded by the Popular Front of India (PFI). These organizations directly spoke of Jihad in India.

The SIMI came into existence on 25 April 1977 in Aligarh district of Uttar Pradesh, India's largest state. Aligarh was the epicenter of the movement for creation of a separate country Pakistan for Muslims. The SIMI has openly declared to convert India into Daru-ul-Islam (the land of Islam) through conversion or violence.[13] It openly called for Jihad. And this organization was not founded by a layman from a Madrasa but a professor of Journalism and Public Relations of Western Illinois University Macomb, Illinois. This was founded as a student wing of the Jamaat-e-Islami-Hind, an outfit of Deoband School of Islam committed to the Sunni sect. The SIMI aimed at establishing a 'Shariate based Islamic rule through Islami Inqilab.'[14] It had no faith in the Indian constitution, no faith in secularism and Osama Bin Laden was a hero for its members! The organization had financial and other links with terrorist outfits like the Jaise-e-Muhammad and the Jamaat-e-Islami of Pakistan, and the Huji, and the Islamic Chhatra Shivir of Bangladesh. It had financial links with Islamic organizations in Kuwait, Riyad, Pakistan and the USA.[15] Before it was banned in 2002 by the NDA government led by Atal Bihari Vajpayee, it had established a solid base in Uttar Pradesh and Kerala, and had engaged in several violent activities. Even after the ban, it continued its activities under different shadow names and activities.[16]

In 2006, the People Democratic Front (PDF) succeeded the National Democratic Front (NDF) of Kerala. Several radical organizations like the Karnataka Forum for Dignity (KFD), the Manitha Neethi Pasarai (MNP) of Tamil Nadu, Goa's Citizen's Forum, Rajasthan's Community Social and Educational Society, West Bengal's Nagrik Adhikar Suraksha Samiti(NASS), Manipur's Lihong Social Forum (LSF) and

Andhra Pradesh's Association of Social Justice later on merged with it.[17] The formation of this forum in fact, started after meeting of Muslim activists and intellectuals of South India to have a common forum to promote social, cultural and political interests of Muslims. But given the leadership that was drawn into it, including the national president of the organization, Abdul Rehman, who happened to be the secretary of the SIMI, speaks volumes about the nature of the organization. It is widely accepted that the PFI is the 'resurrection of the SIMI' with a changed nomenclature and form.[18] The PFI has pan-India presence today, and it has attracted several charges ranging from murder and assassinations to kidnapping,[19] to having links with the ISI to recruiting Muslim youths for the Al Qaida and the ISIS to fight in Syria,[20] from carrying out bomb blasts.[21] It has been found to be involved in promoting love Jihad that seeks to convert Hindu girls into Islam and then use them in religious war,[22] in protests against the Citizens Amendment Act of 2019[23] and riots in different parts of the country including Delhi Riots in March 2020.[24]

The nation was shocked when some members of the PFI chopped off the hand of Professor TJ Joseph in 2010 for allegedly insulting the Prophet! Thirteen members of the PFI were found guilty by the court of the National Intelligence Agency (NIA).[25] The PFI has got footings in several parts of India with a strong presence in Uttar Pradesh and Kerala- the two states which had strongholds of the SIMI. In the last few years, the questionable role of the PFI has figured prominently during debates on radical Islam or Islamic movements or communal violence by Islamists. Intelligence agencies have found the involvement of the PFI in radicalization of youths and for roping them into the world of Jihad.

Earlier, the Indian governments used to assert that Indian Muslims were not involved in Pan-Islamic jihadist activities. While speaking at the 16th Hindustan Times Leadership Summit Union Home Minister Rajnath Singh said that the Indian Muslims should be complimented for resisting radicalization despite several temptations and attempts by anti-Indian forces.[26] His statement was political and intended to discourage the youths from joining the portal of global Jihad. The reality has been a stark contrast. Shahjahan Kandy, a resident of Kannur in Kerala and an active member of the PFI was caught by the Turkey police when he was enroute to Syria.[27] For him, the Al-Qaeda and ISIS fighters were role models. His Facebook posts accessed by the media revealed the connection he had with foreign terrorists. He posted and supported hate posts and used to share and upload those on Facebook and other social media platforms. It was during the third visit to Syria that he was nabbed by the Turkish police.

Now this is clear that people like Shahjahan Kandy are not isolated examples. One can argue that they are minuscule in proportion to the total Muslim population of India. The number of pro-ISIS cases in India was reported to fall somewhere between 180-200 from 2014-18. And Kerala alone contributed nearly 60-70 per cent of the total cases.[28] It has been found that the Muslim dominated areas of North Kerala such as Kannur, Malappuram and Kasaragod have greater concentration of radicalized Muslim youths compared to other regions.[29] Many areas of Bihar, Bengal, Uttar Pradesh, Andhra Pradesh, Maharashtra etc., where Muslims have a dominant presence, are fast turning into breeding grounds for radicalized Muslim youths. West Bengal in the last one and half decades has witnessed several Muslim-Hindu riots where rioters had a field day and Hindu houses were torched off or demolished.

In a Muslim dominated area of Malda district, in January 2016, a crowd assembled to protest against Kamlesh Tiwari, a politician based in Uttar Pradesh, who allegedly had described the Prophet as the first homosexual.[30] The gathering soon turned violent and burnt police vehicle, government buses and police station and Block Development Officer's (BDO) office at Kaliachak-I.[31] Interestingly, the government of West Bengal did not consider this to be a communal riot, despite violent attacks on Hinds by Muslims. The left-liberal media did not come out to criticize it the way they had done on the killing of a couple of Muslim youths in Uttar Pradesh where they had organized a candle march, staged the drama of artists returning awards to protest intolerance, and undertook signature campaign by Left oriented eminent people to oppose what they described as increasing intolerance. This silence on part of the vocal left liberal groups in civil society and intelligentsia to killings of Hindus was perceived to be ideology driven. They even failed to condemn the violence.[32] In December 2016, Muslim crowd went on rampage and destroyed Hindu shops and houses in Dhulagarh in Howrah, just 28 Km away from Kolkata, the State's capital.

The statistics of other states unravel the same picture. Maharashtra has witnessed highest number of Hindu-Muslim riots in post-Independent India.[33] The South Asian Terrorism Portal (SATP) documents in detail the terror networks and their activities in Maharashtra from 2006 to 2018. It explains the deep-rooted radicalization of Muslim youths and their linkages with the terror groups like the ISIS, the Indian Mujahidin etc.[34] The biggest state of India, Uttar Pradesh, keeps hogging headlines for busting of terror modules, arrest of terrorists and radicalization of Muslim youths. In 2001, the State police arrested young Muslims from five centres: Lucknow, Hapur, Saharanpur, Bijnor and Azamgarh.[35] They were all having terrorist links. In April 2001, three terrorists belonging to Jaish-e-Mohammad were killed by the State's Special Task Force in Lucknow. On 30 April 2001, a Pakistan-trained Harkat-ul-Ansar terrorist involved in an explosion in a UP roadways bus at Roorkee bus depot was arrested from a Madrasa in Hapur. Sixteen people were killed in this explosion.[36]

Azamgarh, a small town in UP has earned notoriety since some of its young Muslim residents have found to be connected with terrorist activities. Muslim organizations often allege that security agencies have ascribed a stigma to the city because it is a Muslim dominated town. They ignore the various cases of terrorism with definite links to Azamgarh. One such example is the famous Batla house encounter in Delhi's Jamia Nagar in 2008 in which two young terrorists and a senior police inspector Mohan Chand Sharma were killed. This incident was projected by Muslims and the left-liberal intelligentsia as a case of fake encounter. The terrorists who were killed came from Azamgarh. One Shahzad Khan, who was arrested later, hailed from Azamgarh. The Congress party called it a fake encounter whereas the UPA Government led by the Congress termed it to be a genuine encounter.[37] Salman Khurshid's statement that Sonia Gandhi was restless and wept throughout the night at the killing of those Muslim youths created massive controversy. The issue was how could Sonia Gandhi sympathize with terrorists?

Whether it is Kashmir or Kerala, Maharashtra or Assam, the difference in radicalization is only in terms of intensity. And the spread or extent of radicalization depends on the concentration of Muslim population in the respective areas whether these are districts, blocks or a small town. Delhi, for example, has a Muslim population close to 12 per cent but certain areas of the national capital have earned the epithet of being mini-Pakistan because of high Muslim concentration and reports about nefarious and subversive activities. These areas were key centers of protests against the Citizen Amendment Act, 2019, and subsequent riots in Delhi in March 2020. Seelampur, Jakir Nagar, Jamia Nagar, Jaffrabad and Maujpur are the communally sensitive areas with a sizeable Muslim population. They have often hit headlines because of arrest of people related to violence, terror attacks, espionage etc.

India's situation is quite different from other countries. The Partition of the country was made on the ground that Hindus and Muslims form two different civilizations and they cannot live together. Besides the contiguity principle, the Partition was based on the formulation of strength of religious population: Hindu and Muslim majority areas had to go to India and Pakistan respectively. Muslims had overwhelmingly voted in favour of the Muslim League in the assembly election in 1946. When the Partition was effected, the overall Muslim population in British India was 27.06 per cent as per the 1941 census. Obviously, this excluded the population in the princely states majority of whom were Hindu majority or non-Muslim majority. The Hindu population in post-Partition Pakistan in 1951 was 12.9 per cent but in East Pakistan it was roughly 22 per cent. The population of Hindus in post-Partition India was 84.1 per cent whereas the Muslim population was close to 9.8 per cent. In the last seven decades, the Muslim population rose to 14.2 per cent whereas the Hindu population declined to 78.35 as per 2011 Census. While the Muslim population increased by 5.6 per cent, the Hindus declined by 5.56 resulting in the Muslim population closing the gap by 11.6 per cent in 70 years.

The rising Muslim population has a direct impact on the politics of India. Muslims are not in position to get representation in elected bodies in proportion to their population, but they have used their electoral strength to influence the country's social, cultural and public policies. India sought to implement family planning and population control policy but failed because Muslim community opposed it.[38] The Government could not come out with a Uniform Civil Code despite constitutional mandate under the Directive Principles of State Policy and numerous observations of the Supreme Court.[39] It seems as if the political class has given a blank cheque to the Muslim community on these issues by leaving the decision to their initiatives knowing fully well that they would never come out in support of the cause.

When the Union Government led by Atal Bihari Vajpayee at the Centre decided to deport Bangladeshi infiltrators, Muslim organizations created hue and cry and alleged that community members were being tortured. When the Chief Minister of Assam, Hiteswar Saikia on 10th April, 1992 made a statement regarding the settlement of illegal migrants in Assam, he was forced to withdraw his statement within 48 hours following the threat and intimidation of Muslim leaders that his government would be toppled.[40] As per several estimates nearly 20-30 million illegal migrants from Bangladesh are settled in different parts of India. Sripakash Jaisawal (then Minister of state for home affairs) in a statement in Rajya Sabha on 15th July, 2004 highlighted that till December, 2001 there were 1,20,53,950 illegal migrants were living in 17 states of India. Reiterating about illegal migrants, Kiran Ritju, Union minister of state for home in 2016, in Rajya Sabha mentioned that, "There are reports of Bangladeshi nationals having entered the country without valid travel documents. Since entry of such Bangladeshi nationals into the country is clandestine and surreptitious, it is not possible to have accurate data of such Bangladeshi nationals living. As per available inputs, there are around 20 million (2 crore) illegal Bangladeshi migrants staying in India."[41] The court has directed to deport them yet it has not found resonance with political parties other than the BJP.

When the BJP government under Prime Minister Narendra Modi brought the Citizen Amendment Act, 2019 (CAA) and the government sounded its intention to bring in the citizens' register at the national level, Muslims across the country joined protests which became violent at many places. The protest began from Jamia Millia Islamia University campus and Jamia Nagar. Some members of the mob masquerading as students resorted to violence and police used force to control the situation. Members of the Muslim community sat on Dharna at Shaheen Bagh in Delhi to press for their demands for roll back of the CAA. This was replicated at all India level in many Muslim dominated areas. The protests in Delhi finally culminated into Hindu-Muslim riots in East Delhi. The language of the protests, the slogans used at the protest sites and the participation made it clear that it was a movement led by Muslims and supported by the Communists, the Trinamool Congress of West Bengal and the Indian National Congress. As for example, senior Congress leader and parliamentarian Shashi Tharoor had joined the anti-CAA protests at Shaheen Bagh.[42] The Congress held a rally in Delhi at the Ramlila Maidan on 13 December 2019 and called upon Muslims to hit the street against and openly extended support to this cause.

Sonia Gandhi, the interim president of the party criticized the decision of Narendra Modi government to scrap Article 370. The purpose was to ignite Muslim minds in the wake of series of decisions by the Narendra Modi government and that included abolition of the Triple Talaq, abolition of Article 35A and scrapping of Article 370, and facilitating the construction of the historic Ram Temple at Ayodhya which was opposed by Islamic radicals.

Muslim organizations had realized that the eviction and deportation of those Muslims who had infiltrated illegally would significantly reduce their numerical strength in different states such as West Bengal, Assam, Bihar and Uttar Pradesh. This would severely damage the political gains resulting from enhanced numerical strengths that they had acquired over the last seven decades. Muslim organizations have been using their increased strength to pressurize the political class in different states to extract disproportionate benefits under the cover of minority appeasement. This is evident from the fact that Ms Mamata Banerjee who as a parliamentarian had created ruckus in the Lok Sabha to press the demand for deportation of Bangladeshis Muslims[43] became the staunch votary of their stay in the state. She openly advocated non-application of deportation law in the state. This was political posturing for votes since she knew that the state had no jurisdiction over this matter.

Over the years, Ms Banerjee has tried her best to polarize Muslim voters in the state. She recognized Madrasas, started giving salaries to the Imams and Muezzins, and provided exclusive Islamic townships. She sent hard line SIMI leader Ahmed Haasan Imran to the Rajya Sabha from West Bengal. Over 400 NGOs related to Muslim cause are working in the state and the government recognized over 597 Madrasas. The

NIA has pointed out to the presence of over 500 recognized and 4000 unrecognized madrasas in the state involved in 'indoctrination, recruitment and training of youths in the radical Islam'. But Ms Banerjee has always been trying to stall the proceedings against illegal Madrasas.

Muslims have returned the favours by voting en-block for her party. Earlier they were reported to be loyal to the CPI-M but have now shifted their allegiance to the Trinamool Congress. Bangladesh's Jamaat-e-Islami has canvassed openly for Ms Banerjee's party. The rising Muslim clout in West Bengal due to increase in Muslim population through infiltration from Bangladeshi has emboldened them so much that several Muslim organizations in the State organized a massive rally on 30 March 2013 in support of Bangladesh war criminals of 1971.[44] The war criminals are those who perpetrated crimes against opponents of Pakistani regime in East Pakistan. Jamaat-e-Islami was a part of the protest. This meant support for Pakistani crimes against India supported liberation war of Bangladesh. This did not alert her since she was merely interested in the electoral mathematics that would keep her in power.

West Bengal Muslim population has increased phenomenally like in Assam. In 1998, former IB (Intelligence Bureau) chief TV Rajeshwar and Governor of West Bengal explained in details how illegal infiltration was encouraged by the CPM leadership, specially Muslims, who managed Indian documents such as ration cards and names in the electoral rolls just to increase the numerical strengths of their co-religionists. As a consequence of this, Hindus from border areas of Assam fled to the cities selling their lands and properties even at cheaper rates.[45] Today, Muslims are in position to greatly influence the formation of government in West Bengal because of their capacity to decide the fate of over 130 assembly constituencies in the state out of 294. In the 2016 assembly polls, the Trinamool Congress was ahead in 85 minority-dominated assembly segments.[46] During the first stint of Mamata Banerjee's government in West Bengal, the infiltration rate was up by five times of the earlier.[47]

Similar increase of Muslim population has been witnessed in states like Assam, Bihar and Uttar Pradesh. It is not just the Seemanchal (border districts) areas of Kishanganj, Purnea and Katihar but also other areas that have witnessed drastic increase in Muslim population due to illegal infiltration from Bangladesh. It is precisely the reason that despite difference with the official stand of the JDU, Bihar's deputy Chief Minister and BJP leader Sushil Kumar Modi openly said that infiltration from Bangladesh is the cause of extremism and sought the application of the National Citizen's Register in the state.[48] In fact, three generations of Bangladeshis have settled in different parts of the country and the total influx is counted as close as 30 million. These religious demographics have altered political narratives in many states. In order to assuage the feeling of Muslims, several states like Karnataka, Maharashtra, Uttar Pradesh and Andhra Pradesh came out with bills to give 5 per cent reservation for the community. These bills could not get passed since Indian Constitution does not allow reservations on religious lines.[49]

If both the CAA and the NRC are implemented at the national level, the detection and deportation of illegal migrants is seriously going to dent Muslim political fortunes in many states. This explains why many Muslim organizations have come out openly against the CAA. They are now openly asking for parity between Hindu victims of religious persecution in Pakistan, Bangladesh and Afghanistan and Muslims who may choose India to be their destination. They want to blissfully ignore that Muslims who chose to live in Pakistan had believed in the two-nation theory and the belief that Muslims cannot live together with Hindus. Even on the issue of crackdown on Rohingyas who have migrated illegally to India, these Muslim organizations take stand following the ideology of Pan-Islam. Their much talked about Human Rights for Rohingyas is a ruse to support co-religionists. The same organizations never came out and supported the Human Rights of Kashmiri Hindus who were brutalized in Kashmir in the name of Jihad and forced to evacuate their native places. They never spoke against Islamic terrorism in Kashmir and always supported the existence of Kashmir as a Muslim dominated state. The Muslim leadership in Kashmir did not give the right to citizenship to Hindus who had migrated to the State from Western Pakistan during the Partition, but they had no problem in settling Rohingya Muslims in the state.[50] Most of these 6000 families who were denied their basic rights in Kashmir were Dalits who did menial works. In 2008, then Chief Minister Ghulam Nabi Azad had clarified that "no government can ever do anything for these people for the obvious reason that it could disturb the demographic profile of the state."

The ever increasing population of Muslims and their aggressive posturing in political, social and cultural domains have rung alarm bells in the minds of a large section of Hindus who lean back on history and ponder if it was the same phenomenon that forced the Partition on the country some 70 years back. And nothing has changed in the discourse despite the Partition. The rising terrorism and increase in separatist tendencies and their inclination and attachments to the issues of global Islam and Islamic identity have made the entire issue of Muslim issues far more complex in India than in other democratic countries. Close to 15 per cent Muslim population cannot be thrown out the country and, therefore, Hindus are destined to live with a population whose theological foundations are hostile towards other religions. There are thousands of examples to prove what Muslims have done to the native population and their cultural symbols during their rule of thousand years. Migration of Hindus from Muslim dominated areas in different states of India, including Kashmir, has proved that rising Muslim population creates problems of existence for Hindus and their socio-cultural existence. One is idol worshipper and the other is idol breaker. One is the religion of seekers and the other is the religion of believers.

And the dilemma is that despite involvement of Muslims in over 90 per cent of terrorist activities, politicians have no guts to suggest that Islamic terrorism has roots in theology. The political class and intellectuals in India admit in private the obscurantism and elements of terrorism in Islamic thought, but they do not admit the same in public. The Islamists use the proclivity of political parties to look at issues through the prism of political loss and gains. And this started with India gaining Independence when Nehru rejected the suggestions of many stalwarts of the time in the Congress and outside to exchange Hindu-Muslim population between Pakistan and India. Their argument was based on firm grounds. The Partition had happened due to perennial hostility between the two communities where advocates of Pakistan said that Hindus and Muslims were two nations and they could not live together. The country was divided in the name of religion. Even those Muslims who stayed back in India had voted overwhelmingly in favour of Pakistan.[51] This delivered to Nehru and the Indian

National Congress a band of loyal supporters, those Muslims who stayed in India and saw their survival to the existence of the Congress in power. This created a loyal Muslim vote-bank to the Congress for decades. The Congress and other political parties tied themselves to the idea of secularism through minority appeasement which fed the identity and disintegrative elements of the Muslim population. The appeasement politics has degenerated and has acquired a serious proportion and the Indian state is clueless on how to handle it.

The Western democracies like the USA, the United Kingdom and Australia do not have this kind of problem because Muslim population is those countries are not that strong numerically or otherwise to dominate the political discourse. In Australia, Muslims comprise only 2.6 per cent of the total population and there is hardly any parliamentary constituency which they are able to dominate or singularly affect the electoral outcomes.[52] And, therefore, when the Muslim organizations demanded Sharia laws and Sharia courts in Australia, several leaders in high position of government not only rejected it but made very hostile comments against the community for making such a demand. In 2009, the Australian Finance Minister Peter Costello categorically stated that the immigrants who 'wanted to live under the Sharia law are not welcome in Australia.'[53] The Prime Minister of Australia John Howard had also made similar comments against Muslims in the country.[54]

But this small population has been successful in forcing the society to debate their issues. The way Hizb-ut-Tahrir, a radical Islamic organization, has been welcomed by Muslims there and the way the sound for the Sharia and appreciation of radical Islam is getting strongholds and appreciation in

Australian soil, there are many who think that Australia is no more the same what it used to be a decade ago.[55] There has been increasing unrest in the political class of Australia against the growing radicalization of Muslim youths. Julia Gillard, the former Prime Minister of Australia had criticized the attitude of Muslim immigrants. She said that it is not Australia but the immigrants which will have to learn to adapt. She was very blunt on the exclusivist and intolerant preaching of the Islamic organizations, though the most purported statement attributed to Gillard was wrong.[56]

When it comes to the USA, the threat of Islamic terrorism from outside is real. It also threatens the US interests in different parts of the world. The US thus focuses its energy on preventing it from entering the American soil. Though Islam came to the US in the 17th century with African slave contingent, it did not witness major numerical surge before the end of the Second World War.[57] The second wave of immigrants came from Lebanon and greater Syria in which over 90 per cent were Christians and nearly 10 per cent Muslims. The influx of Muslims started after the Second World War. As there is no religious count in the US Census, the percentage of Muslims is always a guess work or a rough assessment that puts the figure at close to 3.4 million.[58] This is nearly 1.1 per cent of the total US population. This numerical strength does not pose major challenge to the political and cultural space of the US but radicalization of Muslim youths has baffled American security experts and policy makers, more particularly after the attack on Twin towers by the Al Qaida on 11 September 2001, commonly referred to as 9/11.

For the first time, America experienced the taste of Islamic radicalism when two towers, the Pentagon and the WTO, the former symbolizing the country's military might and the latter representing the economic might were razed to the ground on 9 September 2001 in a few minutes by Islamic terrorists. Those who were piloting the civilian planes that crashed into the towers were not misguided laymen but educated professionals who preferred to act as suicide bombers under the influence of hatred and Islamic Jihad. This incident froze the spine of all the nations, particularly the West since they had failed to realise the dangerous repercussions of Islamic terrorism. The theory that educated Muslims or economically empowered Muslims would fight terrorism has proved to be wrong and completely misplaced.

The American State responded to this challenge with both ferocity and caution. The desperation led to comprehensive search operations in mosques and Muslim localities and arrest of radical Muslim leaders and Islamic preachers.[59] Nearly 800 Muslims were arrested and sent to Guantanamo Bay prison near Cuba where America has its military base.[60] They were picked from different parts of the World such as Pakistan, Britain, America and so on. And they were put behind the bar without trial and that too for uncertain period: till the 'war on terror was over.'[61] Although, it created a lot of hue and cry in the liberal democratic space of the US where intellectuals and activists questioned the imprisonment but a large section of the society supported this. The failure of terrorists to repeat the attacks thereafter was seen as a result of this strict vigilance over Islamic centers following the approach of suspicion towards Muslims, particularly the Arab and Asian Muslims.[62] The connotations of 'enemy within' gathered ground and it was essentially attributed to the migrant Muslim community from Arab and Asia. And this is reflected in the conduct and behaviour of the common Americans towards Muslims, in general.

This echoed in media reports as well. The radical ideology of Islam being a religion that created terrorists and a separatist mindset were openly discussed in the editorials, news-reports and headlines of newspapers and Television News Channels.[63] European countries and even China and Russia, that are normally hostile to the US because of power equations, openly sympathized with and supported the US.[64] The headlines of major British newspapers like *The Daily Telegraph* (War on America), *Daily Mirror* (War on the World), *Daily Express* (Declaration of War), *Financial Times* (Assault on America) explain the outrage on the attack.[65] The left-leaning newspapers and media groups depicted such reactions as disproportionate and at the cost of innocent Muslims as a result of Islamophobia but this did not reflect the predominant view of American society. The surveys showed that Western societies were suspicious of Muslims. In 2011, a survey by the Gallup demonstrated that 52 per cent population in the US did not respect Muslims.[66]

This happened in many European countries too, such as Britain, France and Spain and questions were raised on the loyalty of Muslims to the country they have been staying in. Whether the identity of Muslims in America, Britain or other countries is Muslim first and citizen of the country next or vice-versa? This question became significant in the wake of celebration of the 9/11 attacks by certain quarters of Muslims in the US and other countries.[67] Loyalty to the religion or loyalty to the nation became a hot topic of debate while rating the Islamic community. In India also this has been a matter of debate. Late Syed Shahabuddin, Chairman of the Babri Masjid Action Committee (BMAC), who was negotiating with the

Vishwa Hindu Parishad (VHP) on the Ram temple in the early 1990s, used to publish a magazine called 'Muslim India.' The title of the magazine was deliberately and consciously coined in which 'India' came after 'Muslim' and thus, he kept it open for the discourse whether Muslims should give priority to Islam or India. The way he opposed alimony to Shah Bano, despite the Supreme Court order, quoting the non-violability of the Muslim Personal Law. It was clear that constitutional and secular India was secondary for him when it was posited against Islam. There is a great deal of difference between the two connotations because Muslim India leans towards and accords primacy to Islam and India comes next whereas Indian Muslims convey the message of defining and readjusting Islam in which the commitment to the faith does not subordinate national interests and the country identity. Indian Muslim means Muslims who are defined by the characteristics that define an ordinary Indian. The first is easily palpable to slip into the ideology of Pan-Islam. After 9/11, the concepts like good Islam vs Bad Islam, moderate Islam vs extremist Islam and American Muslims vs Muslim Americans or British Muslims have engaged serious attention of scholars and researchers on Islam.

Many American Muslims were uncomfortable with the realization that the position of Muslims would become precarious in the American society. They volunteered and the State and its agencies also encouraged prominent Muslims to come out and publicly denounce terrorism. They not just decried the attack and termed it anti-Islam but also called the perpetrators as murderers and enemies of Islam.[68] Such people started appearing on television channels and in newspaper reports with their statements denouncing violence. Quoting some of them would be giving the sense of discomfort which some American Muslims felt after the attack though there were many who celebrated the same. Farid Zakaria, Shaykh Hisham, Michel Wolf, Hamza Yusuf and many other prominent Muslim intellectuals spent several hours on television channels to convey the message to Americans that how the act was a creation of Wahabi Islam which is not true Islam at all. Some of them even compared Wahhabism to the violent ideology of Communism.[69]

However, this exercise has little impact on the American mind. This is evident from public opinion research in the US. In 2014, the Pew Research Centre published a report on eight major religious communities of the US and it found out that Muslims were at the bottom of it.[70] The 9/11 attacks were carried out in name of Islam and strengthened the image of Islam as a religion that promotes terrorism. Both non-Muslims and the State institutions turned suspicious of Muslim population after the Twin tower attacks. Though it is not reflected as a policy pronouncement, the actions of the state machinery are often suggestive of this. The treatment meted out at airport and public places to people with identifiable Islamic names is indicative of the changed behaviour of the State that once prided itself on equality and non-discriminative practices. This has been understood as growing intolerance in American society towards the non-European immigrants. But Americans do not buy this generalization. There is a growing realization that rising Muslim population is a threat to liberal, democratic and multicultural American society even when public documents may not suggest this.

And it is not without reason. America has its allies in the Central Asia and the Arab world that are predominantly Muslim countries. Some of these countries are the sponsors, nurturer and exporter of Islamic terrorism. The FBI investigation report on the 9/11 incident has not been made public because of security implications but it is widely believed that it has nailed the role of Saudi Arab.[71] Therefore, when George Bush junior decided to invade Afghanistan and Iraq in response to the terrorist attack, he did not blame Islam and dubbed these as 'war on terror.' But the predominant Muslim view considered this to be targeting of Islam by the US. This was realized by President Barack Obama who criticized terrorism but always desisted from criticizing Muslim societies and Islam in particular. He always desisted from using the term 'Islamic terrorism' which according to him was 'sort of manufactured issue.'[72] For him, members of the Al-Qaeda and the ISIS are barbarians who are using the 'mantle of Islam.' He used the conservative logic to justify himself that there are millions of Muslims who are followers of Islam and who do not subscribe to the ideology of these terrorist outfits. To quote Obama "These are people who've killed children, killed Muslims, take sex slaves, there's no religious rationale that would justify in any way any of the things that they do."[73] Obama was largely criticized for his reluctance to openly critiquing Islamic terrorism.

And the Republican President Donald Trump during his election campaign and even after getting elected to the office never minced words in criticizing Islamic terrorism and vowed to eradicate it from the roots. Immediately after getting elected as the President of the United States, Trump proclaimed in his 'America First Foreign Policy' that "defeating ISIS and other radical Islamic terror groups will be our highest priority."[74] He went on to say further, "We're up against an enemy that celebrates death and totally worships destruction – you've seen that. ISIS is on a campaign of genocide, committing atrocities across the world. Radical Islamic terrorists are determined to strike our homeland as they did on 9/11; as they did from Boston to Orlando, to San Bernardino. And all across Europe, you've seen what happened in Paris and Nice. All over Europe it's happening. It's gotten to a point where it's not even being reported and, in many cases, the very, very dishonest press doesn't want to report it. They have their reasons and you understand that."[75] Trump did not celebrate Eid festival in the White House whereas he was very enthusiastic about organizing Deepawali, an Indian festival identified with Hindus. Further, in September 2017, Trump banned entry of nationals of Iran, Libya, Somalia, Syria and Yemen to the US. Though it also listed 'nationals from North Korea and certain government officials from Venezuela' but the step was largely considered as 'banning Muslims.'[76] Trump also openly extended support to India in its fight against Islamic terrorism.

By and large, the American sentiments and approach to tackling political and Puritan Islam also finds echo and reflections in Western societies. Following 9/11, almost all European countries adopted the following five steps in dealing with Islamic terrorism at home. First, they did not accuse Islam per se for the violence and terrorism. They too followed the oft repeated popular phrase that no religion including Islam preaches violence and terror. And therefore, those who are involved in the business of terror and violence are not the true follower of Islam and, thereby, bringing disrepute to a noble and great religion. Thus, instead of attacking the faith they attack the perpetrators of the crime. This is consciously done to avoid annoyance of the Muslim community and the people who have deep spiritual faith in the religion and are no way linked to or endorse the activities of the terrorists. Secondly, they became cautious of the Muslim population and their pockets and accordingly enhance surveillance and monitoring of their activities. Third, they have gone ruthless towards the terror cells by arresting the men and freezing their assets. Fourth, they have, by and large, resorted to the project of secularization of Muslims by identifying and facilitating those who are considered to be the moderate face of Islam and giving them prominence in the public life. Also, they have tried to build interfaith infrastructure to bring the communities together. And finally, they have sought to discourage immigration from Islamic countries. These steps intend to reduce and contain the rise of numerical Islam.

France is a glaring example of this phenomenon. The right-wing party of France and its leader Ms Marine Le Pen has advocated tough measures to tackle political and extremist Islam in the country which she argues poses threat to French civilization and culture.[77] She points out that 150 districts have already slipped into the hands of the Islamists and, therefore, it is time to wake up to this threat and take actions as quickly as possible. Earlier, she was ridiculed for such utterances by her political opponents. But this approach was adopted after Emmanuel Macron was elected the President of France in 2017. Ever since then the French Government has toughened the immigration policies to stop the inflow of migrants for asylum. His administration further took decision to train the Imams in France who could establish a symbiotic relationship between the practice of Islam and following the law of the land. The imams were often linked to Salafism or the Muslim Brothers and "preach against the republic."[78]

His Government announced measures to tighten controls on foreign financing of mosques, to end the nomination by

Algeria, Morocco and Turkey of 300 imams a year for France, and withdrew an year's permission for foreign governments to control language courses for 80,000 pupils learning Arabic, Turkish and other languages from their countries of origin — a system he called "an important vector of separatism" given that many of the teachers did not speak French or care about French culture."[79] France gradually has been trying to stem the threat of radical Islam. Macron supported the Charlie Hebdo magazine that published the cartoon of the Prophet on the ground that "to be French is to defend the right to laugh, jest, mock and caricature, of which Voltaire maintained that it is the source of all other rights."[80] He went to the office of the Magazine to express his solidarity with the journalists who were killed in the office in 2015 by the Islamic Al-Qaeda terrorists.

Almost every country of Europe today has become suspicious of the radicalization of Muslim youths. There is growing resentments against identity assertion by Muslim community. The state and civil society have reached a consensus to handle the menace of Islamic radicalism both by force and by using persuasive liberal policies of exposing Muslim youth to modern education and liberal thoughts.

References:

1 China's treatment of Muslim Uighurs in Xinjiang: 'I had the chills' https://www.dw.com/en/chinas-treatment-of-muslim-uighurs-in-xinjiang-i-had-the-chills/a-52431839. Accessed on 3 July 2020. Accessed on 3 July 2020.

2 China's attempt to change the Quran https://www.dailysabah.com/op-ed/2020/01/09/chinas-attempt-to-change-the-quran

3 This data has been taken from House hearing minutes of the Committee of Foreign Affairs of the House of Representatives, USA, 30 September 2015, N0.114. https://www.govinfo.gov/content/pkg/CHRG-114hhrg96819/html/CHRG-114hhrg96819.htm. Accessed on 4 July 2020

4 Kerimov,Gasym(2008). "Islam and Muslims in Russia since the collapse of the Soviet Union", Pp. 183-192.https://www.tandfonline.com/doi/citedby/10.1080/09637499608431738?scroll=top&needAccess=true. Accessed on 4 July 2020

5 Simons, Greg (February 2019). "Introduction: the image of Islam in Russia". Religion, State and Society, Volume 47, Issue 2, Mar 2019. Pp. 174-179. Online Publication, https://www.tandfonline.com/doi/full/10.1080/09637494.2019.1587936. Accessed on 5 July 2020

6 Sinai, J. (2015). The Terrorist Threats Against Russia and

its Counterterrorism Response Measures. Connections, 14(4), 95-102. Retrieved July 4, 2020, from www.jstor.org/stable/26326421. Accessed on 4 July 2020

7 Ibid.

8 Taneja, Kabir and Siyech, Mohammad Sinan (2019). "The Islamic State in India's Kerala: A Primer", Occasional Papers, Observer Research Foundation, online https://www.orfonline.org/research/the-islamic-state-in-indias-kerala-a-primer-56634/. Accessed on 7 July 2020

9 Johny, Stanly, The ISIS Caliphate: From Syria to the Doorsteps of India, (Bloomsbury India, New Delhi, 2018). Quoted in Taneja, Kabir and Siyech, Mohammad Sinan (2019). "The Islamic State in India's Kerala: A Primer", Occasional Papers, Observer Research Foundation, online https://www.orfonline.org/research/the-islamic-state-in-indias-kerala-a-primer-56634/. Accessed on 7 July 2020

10 Karnataka Forum for Dignity is considered to be the offshoot of the SIMI working in Karnatakaespecially in cities like Mangalore,Dakshina Kannada, Kodagu of Karnataka state and in Kasargod district of Kerala state. In 2006 this merged into PFI.

11 Islamic Sevak Sangh was a radical organization formed in Kerala by Abdul Nasar Madani. He was accused in the Coimbatore Blasts of 1998 aimed at killing RSS people and the Bangalore serial Blasts of 2008. Because of his radical views he outsmarted all other Islamic organizations in Kerala. It is said that Marxists used his posters in the Assembly elections of 2006 to garner Muslim votes and after winning the election the

Assembly passed the unanimous resolutions for his release from the jail the same year.

12 The National Democratic Front was founded in 1994. Later on it was succeeded by the PFI in 2006.

13 https://www.satp.org/satporgtp/countries/india/terroristoutfits/simi.htm. Accessed on 8 July 2020. South Asia Portal.

14 Ibid

15 See for details the Report of Center for Human Security Studies, Hyderabad "Terror Modules in India & Neighbours. http://www.aphrdi.ap.gov.in/documents/Trainings@APHRDI/2018/5_May/cybersecurity/TERROR%20MODULES%20IN%20INDIA%20&%20NEIGHBOURS.pdf. Accessed on 8 July, p. 69.

16 SIMI behind Chennai twin blast in 2014. Times of India News Network, Chennai, 11 July 2016. http://timesofindia.indiatimes.com/articleshow/53155833.cms?utm_source=contentofinterest&utm_medium=text&utm_campaign=cppst. Accessed on 8 July 2020. See for details the Report of Center for Human Security Studies, Hyderabad "Terror Modules in India &Neighbours.http://www.aphrdi.ap.gov.in/documents/Trainings@APHRDI/2018/5_May/cybersecurity/TERROR%20MODULES%20IN%20INDIA%20&%20NEIGHBOURS.pdf. Accessed on 8 July 2020. The Report also quotes the State Police Special Branch, of the State of Andhra Pradesh to conclude that "SIMI is operating under the cover of religious study centres, rural development and research centres. Some of these front organisations were spreading "extremist religious ideals"

among sections of youth in Kerala by acting under the guise of "counselling and guidance centres working for behavioural change".

17 See the Merger declaration of 14 August 2009 at Website of the PFI. http://www.popularfrontindia.org/?q=content/merger-declaration. Accessed on 8 July 2020

18 "PFI, NDF Involved in CPI(M), RSS Cadres' Murders: Kerala" The Outlook, 25 July 2012. https://www.outlookindia.com/newswire/story/pfi-ndf-involved-in-cpim-rss-cadres-murders-kerala/769976. Accessed on 9 July 2020. This was actually stated in the Charge-sheet filed by the Kerala Government in the Court.

19 "PFI, NDF Involved in CPI(M), RSS Cadres' Murders: Kerala" The Outlook, 25 July 2012. https://www.outlookindia.com/newswire/story/pfi-ndf-involved-in-cpim-rss-cadres-murders-kerala/769976. Accessed on 9 July 2020. This was actually stated in the Charge-sheet filed by the Kerala Government in the Court.

20 Prashanth, M P. "Another PFI ex-worker who joined IS `killed' in Syria", The Times of India, 13 September, 2017. http://timesofindia.indiatimes.com/articleshow/60493138.cms?utm_source=contentofinterest&utm_medium=text&utm_campaign=cppst. Accessed on 8 July 2020

21 Chauhan, Neeraj. " Popular Front of India's role in 2011 Mumbai, 2012 Pune, 2013 Hyd Blasts". The Times of India, 31 October, 2017. https://timesofindia.indiatimes.com/india/popular-front-of-indias-role-in-2011-mumbai-2012-pune-2013-hyd-blasts-found-intel-agencies/articleshow/46710055.cms

22 Raghunath, Arjun. " Kerala Church says 'Love Jihad is real". The Deccan Herald, Thiruvananthapuram, 15 January 2020. https://www.deccanherald.com/national/south/kerala-church-says-love-jihad-is-real-claims-christian-women-being-lured-into-is-trap-794814.html. Accessed on 8 July 2020

23 "ED finds 'financial links' between PFI and anti-CAA protests in UP". Press Trust of India, 27 Jan 2020. The TOI, https://timesofindia.indiatimes.com/india/ed-establishes-direct-link-between-violent-anti-caa-protests-in-up-and-pfi-writes-to-mha/articleshow/73662097.cms. Accessed on 8 July 2020

24 PFI-Delhi President, Secretary held for Funding Delhi Riots, The Times of India, 13th March 2020.

25 Philip, Shaju. "13 guilty of chopping Kerala professor's hand". The Indian Express, 1 May 2015, Thiruvananthapuram.

26 "Indian Muslims Deserve Credit for Resisting Radicalization". The Hindustan Times, 05 October 2018. https://www.hindustantimes.com/india-news/indian-muslims-deserve-credit-for-resisting-radicalisation-rajnath-singh/story-W9NeffkhlLT4BmreebTfkL.html, accessed also on 7 March 2022

27 Shekhar, Shashank and Ojha, Arvind. "Meet Shahjahan Velluva Kandy: PFI activist, suspected ISIS sympathiser", Mail Today, 2 November 2017.

28 https://www.orfonline.org/research/the-islamic-state-in-indias-kerala-a-primer-56634/. Accessed on 10 July 2020.

29 Ibid. Also See: https://theprint.in/pageturner/excerpt/god-own-khilafat-why-kerala-is-isis-hotspot-in-india/320945/. Accessed on 10 July 2020.

30 https://zeenews.india.com/news/india/this-is-what-kamlesh-tiwari-said-about-prophet-muhammad-which-infuriated-muslims_1833716.html

31 India Today Web Desk: https://www.indiatoday.in/fyi/story/all-you-need-to-know-about-the-malda-riots-302388-2016-01-06. Accessed on 10 July 2020.

32 https://www.huffingtonpost.in/abhinav-pandya/malda-riots-and-the-shock_b_9004020.html. Accessed on 10 July 2020.

33 Some shocking facts about Maharashtra's Muslims the state does not want you to know https://scroll.in/article/666853/some-shocking-facts-about-maharashtras-muslims-the-state-does-not-want-you-to-know. Accessed on 10 July 2020.

34 https://www.satp.org/satporgtp/countries/india/database/maharashtra_incidents.htm. Accessed on 11 July 2020.

35 https://www.satp.org/satporgtp/countries/india/database/utterpredesh.htm. Accessed on 12 July 2020.

36 Ibid.

37 The then Congress General Secretary Digvijay Singh had said that it was a fake encounter whereas PC Chidambaram and Shivraj Singh Patil called it genuine.

38 There are arguments which debunk this theory and suggest that the higher fertility rate among the Muslims have largely to do with the socio-economic and literacy rather than religious angle and with the rise of awareness this gap between the Hindu and Muslim fertility is narrowing. See; Dharmalingam, A., Navaneetham, K., & Morgan, S. P. (2005). Muslim-Hindu Fertility Differences: Evidence from National Family Health Survey-II. Economic and Political Weekly, 40(5), 429–436.

http://www.jstor.org/stable/4416134. Pp. 429-431.

39 Mahapatra, Dhananjay. "No Steps Taken in 63 Years on Uniform Civil Code, Says SC". The Times of India, 19 September 2019. Justice Deepak Gupta and Aniruddha Bose noted also that Go is a shining example of application of Uniform Civil Code where even the Muslims cannot practice polygamy and verbal divorce.

40 Ragi, Sangit Kumar. "PRICE OF IMDT ACT: MIGRANTS AND ETHNIC POLITICS IN ASSAM." *The Indian Journal of Political Science*, vol. 74, no. 3, 2013, pp. 545–56. *JSTOR*, http://www.jstor.org/stable/24701064. Accessed 5 Dec. 2022.

41 2. Jain, B. (2016, November 16). Two crore Bangladeshi immigrants illegally staying in India, Centre informs Rajya Sabha. *The Times of India*. https://timesofindia.indiatimes.com/india/two-crore-bangladeshi-immigrants-illegally-staying-in-india-centre-informs-rajya-sabha/articleshow/55457903.cms

42 "Shashi Tharoor Addresses Anti-CAA Rally at Jamia". The Statesman, 13 January 2020.

43 Mamata Banerjee insulted the Speaker of the Lok Sabha when she tore off the agenda papers of the house when the speaker refused to initiate a discussion of deportation of Bangladeshi infiltrators in the state.

44 The Muslim groups included the All Bengal Minority Council, the All Bengal Minority Youth Federation, the Madrassa Students Union, the Muslim Think Tank and the All Bengal Imam Muazzin Association.

45 Rajeshwar, TV. The Hindustan Times, 1998.

46 Purohit, Devdeep. "Polarization in Bengal". The Telegraph, 25 May 2019.

47 Thakur, Joydeep. "Infiltration from Bangladesh up 5 times in TMC rule". The Hindustan Times, 23 July 2014.

48 Azad, Nayear. "BJPwants NRC in Bihar to oust Bangladeshis". Deccan Herald, 5 September 2019.

49 "Differences in Maha alliance, this time over Muslim quota". The Times of India, Mumbai, 29 February 2020. "Minister defends Congress promise of quota for backward Muslims", The Economic Times, 25 April 2014.

50 Sharma, Arun. "Refugee vs refugee turns into Kashmir vs. Jammu: Identity certificates spark protests and violence". The Indian Express, 27 December, 2016.

51 Thousands of members of the Jamat-i-Islami and Muslim League who supported the movement of Pakistan did not go to Pakistan. Nearly 72 Lakhs Muslims had migrated to Pakistan in the first phase after partition and they were mainly from Delhi, Punjab, four districts of UP and two princely states of Alwar and Bharatpur whereas Muslims of Bihar, Madhya Pradesh largely stayed back.Khalidi, O. (1998). From Torrent to Trickle: Indian Muslim Migration to Pakistan 1947—97. Islamic Studies, 37(3), 339–352. http://www.jstor.org/stable/20837002.p.320. Accessed on 18 March 2022

52 In 250 members of Popular House and Senators there is only one member from the Muslim community and that too not on the strength of the Muslim population

53 https://www.voanews.com/archive/australian-ministers-comments-sharia-law-anger-muslim-community. Accessed on

14 July 2014

54 Ibid

55 Stapleton, John. (2015). Terror in Australia: Workers' Paradise Lost, A Sense of Place Publishing, Australia.

56 "Most Australians believe in God. This is not some Christian, right wing, political push, but a fact, because Christian men and women, on Christian principles, founded this nation, and this is clearly documented. It is certainly appropriate to display it on the walls of our schools. If God offends you, then I suggest you consider another part of the world as your new home, because God is part of our culture. We will accept your beliefs, and will not question why. All we ask is that you accept ours, and live in harmony and peaceful enjoyment with us". These sentences were attributed to Julia Gillard which she refused to have spoken at all.

57 What is the Truth About the American Muslims? No date, Published by First Amendment Centre, Religious Education Freedom Project, Washington, USA. P. 8. https://www.tolerance.org/sites/default/files/2017-07/What_is_the_Truth_About_American_Muslims%281%29.pdf. Accessed on 14 July 2020

58 New estimates show U.S. Muslim population continues to grow https://www.pewresearch.org/fact-tank/2018/01/03/new-estimates-show-u-s-muslim-population-continues-to-grow/. Accessed on 14 July 2020

59 https://www.newamerica.org/in-depth/anti-muslim-activity/faq/#how-does-the-project-define-the-category-anti-muslim-actions-statements-by-elected-appointed-officials. Accessed on

18 March 2022

60 Sengupta, Sominiand Masood, Salman. "Guantánamo Comes to Define U.S. to Muslims", The New York Times, 21May, 2005. https://www.nytimes.com/2005/05/21/world/asia/guantanamo-comes-to-define-us-to-muslims.html

61 9/11s Anniversary Means 17 Years since the Guantánamo Prison Opened https://www.teenvogue.com/story/911-september-11-anniversary-17-years-since-guantanamo-bay-prison-opened. Accessed on 15 July 2020

62 The FBI investigation has pinpointed towards the Saudi Arabs diplomat but the government has refused to share the investigation with the public depicting it as state sacred as reported by The New York Times Magazine. For details See: https://www.nytimes.com/2020/01/23/magazine/9-11-saudi-arabia-fbi.html.

63 Kellner, Douglas. "The Media In and After 9/11". International Journal of Communication 1 (2007), Los Angeles. Book Review 123-142. https://ijoc.org/index.php/ijoc/article/viewFile/197/102

64 Kellner, Douglas. "The Media In and After 9/11". International Journal of Communication 1 (2007), Los Angeles. Book Review 123-142.https://ijoc.org/index.php/ijoc/article/viewFile/197/102

65 Ibid.

66 Islamophobia: Understanding Anti-Muslim Sentiment in the West https://news.gallup.com/poll/157082/islamophobia-understanding-anti-muslim-sentiment-west.aspx. Accessed on 22 July 2020

67 Pipes, Daniel. "A New Round of Anger and Humiliation: Islam After 9/11", Hoover Press : Brave DP5 HPLEBN0300 04-24-:2 10:02:47 rev1 page 41. https://www.hoover.org/sites/default/files/uploads/documents/0817939024_41.pdf. Accessed on 20 July 2020

68 Hermansen, Marcia. "The Evolution of American Muslim Responses to 9/11" in Geaves Ron, Gabriel Theodore, Hadded Yvonne and Smith Jane Idleman (2004). Islam & the West Post 9/11, Ashgate, England, p. 83-87.

69 Ibid, p. 86.

70 U.S. Muslims Concerned About Their Place in Society, but Continue to Believe in the American Dream. https://www.pewforum.org/2017/07/26/findings-from-pew-research-centers-2017-survey-of-us-muslims/. Accessed on 22 July 2020

71 Cordesman, A. H. (2016). Saudi Arabia and 9/11: Establishing the Truth Behind the Release of the 28 Pages and the "Justice Against Sponsors of Terrorism Act." Center for Strategic and International Studies (CSIS). http://www.jstor.org/stable/resrep23224. Accessed on 18 March 2022

72 Obama: Why I won't say 'Islamic terrorism' https://edition.cnn.com/2016/09/28/politics/obama-radical-islamic-terrorism-cnn-town-hall/index.html. Accessed on 22 July 2020

73 Ibid.

74 "Trump Administration on ISIS, Al Qaeda". Wilson Center, August 15, 2017. https://www.wilsoncenter.org/article/trump-administration-isis-al-qaeda. Accessed on 22 July 2020

75 Ibid.

76 Statistics show that Trump's "travel ban" was always a Muslim

ban. https://qz.com/1736809/statistics-show-that-trumps-travel-ban-was-always-a-muslim-ban/. Accessed on 22 July 2020.

77 Mallet, Victor, "Emmanuel Macron launches campaign against political Islam", The Financial Times, 19 February, 2020

78 Ibid

79 Ibid

80 https://www.ndtv.com/world-news/french-president-emmanuel-macron-says-defend-right-to-laugh-as-charlie-hebdo-attack-trial-begins-2290660.

CONCLUSION

Puritan Islam is interpreted differently by different people. What is puritan for radical elements like the Wahhabis and the Deobandis also varies as it varies for the Shias and the Ahmedias. Also, what is puritan for the Voharas may be not puritan for the Sunnis. However, the notion of Puritan Islam has been an issue of debate. It is more so because all Islamic terrorist organisations have their own notion about Puritan Islam and use these to justify violence on non-believers and also on people from Islamic faith who have not been following their ideals. The Taliban, the Lashkar-e-Taiba, the Al-Qaeda, the Boko Haram and the Hizbul Mujahideen—they all swear by the idea of Puritan Islam to justify killings. Needless to say, the phrase 'Puritan Islam' has become an intimidating doctrine. When the Taliban banned music,[1] films, mobiles and asked Muslims not to shave their beards in Afghanistan, in the areas under its control, it justified the directives in the name of true Islam. Further, when the Taliban destroyed the famous statue of Lord Buddha at Bamiyan in Afghanistan, it was largely depicted as a case of 'Islamic Iconoclasm'[2] and 'cultural terrorism.'[3] There were many in the Muslim world who did not approve of this and called it un-Islamic. When the criticism from all quarters of the world gathered momentum, the Taliban first advanced an egalitarian argument that it retaliated and raged against the European apathy and insensitivity which offered money to protect the old statute but gave scant attention to the Afghani children who were suffering from malnutrition.[4] Initial defence of the Taliban, however, was different and had justified vandalism on the ground that iconoclasm is very much in consonance with the tenets and spirit of Islam. This was in alignment with the common perception of Muslims towards idolatry. Further, the Taliban must have in mind what the Prophet and his disciples did after the victory on Mecca when they destroyed nearly 360 temples of the different pagans around the places in a day. And this was done on instruction of the Prophet. This has also reflected in the holy Quran where idolatry has been despised and reviled.[5]

The actions that got sanctions by the Prophet during his lifetime, and during the time of the four righteous Caliphates after him, messages from the holy Quran, Hadith and Sharia are the ideals that every follower of Islam swears by. When Islamic organisations talk of Puritan Islam, they refer to the Islam that was practiced during the times of the Prophet and the first four Caliphates after him. Iconoclasm which reflects the embodiment of a cult of intolerance and hatred towards the religion and culture of 'the other' thus became the integral and guiding philosophy of Islamic conquests world over. Muslim emperors and rulers practised iconoclasm without remorse wherever they went. One does not need to go too far to see it. India became the classic case of victim of iconoclasm and the religious Islamic adventurism and expansionism. Muslim commanders who invaded India demolished and destroyed temples, smashed idols of Gods and Goddesses whichever roads or streets they passed through. Islamic emperors and rulers who ruled India for centuries continued with this cult of cultural terrorism which subsequently resulted into a permanent conflict between Hindus and Muslims over identity, heritage and history.

There have been several schools of Islam but the three schools that nurtured the most violent and intolerant cults in the last three centuries are the Wahhabis, the Deobandis and the Tablighis. Interestingly, all three of these schools talk about promoting true and puritan Islam. A careful reading of the interpretation of Islam by these schools suggest that Islam essentially is as an exclusivist doctrine which divides entire humanity between believers and non-believers. Believers are those who believe in Allah, Mohammad to be the last Prophet, the last judgement day and commit to theological texts like the Quran, the Hadith and the Sharia. For them, those who do not believe in Islam or do not practice true Islam are Kafirs, and the later deserve punishment. The great Allah is not going to shower mercy on them at all.

These interpretations are not out of context and have full backing of theological sanction. They are ingrained in the religious doctrine itself which finds finest manifestations in the Holy Quran. As per the text, Allah will punish them essentially but the believers also have duty to do so. Believers should not befriend them as that would displease Allah. Waging a war against the Kafirs i.e., Jehad, is their religious duty. Though, religious leaders in Islam reject the interpretations of Jehad the way it is done by the extremists, the most talked about and practiced form of Jehad is the war against enemies of Islam till the whole world is Islamised.[6] The enemies of Islam are all those who do not believe in Islam.

The Wahhabis make a distinction between Dar-ul-Harab, Dar-ul-Islam and Dar-ul-Aman. This needs to be recorded that these terms are not the terms from the Quran or the Hadith. They are post Prophet and post Quranic injunctions largely attributed to imperial growth of Islam where it engaged into battles with non-Islamic regimes. The Dar-ul- Islam is the land of Islam where there is Islamic government and the boundary of the State has common frontiers with some Muslim countries. It is possible where Islam is a predominant numerical majority. The Dar-ul-Harab is the land which is not governed by Islam and, therefore, it is the land of war where Muslims are duty bound wage war against non-Muslims. This is Jihad whose purpose is to turn such land into the land of Islam. Practically, this is possible only when the numerical dominance of Islam gets established. Conversion and increased birth rate are used as tools to achieve this. In a country like India, illegal migration from Islamic countries is being used as a tool to shore up the numbers. Dar-ul-Harab has been enlarged to include those areas that were once under the control of Islam but has been lost to the Western powers and influence. Dar-ul-Aman is the land where Islam is not the governing principles but where followers of Islam can peacefully practice their religion, build their mosques and so on. Needless to say, Wahhabism treats other religions and their followers with a sense of contempt and its ultimate objective is to establish the rule of Islam all over the world.

The Deoband school also seeks to establish and propagate a puritan Islam which was in practice during the times of the Prophet. The Deoband Islam initially began a dialogue with other religionists in India but subsequently got influenced by the Salafi or Wahabi school and the interpretation of Islam by Shah Waliullah who considered Hindus as Kafirs. The Deoband School in Pakistan has never come out to condemn terrorism. Instead, most of the dreaded terrorists from Mullah Umar to Hafiz Sayeed have been products of the Deobandi Madrasas on both sides of the Durand lines. In India, the Deoband school condemns terrorism publicly but it is also true that several terrorists have been arrested from the seminaries of India's Deoband by the security forces.[7] The Tablighis are no way different from the Deobandis. In fact, they want Muslims to practice Islam the way it was practised during the times of the Prophet. Any deviation or dilution is sin for them. And, therefore, they claim to work towards bringing Muslims on roads to true Islam.

This ideology of true and puritan Islam thus becomes the fodder for Islamic terrorist organisations. From the Al-Qaeda, the Boko Haram and the Taliban to the ISIS; they all want to establish the rule of puritan Islam. This can be achieved only when Islamic society and Islamic state is established through Global Jihad. This will help spread Islam and establish a Global Islamic state. These terrorist organisations conclude that global Islam is possible only if Islamic countries practice true or Puritan Islam and emerge as bases from where the mission could be taken to the other parts of the world till the whole world embraces the religion. Obviously, it is not possible all of a sudden, particularly in a country where the followers of Islam are numerically weak or the military base of the Islamic state is not powerful enough to inflict military defeat on the enemy country and force them to adopt Islam. In such a scenario, they have to wait till the right opportunity comes. Till the time they should treat the land as Dar-ul-Sulah. Dar-ul-Sulah is survival strategy for Muslims. It argues that the Muslims should remain peaceful where they cannot force their ideology and religion upon 'others' through fight and assertion. Islamic radicals in India declare it to be Dar-ul-Harab and they aspire to convert Hindustan into an Islamic land. Organisations such as the Students Islamic Movements of India (SIMI) which has been banned openly declared India to be a land of war and expressed its desire to convert the country into an Islamic society.[8] However, in countries like Australia and America where Islam is an insignificant minority they have chosen to adjust with the indigenous cultures and project themselves as a tolerant community. This tolerance is an outcome of necessity since the State is tough and demands absolute loyalty to constitution and culture of the land.

For these terrorist organisations trying to impose puritan Islam, the rulers of Muslim dominated states have lost the paths of the Prophet and turned themselves as apostates and heretics who collaborate with anti-Islamic forces. And, therefore, they need to be overthrown. Since the elements of apostasy has been significantly compounded by the intervention, occupation and exploitation of Muslim lands by the West, particularly the United States of America, they should be treated as enemies of Islam. Force and violence can be used to evict them from Muslim lands. That is why these terrorist organisations target the US and the West in different parts of the world—from Syria to Lebanon and from Afghanistan to Iraq. Thus, they justify all their terror acts on the ground that they are doing all these for sake of restoring the power of Islam which has lost its might and ancient glory. In pursuit of accomplishing these objectives, these organisations have no hesitation in forcing others to accept Islam or inflicting death on refusal to convert to Islam. No one can question the Quran or the Prophet in the land of Islam. Those who dare gets punished.

Fanaticism is not a result of an individual's motivated interpretation of Islam. This is outcome of the core principles stated in the holy Quran in the most unambiguous terms. Violence against the unbelievers is a mandate of the text. Not befriending the unbelievers is a mandate of the religion. And so is to kill and maim them if they are unwillingness to embrace

Islam. Verses are splattered to communicate this, including converting the unbelievers into Islam. Since they are believed to be the divine message from God through the Prophet, Muslims do not dare to question them and reason with them. This leads to creation of rigid closed walls all around in which there is no scope for the fresh air to enter into its ideological and theological space. For the Prophet, the religions that their forefathers and their predecessors practised were the false religion and that is why he commanded them to destroy their deities and temples. And this is what prevents Muslims from respecting other faith systems and their Prophets. This prepares a battleline between Islam and other religions.

In this regard, the Presidential speech of Mohammad Ali Jinnah at the annual session of the All-India Muslim League held in 1940 is worth noting. It is well known to every reader of Indian history that Jinnah was not very fond of Islam and Islamic morality. However, he used it to galvanize Muslims for Pakistan. What he said during this course of journey is interesting. Jinnah said that he too wanted to have a cordial Hindu-Muslim unity but he could not go for it because he was not above the tenets of The Quran and The Hadis.[9] Jinnah stressed that these Islalimc texts do not advocate cordial relationships with the Kafirs and idolaters. Jinnah went further to say that he had read the Quran and the Hadis in depth and discussed the matter with Hakim Azmal Khan and then reached the conclusion that the tenets of Islam did not permit it.

Jinnah was not out of place in interpreting Islam. It looks very medieval, irrational and illogical in modern times but

Islam makes it conditional for a Muslim boy or a girl to marry a girl or boy belonging to other faiths only after they have converted to Islam. This is not the Islam of the Mullah and Maulavis but it is the mandate of the Quran which explicitly says so. There are millions of such examples in India giving rise rise to the controversy of 'Love Jehad'. For common Muslims, it is just a mandate of the Quran, but for the preachers and leaders of other faiths, this is also intended to increase the numerical strength of Muslims. It becomes far more perplexing for a civilization like India which never practised religious imperialism and religious homogenization supported by the state power guided by religious texts. Modern civilization, that accords so much importance to reason, rationality, human rights and individual dignity that it stands diametrically opposed to the fundamentals of Islam.

It appears from religious preachings and practises that Islam and its followers have failed to engage with modernity, science and reason. When juxtaposed with each other, they find a big gap between the theology and the reality making it difficult to make a choice between the two. Christianity too was violent at some point of its evolution and history and Christian nations had launched crusades to achieve expansion and growth. It too resorted to Iconoclasm. It too abhorred science and had sent Galileo to prison for heliocentrism that advocated that the Earth moved around the Sun. The process of Renaissance, Industrialization, Modernity and the onset of Scientism made Christianity engage with science and reason. But the same cannot be said for Islam. Such challenges come to all religions but what is specific and more pronounced with Islam is that it responds to such challenges with violence. Instead of developing arguments and reasons, it shrinks in its shell of theological position because unlike philosophical foundations of Hinduism which propounds its stand on the basis of experiential wisdom, Islam relies on the divine postulations. It is not ready to accept the challenge that comes from science and modernity, and that makes it violent and intolerant.

Further, Islam holds a relatively fix politico-religious world view which makes it closer to the political left. Every ideology that claims to have a revealed and absolute wisdom seeks to govern the entire span of its activities ranging from social to cultural aspects by the same wisdom. Islam, as Maududi argues, is also a complete package as it governs all aspects of Muslims' life. It is not about picking one and negating the others. Since Islam is not an evolved religion but a divine message transmitted through the Prophet by the messenger of the Allah, it produces a rigid Muslim mindset who dares not to go out of the Islamic cultural and religious contours. They refuse to accept and respect the prophets and deities of other religions. It is not just limited to accepting Gods and Goddesses of other religions but seek to imbibe the cultural artefacts of Arabs just because it happens to be land of birth of Islam. They copycat the styles of dresses to names and other components which distinguish their identity not just religiously but culturally also. No wonder, the use of Burqa (veil) among the Muslim women has increased world over, even in the most liberal societies of the West. Hijab has become a point of controversy in India as never before. Arabic attires and style of beard and use of skull cap is on the rise among Muslim men. This brings them in conflict with the predominant majority, as it not just seeks to consolidate its distinct identity in all walks of life but also works towards asserting itself with time.

The ideology of puritan Islam derives strength from an ideology and practices of the medieval age when the new faith as religious and political ideology expanded under the leadership of the Prophet, the founder of Islam, and the first four Caliphates who followed him. These were the most violent times when Islam trampled a vast geographical expanse of Asia and Africa and established Islamic rule wherever they went. It was the time when the Quran came into existence and outrightly rejected them as fake and false. The Prophet made this declaration after the victory of Mecca. Islam declared itself as the only true and divine religion and justified violence and war on infidels as the mandate of the Allah. It was again the time when the Hadith and the Sharia came into existence which presented how true Muslims should conduct themselves. This came to govern the entire range of social, cultural and political life of Muslims. Appeal to Muslims to return to the state of puritan Islam means inciting Muslims, and insisting on them to follow the footprints of the Caliphates who inflicted Jihad to Islamise the entire world. This premise is the root cause behind hostility of Muslims against other religions. It is precisely the reason that Muslim community all over world is at quarrel with followers of other faiths. Its brotherhood, as Dr BR Ambedkar argues, is limited to the Muslims only.[10] It is hostility towards other faiths that made Swami Vivekanand and Rabindranath Tagore to conclude that Islam considers other faiths as its enemies. This hostility poses a threat to co-existence, to democracy and to multi-culturalism. The appeal and insistence by Islamic clerics to Muslims to follow the premises of puritan Islam has unleashed the rise of a new Islamic consciousness which seeks to form and assert its identity parallel, distinct and subsequently in opposition to other communities. The Halal certified goods are far more in demand today than ever before, and more and more Muslim girls and women are wearing Hijabs and Burqas. This phenomenon is on the rise even in the West which hitherto had not seen such dresses on roads and streets. The puritan Islam thus constitute a threat to the World. No wonder, this phrase is so dear to terrorist and radical Islamic organisations.

References:

1 Shiloah, A. (1997). Music and Religion in Islam. Acta Musicologica, 69(2). 143-155. doi:10.2307/932653. Accessed on 9 December, 2020.

2 Flood, F. (2002). Between Cult and Culture: Bamiyan, Islamic Iconoclasm, and the Museum. The Art Bulletin, 84(4), 641-659. doi:10.2307/3177288, p. 641.

3 Jankowski, J. (2011). Bringing Back Bamiyan's Buddhas. Journal of Applied Philosophy, 28(1), 44-64. Retrieved December 9, 2020, from http://www.jstor.org/stable/24356140.

4 Crossette, Barbara, Taliban Explains Buddha Demolitions, The New York Times, 19 March, 2001. https://www.nytimes.com/2001/03/19/world/taliban-explains-buddha-demolition.html.

5 The Quran has criticised Idolatry and suggested actions against the Idolaters.

6 Aaron, D. (Ed.). (2008). Seeds of Jihad. In In Their Own Words: Voices of Jihad- Compilation and Commentary (pp. 37–72). RAND Corporation. http://www.jstor.org/stable/10.7249/mg602rc.8. Also See; Mamdani, M. (2005). Whither Political Islam? Understanding the Modern Jihad [Review of The War for Muslim Minds: Islam and the West;

Globalized Islam: The Search for a New Ummah, by G. Kepel & O. Roy]. Foreign Affairs, 84(1), 148–155. https://doi.org/10.2307/20034214.

7 "UP police bust terror module in Deoband, ATS arrests 2 suspected Jaish operatives". The Hindustan Times, New Delhi, 22 February 2019.

8 https://www.satp.org/terrorist-profile/india/students-islamic-movement-of-india-or-indian-mujahideen. Accessed on 22 February 2022.

9 http://www.columbia.edu/itc/mealac/pritchett/00islamlinks/txt_jinnah_lahore_1940.html. Accessed on 22 February, 2022.

ANNEXURES

■ **COLOUR DENOTES:**

Countries where Active Terrorist Organisations exist

NUMBERS DENOTE:

1 - Luxemburg
2 - Bosnia and Herzegovina
3 - Montenegro
4 - Albania
5 - Macedonia (FYROM)
6 - Moldova
7 - Cyprus
8 - Lebanon
9 - Israel
10 - Kuwait
11 - United Arab Emirates
12 - Djibouti
13 - Gambia
14 - Guinea-Bissau
15 - Sierra Leone
16 - Togo
17 - Equatorial Guinea
18 - Cabinda (Angola)
19 - Rwanda
20 - Burundi
21 - Malawi
22 - Swaziland
23 - Lesoto
24 - Armenia
25 - Bhutan
26 - Bangladesh
27 - Cambodia
28 - Singapore
29 - Brunei
30 - Belize
31 - Honduras
32 - El Salvador
33 - Costa Rica
34 - Suriname
35 - French Guiana

ANNEXURE I

Name of the Country	Religious Demography	Islamic schoolsof Jurisprudence	Terrorist Organisations	Political parties that support Islamic Extremism
Afghanistan	Sunni- 85% Shia – 15%	Hanafi school	Taliban Haqqani Network (HON) Al-Qaeda in the Indian subcontinent (AQIS) Islamic state of Iraqand Syria (ISIS)	Jamiat-e Islami National IslamicFront Hezb-e- Islam Hizb ut- Tahrir Harakat-e-Islami-yi Islamic Dawah Organisation of Afghanistan
Albania	Muslim-58.79% (Majority-Sunni) Christian-16.8%	Maliki school	ISIS Nusra Front (JabhatFateh al-Sham) Al- Qaeda Albanian National Army (ANA)	Justice and Development Party
Algeria	Sunni-96% Ibadis- 1.3% Christen- 1%	Maliki school	Ansar al- Sharia (Algeria) Al- Qaeda in the Islamic Maghreb (AQIM) Al- Mourabitoun Jund al- Khilafah and ISIS	Green AlgeriaFront Harakat-al-Nahda al- Islamiyya (Islamic Renaissance Movement) Harakat Mujtama al-Salim (Hamas) Al- Jabha al Islamiyya li'l- Inqadh (Islamic Salvation Front) Harkat al- Islah al-Watani (Movementfor National Reform)

Azerbaijan	Shia- 85% Sunni- 15%	Ithna Ashair school of Shia Islam	Wahhabists Al- Qaeda Jeyshullah Azerbaijani Jamaat Tovba (Repentance)	Islamic Party of Azerbaijan
Bahrain	Shia- 62% Sunni- 38%	Ja'fari school	Al- Ashtar Brigades	Al Asalah Islamic ActionParty Al Wefaq Jamiyya al- Asala al- Islamiyya (Original Islamic Society)
Bangladesh	Muslim- 90.3% (Majority-Sunni) Hindu- 8.5%	Hanafi school	Harkat-ul-Jihad-al-Islami Bangladesh (HuJI-B) Jagrata Muslim Janata Bangladesh (JMJB) Jamaat-ul-Mujahideen Bangladesh (JMB) Jamaat-e-Islami Bangladesh Purba Bangla Communist Party (PBCB)	Islamic Front Bangladesh Bangladesh Jamaat-e-Islami Purba Bangla Communist Party (PBCB) Islami Oikkya Jote (Islamic Unity Front) Muslim League and Islamic Democratic League
Burkina Faso	Muslim- 60.5% (Majority-Sunni) Christen-23.2%	Maliki school	Jamaat Nusrat al- Islam wal Muslimeen(JNIM) Al- Qaeda in the Islamic Maghreb (AQIM)	----

Chad	Muslim- 58.1% (Sunni- 48% Shia- 21% Ahmadi- 4%) Protestant Christian- 23.5% Catholic Christian- 22.3%	Maliki school	Boko Haram Islamic State in WestAfrica (ISWA) Al- Qaeda in the Islamic Maghreb (AQIM) Islamic State in Greater Sahara (ISGS) Jamaat Nusrat al- Islam wal-Muslimeen(JNIM) Ansar Dine Al- Murabitoun	----
Comoros	Sunni- 98% Christian- 2%	Shafi'i school	Islamic State (ISIS) Al- Qaeda	National Front for Justice
Cote d'Ivoire (the Ivory Coast)	Muslims-42.9% (Majority-Sunni) Christian- 33.9%	Maliki school	Hezbollah Al- Qaeda in the Islamic Maghreb (AQIM) Jamaat Nusrat al- Islam wal-Muslimeen(JNIM) Ansar al- Dine (AAD)	Democratic Party of Cote d' Ivoire
Djibouti	Sunni- 94% Christian- 4.7% Others- 1.2%	Shafi'i school	Al- Shabaab	----
Egypt	Sunni- 90% Christian- 10%	Maliki school	Daesh- Sinai Ansar Bayt al-Maqdis Muslim Brotherhood Hamas Al- Qaeda ISIS- Wilayat Sinai(Sinai Province)	Muslim Brotherhood andFreedom and Justice party Al- Nour Party Fadila Hizb al- Amal(Labour Party) Al- Wasat Party Hizb al- Wafd al Jadid (New WafdParty)

Gambia	Muslim- 96% (majority-Sunni) Christian- 3%	Maliki school	Hezbollah Al- Qaeda in the Islamic Maghreb (AQIM) Al- Mourabitoun	Muslim Congress Party
Guinea	Muslim- 85% (majority-Sunni) Christian- 8%	Maliki school	Boko Haram Al- Qaeda Jamaat Nusrat al- Islam wal-Muslimeen(JNIM) Movement for Unityand Jihad in West Africa (MUJAO)	Rally of the Guinean People
Guinea – Bissau	Muslims- 45% (Majority-Sunni) Christian- 22%	Maliki school	Boko Haram Al- Qaeda Jamaat Nusrat al- Islam wal-Muslimeen(JNIM) Movement for Unity and Jihad in West Africa (MUJAO)	African Party for the Independenceof Guinea-Bissauand Cape Verde
Indonesia	Muslim-87.18% (Sunni- 99%) Protestants-7%Roman Catholics- 2.9% Hindu- 1.69%	Shafi'i school	Jemaah Islamiyah Darul Islam Islamic Defender'sFront Laskar Jihad ISIS affiliated JamaahAnsharut Daulah (JAD)	Prosperous Justice Party Crescent Star Party Reform Star Party National Awakening Party United Development Party National Mandate Party Indonesia Islamic Union Party

Iran	Shia -90% Sunni- 10%	Twelver and Ja'fari school of Shia Islam	Hamas Hezbollah Popular Front forLiberation of Palestine (PFLP) Islamic Revolutionary Guard Corps (IRGC) Taliban Al-Qaeda People's Mujahedinof Iran	Movement of Militant Muslim Islamic CoalitionParty Development and Justice Party Islamic Republican Party
Iraq	Shia- 65% Sunni- 37% Christians- 1%	Iraqi Kurdish Muslims follow –Shafi school	Islamic State of Iraqand Levant (ISIL) Ansar-al- Islam Jaysh Rijal al- Tariqal Naqshabandi (JRTN)	Iraqi Islamic Party Sadr Movement Islamic Dawa Party Islamic Union of Kurdistan National IraqiAlliance Islamic VirtueParty Unified IraqiAlliance
Jordan	Sunni-97.2% Christian- 2.2%	Hanafi school	Islamic State (ISIS) Al- Qaeda Hamas	Muslim Brotherhood andIslamic action Front Wasat Party Zamzam
Kazakhstan	Muslim- 70.2% (Majority- Sunni) Christian- 26.2%	Hanafi school	Al- Qaeda ISIL (Daesh)	Hizb ut- Tahrir Al Islami
Kuwait	Muslim- 86.4% (Majority- Sunni) Christian- 18- 20% Hindu- 7.57%	Hanbali school	Al- Qaeda ISIS Muslim Brotherhood Jemaah Islamiyah Lashkar e- Tayyiba Hezbollah Hamas	Kuwait's Muslim brotherhood and Islamic Constitutional Movement (Hadas) Islamic SalafiAlliance Umma Party Hadas Popular Islamic Association

Kyrgyzstan	Muslim- 88% (Sunni- 83%) Christian- 15%	Hanafi school	ISIS Hizb-ul-Tahrir Al-Qaeda	Hizb ut- Tahrir Al Islami
Lebanon	Shia- 30.6% Sunni- 30.5% Christian- 33.7% Druze- 5.2%	Twelvers Shia school	Hezbollah Al-Qaeda Al- Nusra Front Islamic State of Iraqand Levant (ISIL) Free Syrian Army People's Mujahedinof Iran	Hezbollah The Islamic Society(Jamaa al Islamiyyah) Islamic Action Front (Jabhat alamal al Islami) Al- Jamaat-al-Islamiyya
Libya	Sunni- 91% Ibadism- 6%	Maliki school	Ansar al- Sharia (Libya) Al- Qaeda in the Islamic Maghreb (AQIM) Islamic State of Iraqand ash-sham (ISIS) Majlis Shura Shababal- Islami Abu Salim MartyrsBrigade (ASMB)	Muslim Brotherhood andLibyan Islamic Group Libyan Islamic movement for change Justice and Construction Party Homeland Party
Malaysia	Sunni- 99.8%	Shafi'i school	Malaysian JemaahIslamiyah Al- Qaeda Kumpulan Militant Malaysia (KMM)	Malaysian Islamic Party Islamic Party of Malaysia – Alternate Front
Maldives	Muslim- 98.4%(Majority Sunni)		Al- Qaeda ISIS	Adhaalath Party Islamic Democratic Party

Mali	Muslim- 95% (Majority- Sunni) Traditional African religions- 3% Christian- 2%	Maliki school	Al- Qaeda in the Islamic Maghreb (AQIM) Islamic State in Greater Sahara and Islamic State in WestAfrica Jama'at Nusrat al- Islam wal- Muslimin(JNIM) Ansar al- Dine (AAD)(Defenders of the Faith) Movement for Unityand Jihad in West Africa (MUJAO) Al- Mourabitoun	Rally for Democracy andProgress
Mauritania	Sunni- 100%	Maliki school	Al- Qaeda in the Islamic Maghreb (AQIM)	National Rally forReform and Development Republican Party for Democracy and Renewal
Morocco	Muslim- 93% (Majority- Sunni) Christian- 1%	Maliki school	Moroccan Islamic Combatant Group Al- Qaeda in the Islamic Maghreb (AQIM) Daesh	Justice and Development Party Party of Renaissance andVirtue
Niger	Muslim- 99% (Majority- Sunni) Traditional African religions- 1%	Maliki school	Boko Haram Islamic State of Iraqand Levant (ISIL) Islamic State in WestAfrica (ISWA) Islamic State in Greater Sahara (ISGS) Jamaat Nusrat al- Islam wal Muslimeen(JNIM) Al- Murabitoun Ansar Dine Al- Qaeda in the Islamic Maghreb (AQIM)	National Movement for theDevelopment of Society

Nigeria	Muslim- 53.5% (Majority-Sunni) Christian- 45.9%	Maliki school	Islamic State in WestAfrica (ISWA) Boko Haram Jamaat al Ansar al Muslimina fi Bilad alSudan (Ansaru)	All Nigeria People's Party
Oman	Muslims-85.9% Christian- 6.5% Hindu-5.5%	Ibadi school	Lebanese Hezbollah	--- Absolute Monarchy---
Pakistan	Muslims – 96.28% (Sunni Muslims- 75- 95% Shia Muslims- 5-15%) Hindu- 1.8% Christian- 1.5%	Hanafi Fiqh Sunnischool and Shia Muslims belong toTwelver Islamic school	Al- Qaeda Lashkar-e- Omar Lashkar-e- Taiba (LeT) Jamaat-ud- Dawa (JuD) Jaish-e-Mohammed(JeM) Harkat Ul Mujahideen ISIS- KP (Khorasan Province) Tehreek-e-Taliban (TTP) Sipah-e-Sahaba Pakistan (SSP) Hizb-ul-Mujahideen(HM) Al- Badr Jamait-ul-Mujahideen(JuM) Muslim Mujahideen Islami Inquilabi Mahaz Tehrik-e- Jehad Jammu and KashmirNational Liberation Army Kashmir Jehad Force Islami Jamaat-e-Tulba Al- Jehad Mahez-e-Azadi	Jamaat-e-Islami Pakistan (Islamic Society) Jamiat Ahle Hadith Tehreek-e- Labbaik Pakistan Jamiat-e- Ulema-i-Islam Muttahida Majlis-e-Amal (United Action Council) Tehrik-e- Jafaria Markazi Jamiat-e-Ulema-e- Pakistan Muslim League Islami Jamhoori Ittehad (Islamic Democratic Alliance) Pakistan IslamicFront Mutahida Deeni Mahaz (United Religious Front)

Palestine	Sunni- 86% Jews- 13%	Shafi school	Hamas Palestine Islamic Jihad (PIJ) Palestinian Liberation Front (PLF) Popular Front for the Liberation of Palestine (PFLP) Fatah Al- Qaeda Democratic Front for the Liberation of Palestine (DFLP)	Harakat al-Muqawama al-Islamiyya (Hamas) (Islamic Resistance Movement)
Qatar	Muslims-67.7% (Sunni-90%) Christians-13.8% Hindus- 13.8% Buddhists-3.1%	Hanbali school in Salafi version	Al- Qaeda Jabhat Al- Nusra ISIL Hamas	---Absolute Monarchy----
Saudi Arabia	Sunni- 75-85% Shia- 10-15%	Hanbali school in Salafi version	Daesh (ISIL) Al- Qaeda Taliban	---Absolute Monarchy----
Senegal	Muslim- 95% (Majority-Sunni) Christian- 4%	Maliki school	Jamaat Nusrat al- Islam wal Muslimeen (JNIM) Islamic State in West Africa (ISWA) Boko Haram Al- Qaeda in the Islamic Maghreb (AQIM)	Senegal's Jamaatou Ibadou Rahmane(JIR)

Sierra Leone	Sunni – 78% Ahmadiyya Islam – 10%	Maliki school	Al- Qaeda in the Islamic Maghreb (AQIM)	Sierra Leone's People Party(SLPP) Citizen's Democratic Party
Somalia	Sunni – 90%	Shafi'i school	Al- Shabaab Islamic State of Iraq and ash-Sham (ISIS)	Muslim Brotherhood Peace and Development Party Wadajir Party Somali Revolutionary Socialist Party
Sudan	Sunni – 97%	Maliki school	Hamas Lebanese Hezbollah Palestine Islamic Jihad ISIS	Al- Jabha al- Islamiyya al-Qaumiiyya (National Islamic Front) Hizb al Umma, Janub (Nation Party, South) Hizb al Umma, Imam (Nation Party, Imam) Hizb al Umma, Sadiq (Nation Party, Sadiq) Hizb al Umma al Jadid (New Nation Party) Al- Ikhwan al-Muslimum (Muslim Brotherhood)
Syria	Sunni- 74% Shia- 13%	Shafi'i Madhhab Sunni school and Alawites (offshoot of Shia Islam)	Islamic State (ISIS) Al- Nusra Front Hezbollah Jaish-al- Islam Filaq al- Rahman Free Syrian Army (FSA) Syria Democratic Forces (SDF) and Kurdish Forces	Muslim Brotherhood Movement for Justice and Development(Harakat al Adala wal Bina) Syrian National Movement (Tayyar al Watani al Suri) Kurdistan Democratic Party of Syria Hizb ut-Tahrir

Tajikistan	Muslim- 98% (Majority- Sunni)	Maliki school	Al- Qaeda in the Islamic Maghreb (AQIM) Ansar al- Sharia (Tunisia) Al- Qaeda in the Islamic Maghreb (AQIM)	Al-nahda or Renaissance Party Justice and Development Party Reform Front Party(El Isla)
Turkey	Sunni- 81.5% Alevism- 10.6% Ja'fari Shia- 3.9% Alawis- 1%	Hanafi school	Kurdistan Workers Party (PKK) ISIS Kurdistan Freedom Falcons (TAK) Kurdish Hezbollah Al- Qaeda Hamas Muslim Brotherhood Fethullah Terrorist Organisation Revolutionary People's Liberation Party (DHKP)	Justice and Development Party (AKP) Felicity Party Muslim Botherhood Free Cause Party Rights and Freedoms Party Great Union Party Virtue Party Welfare Party National Salvation Party
Turkmenistan	Muslim- 93.1% (Majority- Sunni) Christian- 6%	Hanafi school	Al- Qaeda ISIS	Turkistan Islamic Party
United Arab Emirates	Muslim- 72% (majority- Sunni) Christian- 12.6% Hindu- 6.6% Buddhism- 2%	Maliki school	Al- Qaeda Lashkar e- Taiba Haqqani Network Taliban Houthis Hezbolllah	Al-Islah and Muslim brotherhood

Uzbekistan	Muslim- 88% (majority- Sunni) Eastern Orthodox- 9%	Hanafi school	Islamic Jihad Union Taliban Tochikistoni Ozod (Free Tajikistan) Al- Qaeda Islamic Movement of Uzbekistan Hizb ut- Taḥrir East Turkestan Islamic Movement	Islamic movement of Uzbekistan
Yemen	Sunni- 53% Shia- 45%	Shafi'i Sunni school and Zaydi Shia school	Al-Qaeda in the Arabian Peninsula Islamic State in Yemen Houthi Rebel group	Tajammu al- Yamini li'l- Islah (Yemini Association for Reform)

ANNEXURE II

World's Most Dominant and Lethal Terrorist Organisations

According to the Global Terrorism Index 2019, Afghanistan becomes the most impacted country by terrorism replacing Iraq, which held that position since 2004.

The four terrorist groups responsible for most of the deaths in 2018 are:

- Taliban
- Islamic State of Iraq and Levant (ISIL)
- The Khorasan Chapter of the Islamic State
- Boko Haram

Taliban

Taliban is a Sunni Islamic fundamentalist organisation in Afghanistan. The Taliban emerged in Afghanistan in 1994 as a reactionary group that combined the Mujahideen that had previously fought against the 1979 Soviet Invasions, and groups of Pashtun Tribesmen. The Taliban wants to turn Afghanistan into what they believe would be the world's purest Islamiccountry.

ISIL (Islamic state of Iraq and Levant)

ISISL's origins trace back to local militant outfits in Iraq in the early 2000s, its most immediate predecessor being the Islamic State in Iraq (ISI). ISIL emerged in 2014 when emir Abu Bakr al-Baghdadi declared Islamic Caliphate in parts of Iraq and Syria. ISIL (Islamic state of Iraq and Levant) is a Sunni Jihadist group with a violent Ideology. IS is working in Middle East and adheres to global Jihadist principles and follows the ideology of Al-Qaeda and other such Jihadist groups related to Wahhabism.

The Khorasan Chapter of the Islamic State

The Khorasan Chapter of the Islamic State is an affiliate of the Islamic State of Iraq and the Levant (ISIL) active in Afghanistan, Pakistan and India. As an ISIL affiliate, the Khorasan Chapter seeks to establish a Caliphate in the Khorasan region, covering parts of Iran, CentralAsia, Afghanistan and Pakistan. Emerging in 2014, the Khorasan Chapter is comprised of local militants including members of Tehrik-i-Taliban Pakistan (TTP) and estrangedmembers of Lashkar-e-Islam.

Boko haram

Boko Haram is a jihadist terrorist organisation founded in North Eastern Nigeria. The organisation was intended to uproot injustice in Nigeria, which it blamed on western influences, and to impose Islamic law or shariah. Therefore Boko Haram is against westernisation, which it views as negatively impacting Islamic values. Boko Haram demographic profile is unique among the terrorist groups in its unusually high proportions of women and children.

Other Dominant Terrorist Organisations in the world

Lashkar-e-Taiba – it is one of the largest and most active terrorist organisation operating mainly in Pakistan. It is a militant group influenced by the Wahhabi sect of Sunni Islam. Itsaim is to establish Muslim rule over the entire Indian subcontinent. It is one of the largest groups operating in Jammu and Kashmir and took part in several attacks targeting non- muslim populations in an effort to create a Muslim state.

Hezbollah is a Shia-Islamist political party and militant group based in Lebanon, this organisation has also a jihadi wing. In 1982 Shia Muslims formed Hezbollah with the goal ofdriving out Israel from Lebanon and establishing Islamic republic.

Hamas – It is a militant Islamic Palestinian nationalist organisation in the west bank and Gaza strip. Hamas is dedicated for the establishment of an independent Islamic state in Palestinian.

Al-Nusra front – it is also known as Al-qaeda in Syria or Al-qaeda in the Levant. It is a Salafist jihadist organisation fighting against the Syrian government. Its aim is to establish anIslamic state in the country.

Al-shabaab – it is a terrorist, jihadist fundamentalist organisation based in east Africa. The organisation describes itself as waging jihad against "enemies of Islam".

The above description manifests that extreme religious interpretation of the Quran and the movement for Islamic revivalism has led to emergence and progression of Violent Jihad incontemporary times. Muslims are the most supportive of terrorist attacks in the name of Islam. The complex interplay between religious understandings and geopolitical events influence Islamic violence and terrorism which poses a serious threat to human lives.

BIBLIOGRAPHY

JOURNALS

1 Ahmad, A. (1979). Conversions to Islam in the valley of Kashmir, Central *Asiatic Journal*, 23(1/2), pp. 3-18.

2 Alexiev, A. "Tablighi Jamaat: Jihad's Stealthy Legions," *Middle East Quarterly*, Vol 12, No.1. Winter 2005, pp. 1-3.

3 Ann B. and Kerrie S.: "Good and Bad Shariah; Australia's Mixed Response to Islamic Law." *UNSW Law Journal Volume* 34(1), p.385.

4 Behuria, A. K. (2008). Sects within Sect: The Case of Deobandi Barelvi Encounter in Pakistan, Vol 32, Issue 1, *IDSA*, New Delhi, pp.57-58.

5 Black, A. (2010). Legal recognition of Sharia law: Is this the right direction for Australian family matters? *Family Matters*, 84, 64-67.

6 Burki Khan, S. "The Tablighi Jamaat: Proselytizing Missionaries or Trojan Horse?" *Journal of Applied Security Research*, Volume 8, 2013 - Issue 1, Taylor and Francis Online pp. 98-117.

7 Choksy, C., & Choksy, J. (2015). "The Saudi Connection: Wahhabism and Global Jihad," *World Affairs*, 178(1), 23-34.

8 Elias, J. (2007). "(Un) making Idolatry: From Mecca to Bamiyan." *Future Anterior: Journal of Historic Preservation, History, Theory, and Criticism*, 4(2), 12-29.

9 Fair, C. (2010). Students Islamic Movement of India and the Indian Mujahideen: An Assessment. *Asia Policy*, (9), 101-120.

10 Ganji, A. (2013). "Who Is Ali Khamenei? The Worldview of Iran's Supreme Leader. Foreign Affairs," 92(5), 24–48.

11 Kane, J. R. (2018). A Life Cycle Analysis of Hezbollah: Where the Group Came from and Where It Is Going. American Intelligence Journal, 35(2), 67–73.

12 Kovacs, A. "Saudi Arabia Exporting Salafi Education and Radicalizing Indonesia's Muslims," *German Institute of Global and Area Studies (GIGA) Focus,* Vol.7. 2014, p.*8.*

13 Kumar, V. (2003). Minorities Right to Run Educational Institutions: TMA Pai Foundations in Perspective. *Journal of the Indian Law Institute, 45*(2), pp.200-238.

14 Lia, B. (2008). "Al-Qaida's Appeal: Understanding its Unique Selling Points," *Perspectives on Terrorism*, 2(8).

15 Maliach, A. "Bin Laden, Palestine and al-Qa'ida's Operational Strategy." Middle Eastern Studies, Vol. 44, No. 3 (May, 2008), Taylor & Francis, Ltd. pp. 353-375.

16 Mamdani, M. (2002). Good Muslim, Bad Muslim: A Political Perspective on Culture and Terrorism. American Anthropologist, 104(3), 766-775.

17 Metcalf, B. (2003). Travelers' Tales in the Tablighi Jamat. *The Annals of the American Academy of Political and Social Science,*

588, 136-148.

18 Mukhopadhyay, A. R. "Tabligh-e-Jamaat Under the Scanner of German Intelligence." *Strategic Analysis,* 29(2), Manohar Parrikar Institute for Defence Studies and Analyses, New Delhi.

19 Nisa, E. (2014). Insights Into the Lives of Indonesian Female Tablighi Jamaat. *Modern Asian Studies*, 48(2), 468-491.

20 Rahman, T. "Jihad as Anti- Colonial Resistance in India: 1831-1920s." *Pakistan Journal of Historical Studies*, no. 2 (2018): 1–42.

21 Rana Muhammad, A. "Tablighi Jamaat: Discourse and Challenges," *Conflict and Peace Studies*, April-June 2009, 2(2), Pakistan Institute of Peace Studies, p. 79.

22 Ragi, S. (2013). Price of the IMDT Act : Migrants and Ethnic Politics in Assam. *The Indian Journal of Political Science, 74*(3), 545-556.

23 Reetz D., "Dār al-'Ulūm Deoband and its Mediatic Self-Representation," *Islamic Studies,* 44(2), 209-227.

24 Şencan, Irfan, & Kuzi, Semanur. (2020). "Global threat of COVID 19 and evacuation of the citizens of different countries." *Turkish journal of medical sciences*, 50(SI-1), 534–543.

25 Sikand, Y. (2008). "Reflections on Deoband's Anti- Terrorism Convention," *Economic and Political Weekly*, 43(12/13), 13-15

26 Sookhdeo, P. (2006). "Issues of Interpreting the Koran and Hadith." *Connections, 5*(3), 57-82.

27 Stewart, A. (2018). "Tabligh Jamaat in China: Sacred self, worldly nation, transnational imaginary," Cambridge

University Press. *Modern Asian Studies*, 52(4), pp. 1194-1226.

28 Tamney, J. (2004). "American Views of Islam," Post 9/11. *Islamic Studies*, 43(4), pp. 599–630.

29 Taylor, J. "Understanding and Engaging with the Tablighi Jamaat," *Lausanne Global Analysis*, 4(6) November 2015.

30 Templin, J. D. (2015). Religious Education of Pakistan's Deobandi Madaris and Radicalisation. *Counter Terrorist Trends and Analyses*, 7(5), 15–21.

31 Singh, U. K. (2004). "Repeal of POTA: What about Other Draconian Acts?" *Economic and Political Weekly*, 39(33), 3677-3680. Retrieved December 8, 2020.

32 Zaman, M. (1999). Religious Education and the Rhetoric of Reform: The Madrasa in British India and Pakistan. *Comparative Studies in Society and History, 41*(2), 294-323.

BOOKS

1. Ahmed, A. (1964). Studies in Islamic culture in the Indian environment, Oxford: Clarendon Press.
2. Ambedkar, B. (1990). Pakistan or the Partition of India. Education Department, Govt. of Maharashtra. Dr. Babasaheb Ambedkar: Writings and Speeches (8).
3. Tayeb, A. M. (2018).*Islamic Education in Indonesia and Malaysia: Shaping Minds, Saving Souls;* Routledge.
4. Basu, S. (2002). Religious Revivalism as Nationalist Discourse: Swami Vivekananda and New Hinduism in Nineteenth-Century Bengal. Oxford University Press. New Delhi.
5. Bearman, P., Peters R. & Vogel, F. E. eds. (2005). The Islamic School of Law: Evolution, Devolution and Progress, Harvard

University Press. Cambridge.

6. Chowdhary, R. (2016). Jammu and Kashmir: Politics of Identity and Separatism. Routledge, New Delhi.
7. Doak, R. S. (2009). Empire of the Islamic World (Great Empires of the Past), Chelsea House Publications. New York.
8. Durant, W. (2014). The Complete story of Civilization, Simon & Schuster.
9. Greaves, R., Gabriel, T., Haddad, Y., Smith, Jane, I., Islam and the West Post 9/11, Ashgate Publications, England, 2004.
10. Kennedy, H. (2007). The Great Arab Conquests: How the Spread of Islam Changed the World We Live In. Philadelphia: Da Capo Press, Print.
11. Madelung, W. (1997). The Succession to Muhammad: A Study of the Early Caliphate. Cambridge, UK: Cambridge University Press.
12. Mani, RVS (2018). The Myth of Hindu Terror: Insider account of Ministry of Home Affairs 2006-2010, Vitasta Publishing, New Delhi.
13. Metcalf, B. D. (1982) Islamic revival in British India: Deoband, 1860-1900. Princeton, NJ: Princeton University Press.
14. Mukherjee, P. (2016). The Turbulent Years: 1980-96. Rupa Publications India, New Delhi.
15. Zacharias P. (2015). Tablighi Jamaat and the Quest for the London Mega-Mosque: Continuity and Change-Palgrave Macmillan, US.
16. Ragi, S. K. (2022). *RSS and Gandhi: The Idea of India* (1st ed.). SAGE Publications Pvt Ltd.

17. Siddiqui, B., Becoming good Muslim: Tablighi Jamaat in the UK and Bangladesh, Springer, Singapore, 2018.
18. Sonn, T. (2009). *A Brief History of Islam*, Wiley-Blackwell. New York.
19. Tikoo, Colonel T. K. (2012). Kashmir: Its Aborigines and Their Exodus. Lancer Publishers LLC, New Delhi.
20. Zakaria, R. (1995). The Widening Divide: An Insight into Hindu-Muslim Relations. Penguin Books.

WEBSITES

1. 'Invasions, Plunders, Loot and Cultural Disintegration: The Chronology of Islam's 800-year-old rule over India,' Organiser, 21 May 2021, https://www.organiser.org/invasions,-plunders,-loot-and-cultural-disintegration:-the-chronology-of-islam's-800-year-old-rule-over-india-1880.html, accessed on May 17 2021.
2. 'Policy Brief 10 – Tablighi Jamaat and its role in the Global Jihad,' South Asia Democratic Forum, 11 December, 2020, https://www.sadf.eu/policy-brief-10-tablighi-jamaat-and-its-role-in-the-global-jihad/. Doi: 10.48251/SADF.ISSN.2406-5625.PB.10, accessed on 6 June 2020.
3. "Co-conspirators in supporting terrorism," Congressional Record Volume 161, Number 182 (Tuesday, December 15, 2015). Pages H9324-H9326. From the Congressional Record Online through the Government Publishing Office [www.gpo.gov], https://www.govinfo.gov/content/pkg/CREC-2015-12-15/html/CREC-2015-12-15-pt1-PgH9324.htm. accessed on 8 June 2020.

4. "Jamiat-Ulama-I-Hind Wanted to Convert India into An Islamic state." 14 March 2016. https://swarajyamag.com/politics/jamiat-ulama-i-hind-wanted-to-convert-india-into-an-islamic-state. Accessed 1 Apr. 2021
5. "Terrorist Groups: An Overview," *South Asia Terrorism Portal*, Institute for Conflict Management, https://www.satp.org/ satporgtp/countries/india/states/jandk/terrorist_outfits/terrorist_groups_j&k.htm accessed on 9 June 2020.
6. "Time for Shias to leave Pakistan - Pakistan - DAWN.COM." 17 Feb. 2013, https://www.dawn.com/news/786738/time-for-shias-to-leave-pakistan. Accessed 1 Apr. 2021.
7. Afsaruddin, A. & Nasr, S. H. "Al ": Encyclopedia Britannica. https://www.britannica.com/ biography/Ali-Muslim-caliph, Accessed on 5 June 2020.
8. Ahmed, N. The Conquest of Sindh. History of Islam- An encyclopedia of Islamic History. https://historyofislam.com/contents/the-age-of-faith/the-conquest-of-sindh/, accessed on 8 June 2020.
9. Ambedkar on Uniform Civil Code in the Constituent Assembly Debates https://indiankanoon.org/doc/870715/
10. Balouch, A. 'Muhammad Bin Qasim: Predator or preacher?' DAWN, 8 April 2014, https://www.dawn.com/news/1098562, accessed on 18 May 2021.
11. Beyler, C. The Jihadist threat in France. Gale Academic OneFile. https://go.gale.com/ps/i.do?id=GALE%7CA348311779&sid=googleScholar&v=2.1&it=r&linkaccess=abs&issn=1940834X&p=AONE&sw=w&userGroupName=anon%7E2813f6b8. Accessed on 20 March 2022.

12. Burton, F. & Stewart, S. (2002). "Tablighi Jamaat: An Indirect Line to Terrorism" World View, Jan 23, 2008. https://worldview.stratfor.com/article/tablighi-jamaat-indirect-line-terrorism, accessed on 11 June 2020.
13. Burton, F. & Stewart, S. (2008). "Tablighi Jamaat: An Indirect Line to Terrorism" https://worldview.stratfor.com/ article/tablighi-jamaat-indirect-line-terrorism, accessed on 13 June 2020.
14. Census Report of 2011 suggests that there has been significant rise in Muslim dominated districts and constituencies in India. https://pib.gov.in/newsite/printrelease.aspx?relid=126326
15. Coynash, H. New weapon of religious persecution and arrests in Russian-occupied Crimea, 4 October 2017, http:// khpg.org/en/index.php?id=1507082183, accessed on 29 October 2021.
16. Dhondy, F. "London Muslims "Celebrate" 9/11." https://www.city-journal.org/html/london-muslims-%E2%80
17. Frayer, L. "The Taliban's Ideology Has Surprising Roots in British-Ruled India", 8 September, 2021, North Carolina Public Radio. Morning Edition, https://www.wunc.org/2021-09-08/the-talibans-ideology-has-surprising-roots-in-british-ruled-india. Accessed on 22 December 2021.
18. Government of India-Ministry of Health & Family Welfare, https://www.mohfw.gov.in/pdf/SocialDistancingAdvisorybyMOHFW.pdf.
19. Haar, K. "Spanish Police Arrest Jamaat al-Tabligh Members in Bomb Threat." The Jamestown Foundation. February 13, 2008. https://jamestown.org/program/spanish- police-arrest-

jamaat-al-tabligh-members-in-bomb-threat/, accessed on 7 June 2020.

20. How to Islamize an Islamic Republic: Jamaat-e-Islami in its own words." 25 Apr. 2017, https://www.brookings.edu/research/how-to-islamize-an-islamic-republic-jamaat-e-islami-in-its-own-words/. Accessed 1 Apr. 2021. https://eeradicalization.com/the-islamist-challenge-in-germany/

21. Khan, E. why did the Pak Maulana visit Deoband? Rediff.com, 18 July 2003, https://www.rediff.com/news/2003/ jul/17pak1.html

22. Latin America's Socialist Islamist Narco Terrorist Alliance https://www.fdd.org/analysis/2017/09/27/latin-americas-socialist-islamist-narco-terrorist-alliance/. Accessed on 10 June 2020.

23. Lipka, M. "Muslims and Islam: Key findings in the U.S. and around the world." Pew Research Centre, 9 August 2017. https://www.pewresearch.org/fact-tank/2017/08/09/muslims-and-islam-key-findings-in-the- u-s-and-around-the-world/. Accessed on 31 December 2022.

24. Mohammad, J. "The Islamist Challenge in Germany", European Eye on Radicalization, 28 August 2019.

25. Musaji, S. (2002). Muslim reactions to September 11th, 'Islâmic Reflections 2002', https://web.archive.orgweb/20021218024208/http://www.crescentlife.com/heal%20 the%20world/muslim_reactions_to_sept_11.htm, accessed on 17 May 2020.

26. Musaji, S. (2002). Muslim reactions to September 11th, 'Islâmic Reflections 2002', https://web.archive.org/

web/20021218024208/http://www.crescentlife.com/heal%20the%20world/muslim_reactions_to_sept_11.htm, accessed on 17 May 2020

27. Population Trends for Major Religious Groups in India from 1951-2011. Table 1.1.22. Socio-Economic and Caste Census, 2011. https://censusindia.gov.in/2011-prov-results/data_files/india/final_ppt_2011_chapter3.pdf
28. Raman, B. "Dagestan: Focus on Pakistan's Tablighi Jamaat", *South Asia Terrorism Portal*, Institute for Conflict Management. https://www.satp.org/satporgtp/publication/idr/vol_15(1)/executive_summary_iii.htm, accessed on 14 June 2020.
29. Ranking of the most significant terrorist acts since 2000 in France 2018 https://www.statista.com/statistics/941657/most-significant-terrorists-acts-since-2000-france/ accessed on 27 December 2015.
30. Razwy, S. A. A. 'A restatement of the history of Islam and Muslims', Uthman, the Third Khalifa of the Muslims, https://www.al-islam.org/restatement-history-islam- and-muslims-sayyid-ali-asghar-razwy/uthman-third-khalifa- muslims, accessed on 17 May 2020.
31. Razwy, S. A. A. 'A restatement of the history of Islam and Muslims', Uthman, the Third Khalifa of the Muslims, https://www.al-islam.org/restatement-history-islam- and-muslims-sayyid-ali-asghar-razwy/uthman-third-khalifa-muslims, accessed on 17 May 2020.
32. Singh, S. B. Man had objected to the cut-off date of 19 July 1948 for those who returned to India by this date. See; https://indiankanoon.org/doc/215406/. Accessed on 7 December, 2020.

33. Statistics Given by the Muslim Council of Britain: https://www.mcb.org.uk/wpcontent/uploads/2015/02/MCBCensusReport_2015.pdf. Accessed on 31 December 2022.
34. "The Rise of Mughal Power - De Gruyter." https://www.degruyter.com/document/doi/10.1525/9780520917774-011/pdf, accessed 1 Apr. 2021.
35. Warren, C. S. (2013). The Hanafi School, Oxford Bibliographies. https://www.oxfordbibliographies.com/view/document/obo-9780195390155/obo-9780195390155-0082.xml#:~:text=The%20Hanafi%20School%20is%20one,Al%2DFiqh%20al%2DAkbar
36. What are Hadith? *Whyislam.org*, https://www.whyislam.org/prophet-muhammad/hadith/, accessed on 17 May 2020.
37. What are Hadith? *Whyislam.org*, https://www.whyislam.org/prophet-muhammad/hadith/, accessed on 17 May 2020.
38. Zahid, F. "Tablighi Jamaat and Its Links with Islamist Terrorism." Foreign Analysis, No.19, March 2015. https://cf2r.org/foreign/tablighi-jamaat-and-its-links-with-islamist-terrorism-2/#_ftn16.Accessed on 5 June 2020.

NEWSPAPER/ ARTICLES

1. 'Coronavirus doubling rate in India now 4.1 days from 7.4 earlier: Health Ministry,' The Print, 5 April 2020, https://theprint.in/health/coronavirus-doubling-rate-in-india-now-4-1-days-from-7-4-earlier-health-ministry/395747/, accessed on 15 May 2020.
2. 'Coronavirus in India Highlights: Delhi reports 183 new cases

in 24 hours; 154 belong to Tablighi Jamaat,' Business Today, New Delhi, 10 April 2020. https://www.businesstoday.in/latest/economy-politics/story/coronavirus-india-live-updates-10-april-cases-deaths-count-lockdown-odisha-mumbai-delhi-254451-2020-04-10. Accessed on 10 May 2020.

3. 'Covid-19: Delhi police releases video of March 23 warning over Nizamuddin Markaz,' Hindustan Times, YouTube, 1 April 2020, https://www.youtube.com/watch?v=HcaSVvjDDjQ&ab_channel=HindustanTimes.
4. 'PM Modi announces 21-day lockdown as COVID-19 toll touches 12,' The Hindu, New Delhi, 24 March 2020. https://www.thehindu.com/news/national/pm-announces-21-day-lockdown-as-covid-19-toll-touches-10/article31156691.ece Accessed on 10 May 2020.
5. 'Tablighi Jamaat: How did the government fail to detect a coronavirus infection hotspot?', Scroll, New Delhi, 1 April 2020, https://scroll.in/article/957891/tablighi-jamaat-how-did-the-government-fail-to-detect-a-coronavirus-infection-hotspot, accessed on 12 May 2020.
6. 'Tamil Nadu is worst-hit by Tablighi Jamaat event, but also seeing men admit participation,' The Print, 7 April 2020, https://theprint.in/india/tamil-nadu-is-worst-hit- by-tablighi-jamaat-event-but-also-seeing-men-admit-participation/396619/, accessed on 16 May 2020.
7. 'Uttar Pradesh: Tablighi links shoot up count to 174,' The Indian Express, 4 April 2020, https://indianexpress.com/article/coronavirus/uttar-pradesh-tablighi-links-shoot-up-count-to-174-6346545/, accessed on 15 May 2020.

8. "A breach of trust - Frontline - The Hindu" 17 December 2004, https://frontline.thehindu.com/world-affairs/article30225764.ece. Accessed 5 April 2021
9. "Jamiat issues fatwa against singing Vande Mataram." Headlines today. https://www.indiatoday.in/latest-headlines/story/jamiat-issues-fatwa-against-singing-vande-mataram-59917-2009-11-03. Accessed on 22 December 2021.
10. "Jamiat-Ulama-I-Hind Wanted to Convert India into An Islamic state." 14 March 2016. https://swarajyamag.com/politics/jamiat-ulama-i-hind-wanted-to-convert-india-into-an-islamic-state. Accessed 1 Apr. 2021.
11. "Questions Remain About How Delhi's Nizamuddin Became a Coronavirus Hotspot," The Wire, 31 March 2020, https://science.thewire.in/politics/government/delhis-nizamuddin-hotspot-coronavirus/, accessed on 10 April 2020.
12. Burnett, Victoria. "14 terror suspects held as Spanish police raid mosque." The New York Times, 20 January 2008. https://www.nytimes.com/2008/01/20/world/europe/20iht-spain.4.9357125.html, accessed on 8 June 2020.
13. Crossette, Barbara, Taliban Explains Buddha Demolitions, The New York Times, 19 March, 2001. https://www.nytimes.com/2001/03/19/world/taliban-explains-buddha-demolition.html.
14. "Digvijaya Singh seeks judicial probe into fake Batla House encounter." 24 May. 2016, https://m.economictimes.com/news/politics-and-nation/digvijaya-singh-seeks-judicial-probe-into-fake-batla-house-encounter/articleshow/52422720.cms. Accessed 5 April 2021

15. Explained: Saudi Arabia's ban on the Tablighi and Da'wah group, Mehr Gill, The Indian Express, 14 December 2021, https://indianexpress.com/article/explained/explained-saudi-arabia-ban-on-tablighi-dawah-group-7670780/, accessed on 17 December 2021.
16. Fadel, L. (2018). "How Muslims, Often Misunderstood, Are Thriving in America", The National Geographic Magazine, May 2018, https://www.nationalgeographic.com/magazine/2018/05/being-muslim-in-america/, accessed on 9 June 2020.
17. Gleditsch, Petterand N. & Rudolfsen, I. "Are Muslim Countries More Violent." The Washington Post. 16 May, 2016. https://www.washingtonpost.com/news/monkey-cage/wp/2016/05/16/are-muslim-countries-more-violent/. Accessed on 26 December 2021.
18. Goel, Sita Ram. 'The Calcutta Quran Petition-Chapter 6: Jihad in Bharat's History.' Hindu Post, 21 April 2020. https://hindupost.in/history/the-calcutta-quran-petition-by-sita-ram-goel-chapter-6-jihad-in-bharats-history/, accessed on 19 May 2021.
19. Hebbar, N. "PM Modi announces 21-day lockdown as COVID-19 toll touches 12", The Hindu, New Delhi, 24 March 2020, https://www.thehindu.com/news/national/pm-announces-21-day-lockdown-as-covid-19-toll-touches-10/article31156691.ece.
20. Ibrahim, Y. M. "The Mideast Threat That's Hard to Define. Washington Post, August 11, 2002.
21. Iqbal, S. (2018). Setback to Tablighi Jamaat Plan to Build a

'Mega Mosque' in London, The Dawn, Pakistan, 30 January 2018. https://www.dawn.com/news/1386043, accessed on 29 October 2021.

22. Mallet, V. "Madrasas: behind closed door"', Financial Times, 30 0ctober 2015, https://www.ft.com/content/ d807f15a-7db0-11e5-98fb-5a6d4728f74e
23. Marino, F. (2020). Tablighi Jamaat, an 'antechamber of terrorism' in Europe? 02 April 2020, https://www.aninews.in/news/world/europe/tablighi-jamaat- an-antechamber-of-terrorism-in-europe20200402214459/, accessed on 7 June 2020.
24. McManus, J. 'Have pictures of Muhammad always been forbidden?' BBC News, 15 January 2015. https://www.bbc.com/news/magazine-30814555
25. McNeil Jr. & Donald G. (2001). "A Nation Challenged: The Foreign Soldier; Body Confirms Suspicions About Frenchmen in Al Qaeda." The New York Times, 28 Dec 2001, https://www.nytimes.com/2001/12/28/world/nation-challenged-foreign-soldier-body-confirms-suspicions-about-frenchmen-al.html, accessed on 12 June 2020.
26. Mouza hem, H. "Saudi Wahhabi Sheikh Calls on Iraq's Jihadists to Kill Shiites", AL monitor, 28 April 2013. Darul Islam and Darul Harab categorization in the Islamic texts
27. Nazish, K. (2015). "Is Pakistani religious school a terrorist breeding ground"? USA Today, 12 December 2015, https://www.usatoday.com/story/news/world/2015/12/12/pakistani-religious-school-terrorist-breeding-ground/77149880/, accessed on 9 June 2020.

28. P Worrall, 'Sharia Law in the UK' (Channel 4, 14 July 2014). https://www.channel4.com/news/factcheck/ factcheck-qa-sharia-law-uk> accessed 23 January 2022.
29. Parvaz, D. "Iran 1979: the Islamic revolution that shook the world." Aljazeera, 11 February, 2014, accessed on 14 June 2020.
30. Pathak, V. 'Century not out, Jamiat still bats for an India with a composite culture', The Hindu, 23 June 2018, https://www.thehindu.com/news/national/century-not- out-jamiat-still-bats-for-an-india-with-a-composite-culture/ article24242019.ece
31. Rashid, O. & Kumar, A. '6 Tablighi Jamaat-linked persons to be booked under NSA for misbehaving with nurses in Uttar Pradesh's Ghaziabad', The Hindu, 3 April 2020. https://www.thehindu.com/news/national/other-states/6- tablighi-jamaat-linked-persons-to-be-booked-under-nsa-for-misbehaving-with-nurses-in-uttar-pradeshs-ghaziabad/ article31247168.ece, accessed on 30 October 2021.
32. Revesz, R. "US Islamophobia: Threats and acts of vandalism against mosques double so far in 2017." The Independent, 15 March 2017, UK.
33. Sachs, S. "A Muslim Missionary Group Draws New Scrutiny in U.S" The New York Times, July 14, 2003. https:// www.nytimes.com/2003/07/14/us/a-muslim-missionary- group-draws-new-scrutiny-in-us.html, accessed on 6 June 2020.
34. Serhan, Y. (August 2016). "France Disappearing Mosques." The Atlantic. https://www.theatlantic.com/ news/archive/2016/08/french-mosques-islam/493919/. Accessed on 27 December 2021.

35. Singh, N. K. 'Tablighi Jamaat Should be Banned.' The Sunday Guardian, 4 April 2020. https://www.sundayguardianlive.com/opinion/tablighi-jamaat-banned, accessed on 4 June, 2020.
36. Smit, C. S. "Muslim Group in France Is Fertile Soil for Militancy", The New York Times, 28 April 2005.
37. Sunni Conference: Neither the Leadership nor the Imamat of Wahabi is accepted. Sunni News. 6 January 2010. https://sunninews.wordpress.com/2010/01/06/sunni-conference-neither-the-leadership-nor-the-imamat-of-wahabi-is-accepted/, accessed on 7 June 2020.
38. Tablighi Jamaat: Muslims from China were involved, ABP Special, 02 Apr 2020. https://news.abplive.com/videos/news/india-tablighi-jammat-muslims-from-china-were-involved-abp-special-1188010, accessed on 30 October 2021.
39. Tell the 'gate of terror' that the noose has been tightened on the Tablighis, now Saudi Arabia will also stop terror funding? Hindustan News Hub, 12 December 2021. https://hindustannewshub.com/india-news/tell-the-gate-of-terror-that-the-noose-has-been-tightened-on-the-tablighis-now-saudi-arabia-will-also-stop-terror-funding/. accessed on 19 December 2021.
40. Time for Shias to leave Pakistan - Pakistan - DAWN.COM." 17 Feb. 2013, https://www.dawn.com/news/786738/time-for-shias-to-leave-pakistan. Accessed 1 Apr. 2021.

INDEX

C

D

E

G

H

I

J

O

P

Q

R

S

T